Andrea Palladio's
Teatro Olimpico

Theater and Dramatic Studies, No. 8

Bernard Beckerman, Series Editor

Brander Matthews Professor of Dramatic Literature
Columbia University in the City of New York

Other Titles in This Series

No. 1   *The Original Casting of Molière's Plays*   Roger W. Herzel

No. 2   *Richard Foreman and the Ontological-*
Hysteric Theatre   Kate Davy

No. 3   *The History and Theory of*
Environmental Scenography   Arnold Aronson

No. 4   *The Meininger Theater: 1776–1926*   Steven DeHart

No. 5   *Shakespeare Refashioned:*
Elizabethan Plays on Edwardian Stages   Cary M. Mazer

No. 6   *The Public and Performance: Essays*
in the History of French and German Theater,
1871–1900   Michael Hays

No. 7   *Richard Boleslavsky: His Life and Work*
in the Theatre   J.W. Roberts

No. 9   *Georges Feydeau and the Aesthetics of Farce*   Stuart E. Baker

No. 10   *The Theatre Director Otto Brahm*   Horst Claus

Andrea Palladio's
Teatro Olimpico

by
J. Thomas Oosting

UMI RESEARCH PRESS
Ann Arbor, Michigan

Produced and distributed by
UMI Research Press
an imprint of
University Microfilms International
Ann Arbor, Michigan 48106

Library of Congress Cataloging in Publication Data

Oosting, J. Thomas
  Andrea Palladio's Teatro Olimpico.

  (Theater and dramatic studies; no. 8)
  Revision of thesis (Ph.D.)—University of Iowa, 1970.
  Bibliography: p.
  1. Teatro Olimpico (Vicenza, Italy) 2. Palladio, Andrea,
1508-1580. 3. Vicenza (Italy)—Theaters. 4. Architecture,
Renaissance—Italy—Vicenza. I. Title. II. Series.

NA6840.I82V535   1981   725'.822'0924   81-16303
ISBN 0-8357-1252-4   AACR2

Contents

List of Figures   *vii*

List of Tables   *xi*

1   Introduction   *1*
      The Olimpico as Roman Model
      The Olimpico as Roman Model Tempered by Renaissance Culture
      Evidence
      Methodology

2   Palladio's Archaeological and Architectural Learning   *27*

Figures   *53*

3   Palladio's Theatrical Occupations   *101*

4   The Teatro Olimpico Design   *115*

Conclusions   *145*

Tables   *149*

Appendices   *159*
      A   *Sofonisba* Description
      B   Olimpico Design Transactions
      C   Olimpico Iconography

Notes   *179*

Bibliography   *209*

Index   *215*

List of Figures

1. Montenari, elevation of Olimpico *cavea*   55

2. Bertotti Scamozzi, Olimpico section   56

3. Bertotti Scamozzi, schematic of Vitruvian method in Olimpico   57

4. Fresco, Olimpic Stadium   58

5. Fresco, *L'Amor costante*   58

6. Fresco, *Sofonisba*   59

7. Fresco, *Edippo*   59

8. Fresco, Japanese envoy   60

9. Fresco, *torneo*   60

10. Berga theatre, Vicenza   61

11. Schematic of Barbaro-Palladio Roman theatre   62

12. Schematic of modern interpretation of Roman theatre   62

13. Barbaro-Vitruvius, *cavea* section   63

14. Barbaro-Vitruvius, *cavea* exterior elevation   63

15. Barbaro-Vitruvius, plan of Greek theatre   64

16. Jocondus-Vitruvius, plan of Roman theatre   65

17. Cesariano-Vitruvius, plan of Roman theatre   *65*

18. Cesariano-Vitruvius, *cavea* exterior and interior   *66*

19. Peruzzi, Marcellus theatre   *67*

20. Sangallo the Younger, Marcellus theatre   *67*

21. Ligorio, Marcellus theatre   *68*

22. Serlio, plan of Marcellus theatre   *69*

23. Setezone "scena," Palladio autograph   *70*

24. Teatro Olimpico *frons-scenae*   *71*

25. Casa Raphael   *71*

26. Palazzo Valmarana   *72*

27. Conjectural reconstruction of *Sofonisba frons-scenae*   *73*

28. Vicentino, Henry III entry, Venice   *74*

29. Artist unknown, Henry III entry, Venice   *75*

30. Triumphal arch of Septimus Severus, Rome   *76*

31. Braun and Hogenberg map of Vicenza, ca. 1540-50   *77*

32. Teatro Olimpico *cavea*   *78*

33. Bertotti Scamozzi, *frons-scenae* elevation   *79*

34. Bertotti Scamozzi, *cavea* section   *79*

35. Bertotti Scamozzi, order detail drawings   *80*

36. Montenari, Olimpico ground plan   *81*

37. Dumont, Olimpico ground plan   *82*

38. Bennasuti, Olimpico ground plan   *83*

39. Bennasuti, Olimpico *frons-scenae* elevation   *84*

40. Magrini, Olimpico *frons-scenae* elevation, *cavea* section and ground plan   *85*

41. Sonrel, Olimpico *frons-scenae* elevation   *86*

42. Sonrel, Olimpico ground plan   *86*

43. Sonrel, Olimpico section   *87*

44. Bertotti Scamozzi, Olimpico ground plan   *88*

45. Barbaro-Vitruvius, *frons-scenae* elevation   *89*

46. Berga theatre plan and elevations, Palladio autograph   *90*

47. Barbaro-Vitruvius, Roman theatre ground plan   *91*

48. "London Studio," Palladio autograph   *92*

49. Roman study of theatre, Palladio autograph   *93*

50. Verona theatre plan, Palladio autograph   *94*

51. Verona theatre section, Palladio autograph   *95*

52. Verona theatre section and elevation, Palladio autograph   *96*

53. Pola theatre ground plan and elevation, Palladio autograph   *97*

54. Olimpico *frons-scenae* elevation, Albanese autograph   *98*

55. Olimpico drawings, Orefice, 1620   *98*

56. Olimpico *cavea*   *99*

List of Tables

1. Barbaro-Palladio Roman Theatre: The Plan   *151*

2. Barbaro-Palladio Roman Theatre: The Elevation   *151*

3. Comparison of Palladio's Berga Theatre and Roman Study with the Barbaro-Palladio Vitruvius   *152*

4. Comparison of Palladio's Verona and Pola Theatre Drawings   *153*

5. Comparison of London Studio and Present Teatro Olimpico: *Cavea*   *154*

6. Comparison of London Studio and Present Teatro Olimpico: Stage   *154*

7. Comparison of London Studio and Present Teatro Olimpico: *Frons-Scenae* Orders   *155*

8. Comparison of London Studio and Present Teatro Olimpico: *Frons-Scenae Aediculae*   *156*

9. Comparison of the *Frons-Scenae* Plans in the Right London Studio with the Present Theatre   *157*

Acknowledgments

To Dr. David Thayer for his advice and encouragement; to the Centro Internazionale di Studi d'Architettura "Andrea Palladio" Vicenza and the Center's Executive Secretary, Professor Ranato Cevese, for considerable assistance and access to the Teatro Olimpico's 1965 Building Survey and the Centro's photographic archives; to Mr. Luigi Rossi of the Teatro Olimpico, the Biblioteca Bertoliana of Vicenza, and the Royal Institute of British Architects, London, for their generous assistance and materials; to my translator, Alba Shank, who led me through many a difficult passage; and to c-j, m-s, and m-n-o, who have made this study worthwhile.

1

Introduction

It is generally acknowledged that the theatres of the Italian Renaissance played a primary role in the history of theatre architecture. During the Italian Renaissance, the theatrical concepts of illusionistic stagecraft and mechanical spectacle and their architectural counterpart, the proscenium theatre, were formulated. There is no denying the causal importance of Italian Renaissance theatre on much of today's theatre architecture and practice. Largely because of their accidental existence, two late Italian Renaissance theatres, Scamozzi's theatre at Sabbioneta (1589-90) and Aleotti's Teatro Farnese at Parma (1619), have enjoyed considerable scholarly attention as ready examples of that importance.

Like the theatres at Sabbioneta and Parma, the Teatro Olimpico at Vicenza (1585) is equally accidental in its existence. As the first permanent theatre in continental Europe built especially for the performance of plays, writers have felt compelled to give the Olimpico a crucial role in the history of theatre architecture. But unlike the effective role attributed to the theatres at Sabbioneta and Parma, the Olimpico produced no apparent subsequent effect on theatre architecture. Its production career is similarly terminal. After an inaugural performance of *Edippo re* in 1585 (just four years before the Sabbioneta was opened), thirty-three years passed before the Olimpico's next production, Torquato Tasso's *Torrismondo* (1618). The seventeenth century records reveal no subsequent theatrical use.

In spite of its terminal character, the Olimpico has continued to receive scholarly attention as an example of Renaissance academic theatre. Viewed as the product of the propensity in the Italian Renaissance to revere the ancients, the Olimpico serves as a microcosm of that cultural phenomenon. In keeping with their avowed humanistic purpose, the Academia Olimpica commissioned their co-academician, Andrea Palladio, to design and build a theatre for the production of classical plays and imitations. Palladio died in 1580 during the early stage of construction; the theatre was completed under the supervision of the academy and Palladio's son, Silla.

Most writers agree that the Olimpico was a sophisticated attempt at reconstructing the theatre of the ancient Romans. But even though scholars agree about the general motive which produced the Olimpico, there is no unanimity of opinion about either the quantitative identification of the theatre's design sources or their qualitative imprint on the theatre's design and execution. The variety of opinions regarding the theatre's design sources has been conditioned largely by the writers' assumptions about Palladio's role as Renaissance theatre architect. Three basic assumptions can be identified. On the assumption that Palladio was intent on explicitly imitating the theatre of the ancient Romans, the causal explanation for the Olimpico's design becomes a matter of isolating Palladio's concept of the ancient Roman theatre and demonstrating the presence of that concept in the executed design. The second assumption is a refinement of the first. Arguing that so-called classical imitation in the Italian Renaissance was really an interpretive mutation of classicism, Palladio's concept of the ancient Roman theatre is presumed to be influenced by his contemporary culture as well. Not only is Palladio regarded as a humanist theatre archaeologist-historian, he is also regarded as a practicing Renaissance architect with his own set of stylistic and aesthetic biases. This view suggests that, like lovers, imitative artists see only what they elect to see. The third assumption is a historical perversion of the second and is argued by a small and dated group of writers who feel compelled to give the Olimpico an effective role, like the theatres at Sabbioneta and Parma, in subsequent theatre architecture. They admit that the Olimpico is derivative of the ancient Roman model but hasten to point out its use of illusionistic scenery as a sure sign of the theatre's acquiescing to the so-called Renaissance stagecraft.

Implicit in each of these assumptions is a theory about Palladio's architectural motives. Yet each theory has been asserted in the absence of a systematic analysis of the theatre's sources. And those sources that are analyzed as significant do not supply sufficient causal explanation for a thorough-going understanding of the design of the theatre.

This study undertakes to identify and substantiate the potential influences on the Teatro Olimpico's design and execution.

The Olimpico as Roman Model

By far the longest lived theory of the Olimpico's design asserts that Palladio designed the theatre according to his concept of an ancient Roman theatre. The assertion is not difficult to understand; generally the method is to posit the physical features of the ancient Roman theatre, and then, feature by feature, show their presence in the Olimpico.

The earliest published document mentioning the Olimpico is Marzari's *La historia di Vicenza* (1590). He writes that all those who now see this magnificent building, that isn't yet fully completed, are no less satisfied than they are amazed since it can be compared with any other building, both ancient and modern, built for performances.[1]

Marzari's brief notice, which includes a reference to the theatre's "oval form,"[2] serves as a keynote to the interpretive confusion that has beset the study of the theatre. Marzari's comparison of the Olimpico to both the ancient and modern theatres is obscure. Conceivably his comparison merely means that the Olimpico is as good a theatre as ever was built. Or perhaps his comparison is formal; like the ancient theatre, the Olimpico has classic features in its orchestra and formal *scena;* like the modern theatre, the Olimpico has modern features in its perspective scenery and its roofing. If Marzari's comparison is formal, he begins a long tradition of writers who recognize the theatre's dual personality. Curiously missing from Marzari's short notice is the identification of Palladio as the theatre's architect. In a later section of the book which includes brief biographies of famous Vicentine men, Palladio is cited as an architect of "especially public and private palaces"; Vicenzo Scamozzi is linked to the "scena del Teatro [Olimpico] per la Tragedia" and to the design of the Gonzati theatre in Sabbioneta.[3] Marzari's omission of Palladio's design role is probably accidental. But twentieth century writers will introduce the notion that Palladio's death in 1580 allowed the execution of the Olimpico according to non-Palladian designs.

If the Olimpico were modelled after the ancients, how much did it imitate them? It is not surprising that, chronologically, the first attempt at explicating the Olimpico as Roman model came out of the eighteenth century. We are reminded that the eighteenth century historian was in the midst of changing philosophy about the business and methods of history.[4] Chiefly influential was the extensive expansion of available documents, publications, and antiquarian interest. Italians turned to the recording of the Olimpico for posterity. Taking advantage of all that previous classical scholars had left in the form of editions of the ancients, Academy members, neoclassic practicing architects, and art historians became archaeologists.[5] The works by Montenari and Bertotti Scamozzi are representative.

Montenari states his thesis about the origin of the Olimpic design: "This theatre was formed according to the ideas that we have from Vitruvius."[6] His method is simple: (1) identify a Vitruvian element in the Olimpico and describe it, (2) quote Vitruvius, and (3) cite other Roman authors who corroborate the element's location or function. The limits of Montenari's method are illustrated with only a few specifics. In discussing the *scena* or *frons-scenae,* Montenari observes that like the Olimpico, the Romans also had a *scena.* He quotes from Cassiodoro, Agatarco (Agatharcus, mentioned in Vitruvius' introduction to Book VII), Suidas, Plutarco, Tacito, and Plinio for four pages, never once supplying a visual image of the Roman *scena* nor comparing it with the Olimpico's *scena*.[7] As in the Greek theatre in Athens, Montenari finds an odeo attached to the Olimpico (figure 44). He supplies us with the information that an odeo was a small theatre and music recital hall attached to the left of the theatre (Vitruvius, V.ix.l.).[8] There is a room to the left of the Teatro Olimpico auditorium and one wall of the odeo is pierced by three openings—just like the *scenae* of a theatre. What Montenari does not tell us is that an odeo was generally attached to a Greek theatre and the Olimpico is, if anything, a Roman model. There is no evidence to support the conclusion that Palladio ever envisioned the existence of the so-called odeo in the Olimpico.

Montenari does recognize that the elliptical plan of the Olimpico *cavea* (auditorium) and orchestra is physically dissimilar to the Roman model, but his explanation of Palladio's use of the elliptical shape is unsatisfactory, in spite of his identification of key factors relevant to the design of the unique plan. His method falls apart from uncritical use of evidence and an unwillingness to make discriminating inferences. Recognizing that Palladio was limited by property in the shape of a rectangle,[9] Montenari argues that Palladio would not have built a satisfactorily large theatre if he had used the circular plan stipulated by Vitruvius (V.vi).[10] He reasons that Palladio, knowing of Vitruvius' permission to deviate from the ideal (V.vi.7), selected an ellipse so as more efficiently to use the space allotted. At this point Montenari admits he cannot explain how Palladio applied the ellipse:

> He left no record of how he had directed it, but he has left the sight of an elliptical figure, the marvelous fruits of his knowledge, with all the parts of the Roman theatre in like proportion as Vitruvius with the circular.[11]

Obviously, the presence of the ellipse undercuts Montenari's thesis. Yet, he does not offer an explanation for the introduction of this nonclassical element. Worse is Montenari's assertion that the parts of the Olimpico are in "like proportion as Vitruvius with the circular"; he could not make this assertion without first determining the Vitruvian edition that Palladio was following. Although we know that Palladio was intimately involved in the Barbaro edition of 1556,[12] Montenari elects to use the Philandri edition of 1543.[13] And, Montenari is aware of potential differences of interpretation.[14]

Not only is Montenari guilty of being methodologically uncritical, his handling of evidence is questionable. He misrepresents evidence, not by error but by commission.[15] Citing *Tito Livio*, which says that the first fourteen rows of seats were reserved for senators of the equestrian order, Montenari notes that because the Olimpico was used by noble persons (a stretching of the evidence) there were fourteen rows of seats (figure 1).[16] There have always been only thirteen rows of seats in the Olimpico.

Montenari's study did not live unscathed even during his own lifetime.[17] Ottavio Bertotti Scamozzi, another architect-archaeologist, severely criticizes Montenari's analysis. While he admits that Montenari is an erudite scholar of antiquity, he notes that although Montenari recognizes the chief difference between the Olimpico and the Roman theatre, namely the ellipse, Montenari fails to advance a method for reconciling the resultant proportions with those set down by Barbaro in his edition of Vitruvius (1556).[18] Seemingly, Bertotti Scamozzi is on the right track to an analysis of the Olimpico as Roman model. He notes only two features present in the Roman theatre missing from the Olimpico: the rain shelter portico behind the stage area and the acoustical vessels (figure 2).[19] Bertotti Scamozzi's perceptions are telling; bent on showing Roman imitation, he fails to consider whether inclement weather and acoustical augmentation were relevant design considerations in a Renaissance theatre.

Bertotti Scamozzi's study has two thrusts: to rectify the problems he sees in Montenari's study and to physically describe the elements of the theatre. Of interest to us is his analysis of the theatre's design sources. Arguing totally from Vitruvian instruction, Bertotti Scamozzi establishes the Barbaro edition (1556) as Palladio's guide book. He recognizes that Palladio was familiar with Roman theatre ruins, especially the Berga theatre in Vicenza;[20] he sees this archaeological experience as totally reflected in the Barbaro edition and rejects any possibility that Palladio's interpretation of Vitruvius might have changed when he designed the Olimpico or that the archaeological experience might have had an independent influence on the design of the Olimpico. An example of Bertotti Scamozzi's method will illustrate the limits of his analysis.

Bertotti Scamozzi begins his analysis by asserting that Palladio was instructed, by the Academy, to build a theatre like the ancient Romans.[21] His method is both schematic and mathematical. He argues that "if Palladio had been granted a large space of land to construct a theatre, he would probably have followed the direction of the plan of Vitruvius."[22] However, the restricted property would not allow him to apply "a perfect circular shape to his plan according to Vitruvius' preparation" since

in the narrow and irregular piece of land that was actually granted to him, it would have resulted in neither a big enough nor a comfortable theatre, not only for the population of Vicenza, but also for a less populated town than ours.[23]

Establishing, on the one hand, that the elliptical shape was not Vitruvian, he proceeds with a purely Vitruvian analysis of the theatre. He shows schematically how the Olimpico fits Vitruvius (figure 3). First, he lays out an outline of the *cavea,* orchestra, and *frons-scenae.* Next, he continues the *cavea* and orchestra semiellipses into two full ellipses. Third, he draws one large and one small circle in the respective ellipses whose diameters equal the lengths of the respective ellipse minor axes. Fourth, he draws three additional circles inside the *cavea* ellipse; their diameter equals half the length of the major axis of the ellipse. Last, he inscribes four triangles (as Vitruvius instructs [V.vi.1]) into the larger circle (C,C,C,C);[24] these triangles locate the placement of *frons-scenae* openings, the *versurae* (the wings which abut perpendicularly to the *frons-scenae*), the steps in the *cavea,* and the stage depth.[25] We must admit that Bertotti Scamozzi's method yields a Vitruvian comparison. But what about that third step? Why are the circles inscribed within the minor axes and not given diameters equal to the lengths of the major axes? Circles inscribed about the major axes would generate an unreal *frons-scenae* position. What about the three circles in the fourth step? What is their significance? Vitruvius gives no procedure that uses circles whose diameters are equal to half the orchestra diameter in any application. Conceivably Bertotti Scamozzi sees them as forming the beginning of the ellipse curve. But then we ask, why not three circles whose diameters are equal to a third of the orchestra diameter (or four circles, each a fourth of the diameter) and which orchestra diameter, the major or the minor axis? Then the ellipse would have a different curve and yield a different theatre shape; Bertotti Scamozzi's argument is circular. Maybe there is no logical answer. If not, one should not be invented. Whatever the case, there are non-Vitruvian sources present.

Bertotti Scamozzi does not stop at schematic speculation. Consider, for example, his analysis of how Palladio generated the length of the *frons-scenae*. He acknowledges that the length of a *frons-scenae* is equal to twice the diameter of the orchestra (Vitruvius, V.vi.6; the diameter of the Roman theatre orchestra was used as a measurement module—1d.—to determine other feature measurements in the theatre). If Palladio had doubled the diameter of the orchestra (the orchestra major axis equals 50'-8" Vicentine[26]), the *frons-scenae* would have been 101'-4" Vicentine. Noting this discrepancy, Bertotti Scamozzi says "it is not so easy to guess . . . by which rule Palladio had determined to establish the length of the *scena.*"[27] He hypothesizes that Palladio had added the major orchestra axis (50'-8" Vicentine) to half the minor orchestra axis (18'-7" Vicentine) to achieve a quantity (69'-3" Vicentine) that falls barely short of the final *frons-scenae* length (70'-4" Vicentine).[28] Bertotti Scamozzi suggests the difference (1'-1" Vicentine) "could be the result of a mistake in the execution, and it is a difference which causes no or very little alteration in the proportion of the parts."[29] The "rule" that Bertotti Scamozzi discovers is no rule at all in a Vitruvian system. For him to argue that there is "no or very little alteration in the proportion of the parts" is somewhat of an acceptable rationalization since the Vitruvian aesthetic was based on proportional harmony of building parts. Yet, the fact remains that in adding a whole diameter to a half diameter, Bertotti Scamozzi yields an un-Vitruvian solution; Vitruvius' instruction is to double the diameter. His analysis is deficient because he does not identify his "rule" as speculation, and because he refuses to admit to the evident operation of non-Vitruvian influences. For example, although Bertotti Scamozzi says the unusual shape of the theatre's site had an effect on the theatre's planometric shape, he asserts that practicality was made "subservient to the design."[30] He does not advance a method for demonstrating that Palladio controlled the practicality rather than that the practicality controlled Palladio.

Besides Bertotti Scamozzi's tendency to look only to Vitruvius and ignore practicalities as an equally telling influence, he ignores the possible influence of Palladio's previous theatre architecture and he breezes over the Scamozzi vistas without questioning whether they are organically related to Palladio's apparent design intention.[31]

The methods of Montenari and Bertotti Scamozzi demonstrate a praiseworthy ingenuity. However, as thorough analyses of the design they tend to be narrow in their interpretation of evidence, ignoring alternate sources of design.

In the twentieth century scholars have carried on the argument that the Olimpico is best identified as a Roman derivative. The majority of writers who take this stance do not elaborate on their hypothesis. The Olimpico's existence in the history of theatre architecture is contrasted with the Peruzzi-Serlio development of scenic illusionism and the evolution of the proscenium arch.[32] The thrust of the argument is that the Olimpico was out of phase with other theatrical design activity of the same period and geographic area. This polarization of the Olimpico and the Perruzzi-Serlio traditions, while largely accurate, is a presupposition which affects the perception of potential design sources. Kindermann, for example, argues that Palladio had planned to use *periaktoi* (a classical theatrical machine) behind the openings of the *frons-scenae,* and that Scamozzi's scenic vistas were a significant change from the initial design.[33] There is evidence that Palladio had *periaktoi* on his mind, since he located them behind the *frons-scenae* openings in the 1556 Barbaro edition of Vitruvius. There is also evidence that Palladio had used three-dimensional perspectives behind the *frons-scenae* openings in his temporary theatre in the Vicenza Basilica (for Trissino's *Sofonisba,* 1562) and had intended them in the Olimpico design.[34] Depending, then, on the significance assigned to this evidence, Palladio's Olimpico becomes more or less a Roman theatre, or a Roman theatre influenced by Renaissance theatrical convention. Kindermann's polarization forces a hasty interpretation of the evidence.

Thomas E. Lawrenson probably best exemplifies the attitude that the Olimpico was out of phase with current theatrical developments. Lawrenson believes that Italian Renaissance theatre architecture and stagecraft were the product of inaccurate readings of Vitruvius and Alberti. But with "the drawings of Barbaro [prepared by Palladio] and the Olimpico theatre at

Vicenza by Pallidio (and Scamozzi)," a more accurate concept of Vitruvius was posited, ending "the spate of ancient-modern fusion."[35] Lawrenson goes on to argue that the Olimpico "had an immense negative significance"[36] on the subsequent development of theatre architecture.

> The Olimpic theatre, wherever with more or less fidelity it reproduced the Roman theatre (of necessity in miniature), was appealing architectonically, to social conditions which no longer existed. In reconstructing an archaic archaeological form, its architect built something which reflected a dead society. It solved no theatrical problem of the times, whatever absolute architectural merit it may be held to possess.[37]

Lawrenson's position is appealing in terms of a general view of the evolution of theatre architecture. He makes two assertions, however, that point to the problems that develop when intentions are inferred without a total evaluation of all the potential influences. Lawrenson sees an explanation for the elliptical Olimpico *cavea* as "partly a memory of those slightly truncated Roman auditoria that Palladio had himself inspected. (Pola, Berga, and Aosta are examples.)"[38] The errors in Lawrenson's identification are that the "auditoria" of Berga and Pola are full half-circles and not truncated and that there is a geometric difference between a truncated half-circle and an ellipse. There is no evidence to suggest that Palladio had seen or that he knew of the ruin at Aosta. If Palladio were inspired by truncated half-circles, why did he use an ellipse?

Lawrenson asserts that the Olimpico is praiseworthy on one count; it manages a more intimate actor-audience relationship than other theatre buildings (temporary and permanent) of the period.[39] Apparently what Lawrenson means by intimate is that physically the audience is closer to the Olimpico stage than, for example, the audience in the Teatro Farnese at Parma. Implicit in Lawrenson's praise of the intimacy of the Olimpico is the assumption that one of the design motives was to achieve that intimacy. There is no evidence that the Olimpico was designed according to this theatrical principle. Lawrenson is applying a twentieth century sensibility.

One last advocate of the theory that the Olimpico is a product of the motive to imitate the classic theatre is George Kernodle. He argues that "while typical of neither school nor court theatre, it [the Olimpico] borrowed from both—an arcade screen from one and perspective settings from the other."[40]

> The modern historian has taken too literally their [Palladio et al.] own estimate of what they were doing. He has considered the Teatro Olimpico as merely a direct imitation, a reproduction of the ancient facade. We now see that the architects for the Teatro Olimpico really created in the patterns of their day as surely as if they had set out to produce the most up-to-date theatre. The Teatro Olimpico might have been exactly the same if neither Vitruvius nor the ancient theatre had ever been rediscovered.[41]

The theatrical "patterns of their day" to which Kernodle refers are the Terence arcade stages. Kernodle is differentiating between the motive to imitate the classic stage directly and the motive to interpret the classic stage. As I have been arguing, to even suggest that Palladio *directly* imitated the Roman theatre is to imply that Palladio had an extant model. But Kernodle does not look to Vitruvius and archaeology; in fact he denies the viability of these considerations as sources. Kernodle, on the contrary, argues that the facade of the Teatro Olimpico is best explained as "the crowning glory of the Terence School tradition."[42] The "Terence School tradition" is generally regarded as that group of late fifteenth and early sixteenth century attempts at producing the plays of Plautus and Terence. These productions can be documented with some degree of certainty, chiefly in Rome (c. 1485, 1497, and 1502) and Ferrara (1485, 1487, 1491, 1499, and 1502); the productions were largely superseded in the sixteenth century by those of contemporary playwrights (e.g., Ariosto's *La cassaria,* Ferrara, 1508, and Bibienna's *La Calandria,* Urbino, 1513).[43] Descriptions of these productions become the key to Kernodle's argument since their stages must be interpreted to resemble curtained, arcade-backed stages as illustrated in woodcuts in Terentian and Plautine editions (Ulm, 1486; Lyons, 1493; Strasburg, 1496; Venice, 1497; Venice, 1518; Venice, 1524; Venice, 1545). None of the illuminations of so-called Terence arcade stages have ever been associated with any theatrical performance, and there is good reason to believe that the illuminations have no relationship to theatrical technique of the times.[44] Kernodle has neither demonstrated Palladio's awareness of these illuminations nor rejected other possible sources of influence.

We might note that Kernodle's "tradition" is at least fifty years removed from the design of the Olimpico and that Kernodle has not shown his type of stage to be in use in Italy during the design of the Olimpico. Other questions arise regarding the descriptions of the productions at Rome and Ferrara. If the stages used were attempts to realize classical stages, guided by Vitruvius and Alberti (Kernodle denies the influence on Palladio of the former and ignores the latter), the arcade stage is synonymously a concept of the *frons-scenae.* Interpretation of the *frons-scenae* matures as archaeological study improves, resulting in the knowledgeable reconstruction by Palladio and Barbaro in 1556; therefore, the Terence and Plautus arcade stages become irrelevant considerations.

Concerning the question of the multiple vanishing-point scenery behind the Olimpico *frons-scenae,* Kernodle writes:

> The use of illusionistic settings on inner stages behind the facade was in no wise due to the Romans. Indeed, Vitruvius said the perspective settings should all tend to the same vanishing point. Nor was it a new invention of the architect. Already suggested in the

illustrations of Barbaro's edition of Vitruvius in 1567 it carried a little further the tendency developed in the Terence school tradition of placing separate scenes behind the arched openings.[45]

Twentieth century archaeology might allow Kernodle to assert that there is no evidence to suppose that the Romans used multiple vanishing-point illusionistic scenery. Yet, he forgets that what we know now is different from what the Italian Renaissance archaeologist and scholars of Vitruvius *thought* they knew. And, though Kernodle thinks he sees multiple vanishing-point scenery in the 1567 Barbaro edition *frons scenae* elevation, there is no indication of multiple vanishing-point scenery in the 1556, 1567, or 1584 editions by Barbaro. See, for example, the first edition, 1556, *frons-scenae,* (figure 49). Moreover, Kernodle seems to assume that the perspective scenery is organically related to Palladio's design concept; he implies that the elliptical *cavea* was designed with the multiple vanishing-point scenery in mind.

> It is probably significant that this theatre of a club of equals follows, both in its auditorium and in its stage, a different tradition from that of the court. Here the auditorium is not dominated by the royal box; instead, all seats are of about equal importance. Hence, the architect could not build a unified perspective setting but followed the form of the arcade screen—its main axis parallel to the front of the stage. Yet, for this aristocratic academy, elements of the court stage—the perspective setting—were borrowed and placed behind the formal openings in the facade. They were so cleverly arranged, however, that every seat in the house afforded a vista down one of the long streets in perspective—a most successful device to make each of the spectators feel as important as a prince.[46]

In view of Kernodle's rejection of Vitruvius as a design source, he can inject such logic that a "club of equals" would not follow the court "tradition" where the auditorium and scenery design were "dominated by the royal box." But Kernodle's argument is a post facto explanation for the results, as he sees them, rather than an explanation based on an evaluation of the motives which produced the theatre. Kernodle implies that the *cavea* shape and scenery arrangement were designed coordinately. Yet, if there is an un-Palladian feature in the Olimpico, it is the radial *arrangement* of the scenery.

The Olimpico as Roman Model Tempered by Renaissance Culture

We cannot ignore the idea that Palladio was an artist as well as an architect of a theatre. More recent scholars have argued from several premises: the Teatro Olimpico is the product of a combination of sources, manifested in the motive to imitate the Roman theatre according to Renaissance architectural stylistics and the humanistic goals of an academy; the Olimpico reflects a compromise of Palladio's intentions through foreign elements introduced after his death; and the Olimpico's design is best evaluated organically (on the ability of the theatre's parts to fit together as a whole, to cohere).

Antonio M. Dalla Pozza was the first twentieth century art historian to engage in an artistic analysis of the Olimpico's design sources. Dalla Pozza is critical of writers who have regarded the Olimpico "more as a scholarly curiosity than as a real problem of art," searching for a historical model in an effort to guarantee the Olimpico "a high cultural interest."[47] He disparages the previous Olimpico architectural criticism for its imbalanced attention to Vitruvius and archaeological ruins. As he points out,

> it is not hard to detect in the Olympic theatre some structural precedents and forms derived from similar monuments of antiquity, but it seems to us a needless trouble to identify in the Berga theatre or in any other Roman theatres an almost indispensible model.[48]

He admits that the basic ground plan features of the Olimpico are identifiable in Vitruvius and the archaeological remains of Roman theatres. And he accepts the probability that Palladio's concept of Virtruvius was dependent on Palladio's knowledge of the Berga theatre in Vicenza and the Barbaro edition of Vitruvius (1556). But as Dalla Pozza sees Palladio's design motives,

> the Olimpic theatre is not an erudite archaeological reexhumation but a way to revive antiquity, according to the artistic mind and dreams of the Renaissance. Palladio did not want to reconstruct an ancient theatre, but he wanted to make a theatre in the same style as the ancients. Therefore, in a broad sense, the ancient elements of plane geometry and structure were adapted for the Olimpico, but also transfigured and made according to the individual sensibility of the artist no different from what he did in any other building that he planned and that was expressed with the use of orders.[49]

Referring to the only extant Palladian design for the Olimpico, Dalla Pozza points out that this drawing, called the "London Studio" (figure 52), contains alternate solutions to the *frons-scenae* height and other differences from the executed Olimpico.[50] Dalla Pozza asserts that Palladio redesigned the London Studio, favoring the right half of the drawing. He argues that the solution represented on the left half of the drawing, with its third Corinthian order, yields a "slow rhythm which would have given too much prominence to the plastic forms inserted in the intercolumnations."[51] The right-hand solution, with its attic "occupied by a series of bas-reliefs, scanned by a series of *lesene* [pilasters], became like an area of tranquility necessary after such a crowd of ascending lines."[52] Dalla Pozza then argues that this "area of tranquility" was improved further by increasing the height of the *frons-scenae* from the dimension represented in the Studio drawing.[53] Other adjustments from the Studio drawing to finished product are indicated, each with the result of decreasing the plasticity of the elements and decreasing the degrees of reflected light intensity. For example, of the change from freestanding columns on either side of the first and second order pavilions *(aediculae)* to engaged pilasters, Dalla Pozza admits the loss of "pronounced plasticity" but sees the gain of "an exquisitely pictorial value."[54] And the columns that impost the central portal arch are freestanding in the Studio drawing and engaged pilasters in the finished theatre. Dalla Pozza reasons that the freestanding columns

> delayed the transition of tones between the luminosity of the wall masses and the deep darkness of the arcade, with the various actions of the light on the curved surfaces of the shafts of the columns.[55]

Dalla Pozza's analysis, thus far, is faulty because of his numerous untested arguments. His explanation of why Palladio apparently selected the London Studio right-hand solution is based on a mechanistic aesthetic. Yet, Dalla Pozza has not established that Palladio's architectural aesthetic was mechanistic.[56]

Dalla Pozza erroneously argues that Palladio increased the height of the *frons-scenae* from the dimension executed in the Studio. In fact, the present Olimpico *frons-scenae* height is less than in the right-hand Studio drawing. In the minor door opening of the right-hand Studio drawing, in Palladio's hand, is written "alto in tuto piedi 43 1/2." This dimension confirms the scale of the drawing. Yet, Dalla Pozza says the right-hand side measures only 40'-0" Vicentine. The height of the executed Olimpico *frons-scenae* is 41.44' Vicentine (14.38 meters). According to Dalla Pozza's mechanistic analysis, rather than the asserted increase in height improving the "area of tranquility," the actual decrease in height would damage the effect of the "area of tranquility."

He also asserts that the change from the London Studio freestanding columns to the executed engaged pilasters decreases light-play and plasticity. Admittedly he has described the results of the change, but the explanation of Palladio's motives is illogical in light of Dalla Pozza's belief that Palladio was intrigued with creating boundless space within physical limits.[57] There is no doubt that Palladio experimented with real and implied space. We can see this experimentation in Palladio's execution of the columns which serve as a screen between the choir and the altar in San Giorgio Maggiore (Venice, 1565) and Il Redentore (Venice, 1576-77). In each church a curved screen of freestanding columns, by nature of their spacing, does not allow the viewer to ascertain the actual physical limits of the choir. The effect is a choir of larger size than is really there. If Palladio were asserting his artistic individuality as the chief design motive, as Dalla Pozza suggests, then his engaging of the columns around the central portal goes against his own stylistic practice. It does not occur to Dalla Pozza to compare the Studio *frons-scenae* length (79'-0" Vicentine) with the executed *frons-scenae* length (72'-0" Vicentine), or to consider whether the shortening process was the practical cause for the engaging of the central portal columns.

Of the elliptical *cavea* and orchestra, Dalla Pozza believes the shape was not due "to the narrowness of the place" but "reflects in our opinion the conscious or unconscious desire of the architect to surmount any static position in the movement to escape the finite by suggesting the boundless."[58] Apparently what is meant is that the seats in an elliptical auditorium are not oriented to a single focal point. Implicit in the statement is an acceptance of the theory (also espoused by Kernodle) that Palladio intended real space beyond the *frons-scenae* and that the vistas would have a multiple vanishing-point radial orientation.

Dalla Pozza claimed that the Olimpico was designed as "a way to revive antiquity . . . . a theatre in the same style as the ancients." Implicit in this claim is the reference of the design to antiquity, yet Dalla Pozza has not submitted any concept of theatrical antiquity for comparison. For example, his analysis of the Olimpico *frons-scenae* is devoid of any detailed reference to a classical source such as the Roman *frons-scenae* described by Virtruvius (V.vi.6). To assert the dominance of artistic individuality in the design process, one must substantially eliminate the imitation of nonautographic elements as a source. Moreover, an analysis must account for the influence of practical limitations on that individual expression. While Dalla Pozza indicates a line of thinking that might yield an understanding of Palladio's motives, his analysis describes only the results and not the causes.

The same and other methodological problems are apparent in two largely similar works by Licisco Magagnato.[59] Magagnato begins his analysis by establishing the progressive growth of two types of theatres in sixteenth century Italy: the one, resulting from a humanistic endeavor to study the ancient Roman theatre archaeologically, was largely limited to speculations on paper, while the other was the development of practical theatre emphasizing scenic illusion and mechanical spectacle. By 1565 the Vasari theatre at the Medici court in Florence stabilized the basic structural features of the late Italian Renaissance theatre: "proscenium arch, illusionistic setting, rectangular auditorium. *And against all this Palladio reacts.*"[60] Palladio's reaction, and I assume that Magagnato sees this as a conscious reaction, is manifested in the Olimpico. Magagnato proposes a complex of motives behind the design of the Olimpico. He admits "that what was decisive for his choice of structure was his desire to erect a theatre in the Roman way."[61] But he warns,

to pursue too exclusively and insistently one or the other hypothesis on the sources of the Olimpico is to reduce Palladio to a copyist of the Terence illustrations [with reference to Kernodle] or Vitruvian reconstruction and to neglect the central motive of the work, the motive that controlled the choice and modification of whatever scheme. Here, as always, Palladio's creation is a complex one; various and subtly connected attitudes are gathered up in it, justified and harmonized in the solution of an architectural problem. The central motive is the wish to solve an architectural problem: conceptions of stage and theatre given

by tradition and education are the elements he uses. That Palladio's problem was an
architectural one concerned with the organization of internal spaces is worth emphasizing:
for this was the first time in the century that the making of a theatre had been seen in this
way. [That is, the Olimpico was built from 'scratch' rather than adapted inside an existing
structure.] Until now the problem had been one for painters and scene designers.[62]

In comparison to the Peruzzi-Serlio-Vasari type of theatre and stagecraft,
Palladio's theatre "may be viewed as an anachronistic experiment."[63] Viewed
as an attempt to solve the architectural problems inherent in the illusionistic
theatre, namely the gulf between the actor and spectator created by the
proscenium arch, Magagnato sees Palladio's reaction as an attempt to "find
an organic and unitary solution to them [actor-spectator split] in the terms
proper to his art and no other."[64] Magagnato claims to discover in his
researches "what parts in his [Palladio's design] decision were played by
respect for local usages, by desire to recreate the antique, and by his own
artistic individuality."[65] He hypothesizes three sources (the remainder of his
analysis seeks to affirm the operation of these sources on Palladio's "organic
solution" and the *frons-scenae* as "central element"):

Respect for local usage. Magagnato recites the evidence of Palladio's pre-
Olimpico theatrical designs and the Academy's production program. Because
of the Academy's production of classical and classically modelled plays and
because the evidence suggests that Palladio's earlier theatre designs used a
classical *frons-scenae,* Magagnato concludes that Palladio's motive was
archaeological humanism.

Desire to recreate the antique. Palladio's activities in archaeological
research and his participation in the Barbaro edition of Vitruvius "must have
had no small part in stimulating him to propose the construction of his various
theatres in the style of the ancient ones."[66] Yet, admitting Palladio's
knowledge of the antique, his examination of theatres in Verona, Pola, Berga,
and Rome, and his knowledge of the Peruzzi, Serlio, and Caroto studies of
antique theatres,[67] these materials were only one source for Palladio's "artistic
intuition."[68]

Artist's individuality. Therefore, the key to understanding the Olimpico's
design sources depends upon an understanding of Palladio the artist. The
design of the *frons-scenae* was problematic to Palladio since he had no model
from which to work. His temporary theatres in Vicenza (1561 and 1562) and
Venice (1565) used *frons-scenae* similar to the Olimpico. On that assumption,
Palladio's concept of a *frons-scenae* must both have predated and evolved
with these initial theatre designs; it was the product of a careful reading of
Vitruvius (V.vi.6), assimilation of the ideas of other Vitruvian commentators
and illustrators,[69] and the inventive application of the triumphal arch as a
formal analogy to the *frons-scenae.*[70] Magagnato sees the triumphal arch
motif as

an element of reference to the classical world to which he [Palladio] was sentimentally attached, but above all an architectural element that was more suitable than the scenic arch to become one of the walls of that larger inner space.[71]

Palladio's *frons-scenae* does not escape Magagnato's criticism, for he sees a decadence in Palladio's handling—"a certain over-emphasis which the three orders give the proscenium is typical of Palladio's final manner."[72]

As the "central element" which organizes the Olimpico, the *frons-scenae* links the auditorium to the scenery by acting as a sculptural screen or architectural curtain.[73] Beyond the architectural curtain Magagnato argues that Palladio had envisioned a scenic handling much like Scamozzi finally produced. He reasons that Palladio's concept of placing the classically derived *periaktoi* behind the *frons-scenae* openings, while a misinterpretation of Vitruvius' directions, was the beginning of the idea. Citing a contemporary account of Palladio's theatre for the academy production of Trissino's *Sofonisba* (1562) and the recorded academy reference to a model and perspective design done by Palladio for the Olimpico, Magagnato reasons that Palladio had conceived of some kind of three-dimensional scenery behind the *frons-scenae* openings.[74] The motive behind the scenery was classical; Magagnato believes that this arrangement of space within space was part of Palladio's late stylistic tendency toward the "scenographic stressing of the interlocking of spaces into spaces."[75] Magagnato notes the presence of such spatial arrangements in San Giorgio Maggiore and Il Redentore in Venice. In effect Scamozzi's contribution is small, although Magagnato finds the Scamozzi vistas distracting.[76]

The thrust of Magagnato's analysis is that regardless of substantive sources (e.g., Vitruvius, theatre ruins) we eventually must understand Palladio's conception in terms of his role as an artist solving a design problem. As reflected in the title of one of Magagnato's studies, "The Genesis of the *Teatro Olimpico*," he is interested in identifying and analyzing the causes of the Olimpico. Yet chiefly absent from the analysis is an awareness that the Olimpico was intended to be a functional theatre. Magagnato inadvertently admits the narrowness of his analysis when he writes, "as every real architectural work, the Olimpico was a place that was created to live in the daylight"[77] and "to us this genesis seems the model if we want to capture the spirit of Palladio's poetry."[78] Suddenly the Olimpico is a piece of daylighted sculpture and not a theatre.

Magagnato has begun with a theatrical thesis—that Palladio wished to join actor and spectator organically. But without documentation of this sensibility in Palladio's motives, the sensibility remains a product of the twentieth century, and the Olimpico remains merely an anachronistic imitation of the ancients. To suggest, in fact, that Palladio "reacts" against the

Serlio type of theatre because of its inherent actor-audience split is to misunderstand (or naively impose an assumption on) Serlio's productions with their elephant and chariot intermezzi.[79] Such a view is unsympathetic to Serlio.

Magagnato further corrupts his analysis by not fully accepting the Academy as Palladio's client. Certainly we can declare the Olimpico or even Trissino's *Sofonisba* as anachronistic from our twentieth century vantage point; but can we say that in Palladio's cultural context he built an anachronism? The details of Palladio's classical studies are not explored as a potential influence on the Olimpico's design. We cannot know that Palladio was interpreting ruins according to his own stylistics without a better picture of what Palladio's understanding of the ruins was.

Magagnato argues that the Olimpico *frons-scenae* is based on the triumphal arch.[80] Formally, he may be correct; like a triumphal arch, the *frons-scenae* is pierced with openings and decorated with celebratory sculpture. Physically, however, a triumphal arch is taller than it is wide and frequently has only one opening. Neither feature is comparable to the Olimpico. The limits of a formal analysis are obvious. If Palladio really did look to the formal triumphal arch as a source, must we conclude that Palladio's knowledge of Vitruvius' description of the Roman *frons-scenae* and classical ruins were irrelevant sources?

We are reminded that Magagnato speaks of an "organic solution" in the Olimpico. Yet we are not given a thorough analysis of the whole building, only a formal analysis of the *frons-scenae*. No aesthetic system practiced by Palladio is described nor is it ever explained how the theatre operated as an organic whole. Sources are described and influences identified, their presence in the theatre is noted, but no rationale for their presence and mixture is advanced.

Set on demonstrating the presence and predominant influence of artistic individuality, Magagnato has posited a narrow view. To fully understand the Olimpico's role in theatre history, we must do precisely what Magagnato says he sees no point in doing—"pursuing the abstract search of the sources of his creation."[81]

Two writers remain who are particularly interested in explaining the motives behind the design of the Olimpico. On the whole these writers reflect the assumptions made by Dalla Pozza and Magagnato and for that reason will be only briefly reported. Their importance lies in their stance that the Teatro Olimpico, while begun by Palladio, suffered significant design changes after his death in 1580. Their argument is that the Olimpico is an unsuccessful work of art because of the introduction of foreign elements. As with previous writers, the ideas advanced have an important bearing on a thorough understanding of the sources of the Olimpico design, yet in the end the analysis is harmed by narrow methodological assumptions.

Both Roberto Pane and Lionello Puppi[82] begin with several acceptable assumptions: the Olimpico is basically modelled after the ancient Roman theatre, the presence of Palladio's individual artistic vocabulary and aesthetic is apparent, and, until proven otherwise, the designer operated from an organic aesthetic. Both writers recite the same catechism of evidence: the research into ruins, Palladio's knowledge of Vitruvius, the Barbaro commentary, Palladio's pre-Olimpico theatrical endeavors, and the original limitations of the Olimpico property. Both regard these hypothetical sources of influence as viable considerations. There are differences too; Pane believes the Olimpico is best regarded as an imitation of the Roman theatre and allows only minor influences from the other proposed sources;[83] Puppi, more akin to Magagnato, sees the Olimpico as a mélange of influences affected by Renaissance architectural stylistics.[84] Actually the difference is subtle. To Pane, the Olimpico, as a work of antique intention, is structurally faulty—as an organism—because it satisfies neither the "classicist spirit" nor the contemporary "rationalist spirit."[85] To Puppi, the Olimpico design is a personal "restoration based, guaranteed, and determined by a conscious cultural choice in the frame of an authentic architectural scheme" rather than a "pedantic reconstruction of archaeological ruins."[86]

The Teatro Olimpico, Pane explains, has been acclaimed because it is Palladio's last work; he despises the "reverential fear"[87] of writers who will not say critical things about the building. Essentially there is a design compromise in the Olimpico: the stage and the *cavea* are two spaces and not one; the separation is caused by the "two transverse walls," and this separation is reflected "above with two different ceilings."[88] In ground plan Pane accepts the rationale advanced by Bertotti Scamozzi which shows the Vitruvian instructions operating in the Olimpico;[89] like Bertotti Scamozzi, Pane does not suggest an aesthetic system or rule which accounts for the Olimpico's unique design elements.

Regarding Vincenzo Scamozzi's scenic vistas, Pane calls them "pleasant and odd in their mannerist aspect."[90] He criticizes them for causing a visual conflict with the *frons-scenae* and for producing a "dense and whimsical succession of different episodes."[91] Here Pane is simplistic; he argues that Scamozzi's scenery is an autonomous addition,[92] and that Palladio would probably have used a system like the scenery represented in the Barbaro edition of Vitruvius. Pane does not say whether he thinks Palladio intended *periaktoi* nor does he incorporate the evidence of perspectives used in Palladio's temporary theatre for *Sofonisba* (1562). What he seems to mean is that Palladio's scenery would have been less detailed, as suggested in figure 49.

Pane's chief complaints concern the distribution of space in the theatre, the dual nature of the ceiling treatment, and the separated *cavea*-stage relationship. He blames Palladio for the poor handling of the *cavea*-stage space ratio, calling it an "enormous disproportion."[93] One wonders from what critical criteria Pane is operating. Apparently Pane is setting up an ideal against which he compares the finished product; while he recognizes Palladio's property limits,[94] the criticism implies that Palladio could have solved the problem, if indeed Palladio conceived it as a problem.

From the definition that the purpose of art (in architecture) is "to give life to a fiction,"[95] Pane postulates that Palladio's problem was to erect a Roman theatre, a meaningless fiction in the Renaissance, and give it life or meaning. Beginning with the portico which surmounts the *cavea,* he notes that its existence is anachronistic in purpose;[96] the Vitruvian portico was for protection from the rain, and the Olimpico is fully roofed. Pane argues that Palladio could not build a theatre during the Renaissance that was not covered; for functional reasons he could not do without the roof and for formal reasons he could not do without the Vitruvian portico. As an artist he had to make the "fiction" acceptable. The solution is not satisfactory (figure 56). The niches, statues, columns, and surmounted balustrade and statues of the portico are real until they reach the two transverse walls. On these wall surfaces the niches and statues are real and the other elements are painted on the surface. As the joint between the *cavea* and the stage, the painting on the transverse walls calls attention to the fiction and thus it is unacceptable.

The ceiling is another example of a poorly handled fiction. Pane seems to favor the theory that the whole theatre ceiling (*cavea* and stage) should be a *painted* representation of a stretched canvas—like the *velarium* that is said to have shaded spectators in the Roman theatre. In this manner, both the functional ceiling and the fictional open air quality are maintained. But the present ceiling treatment over the stage, in the Ducal style, calls attention to the ceiling's fictional function.

As indicated, Pane sees the transverse walls which separate the stage from the *cavea* as an alien intervention into Palladio's intentions. He believes that Palladio was not responsible for either the transverse walls or the features painted on them since Palladio would have managed to de-emphasize the fiction. Pane believes there are clues in the Olimpico which suggest how Palladio originally planned the junction of the *cavea* to the stage. He argues that the portico should have grown into the face of the stage wing (*versurae*) without the transverse walls.[97] He cites as further evidence that the roof joists run perpendicularly to the stage front and thus the transverse walls are not relevant to the roof's statics (figure 3).

Pane's speculation makes some sense. There are problems however; the *versurae* second order cornice does not align with the portico cornice and the real columns, statues and balustrade would have to be engaged to the wall surface which joins the portico to the *versurae*. In other words, there would still be a transverse wall; it would just not thrust out from the *versurae* surface (figure 44). The existence of the transverse walls is, to Pane, "the merely intellectualistic intention to separate the two images [*cavea* and stage];"[98] the walls are the intervention of a "rationalistic spirit." Implicit in Pane's argument is that the classical spirit of modelling the Roman theatre lost out to motives which attempted to frame the stage of the Olimpico in the manner of contemporary developments in theatre architecture. Curiously, Pane declines to say whether the "rationalistic spirit" was Palladio's or that of another designer involved in the construction after Palladio's death.[99] If Pane's theory is correct, some attempt must be made to ascertain responsibility. Only then can we legitimately talk about the Olimpico as Palladio's theatre or another's.

Pane equivocates on the responsibility for the perceived spatial disorientation of the *cavea*-stage relationship. Lionello Puppi lays the responsibility squarely on the persons responsible for the completion of the theatre after Palladio's death. The Teatro Olimpico, as it appeared for the inaugural production of *Edippo* in 1585, was not built according to Palladio's design.[100] Asserting an organic aesthetic, Puppi argues that Palladio would have better united the elements of the theatre. He cites the two elements of the *frons-scenae* colonnade and the portico above the *cavea* as evidence of the unitary failure. Each element has the potential for creating a rhythm of real openings, false spaces, and column shafts along their surface. But the changes from the Studio *frons-scenae* to the finished theatre destroyed any rhythm of real and false space there. And the *engaged* columns and niches substantially destroyed any rhythm in the portico. If the rhythm had been maintained, the *cavea* would have been better unified with the *frons-scenae*. The unity is further destroyed by the painted portico on the transverse walls which join the *cavea* to the stage. Clearly, according to Puppi, a "foreign mind" is present and that "foreign mind" did not understand Palladio's initial conception.

The "most violent" disruption that "compromises" the goal and unity "is present in the relief that the perspectives obtained."[101] The vistas, because they diverge from the optical axis, tend to unsettle the appearance of the whole building rather than unify it. Palladio would not have left such a plan; the blame is certainly Scamozzi and Angelo Ingegneri's.[102] They enlarged the size of the minor *frons-scenae* openings (*hospitalia*), they used a curtain at the forward edge of the stage for the *Edippo* production, and they used the jutting piers of the transverse walls as proscenium-like tormentors.[103]

Puppi's concept of an intervening "foreign mind" raises some intriguing points. The Olimpico, in the form it was finished, is anti-humanist in the sense that Scamozzi and Ingegneri were trying to adapt an impractical Roman model to the production requirements of the times by executing a primitive proscenium arch. Palladio, as theatre architect, initially designed an unsatisfactory anachronism in terms of current production demands. If Puppi is correct, we need to begin thinking about the Olimpico as a design compromise; in effect there is Palladio's theatre, and there is the theatre completed by others. However, to confirm Puppi's position these design features must be shown as foreign to Palladio's apparent design motives.

Puppi operates on an organic assumption, as did Palladio. However, Puppi is obliged to establish that aesthetic as Palladian and demonstrate in other Palladio works the practical operation of spatial linking of structural elements. The analysis of the portico treatment so essential to Puppi's argument is also lacking. No mention is made of the property limits' effect on the Olimpico design, specifically with regard to the less than ideal treatment of the Olimpico portico. Puppi has asserted the presence of a "foreign mind" on the assumption that had Palladio lived, he would have had another solution for the portico. Yet, there is evidence to suggest that each so-called design compromise was Palladian and practically motivated.

Puppi's importance lies not only in the questions his theory raises but in his convincing argument which links Scamozzi to the design of the Olimpico scenery. His major opponent is Zorzi;[104] the details of this controversy will be covered in chapter 4.[105]

Many questions have been raised and many criticisms have been made in this lengthy review of the literature concerned with describing and analyzing the motives behind the Olimpico design. For the most part, the descriptive half of the existing research has been found to be perceptive by virtue of its collective identification of the most probable sources of influence on the design of the Olimpico: Vitruvian theatre construction canon, Roman theatre archaeology, the Olimpic Academy as architect's client, compromising practical limitations, Palladio's pre-Olimpico theatrical occupations, the theatrical practice of the times, and Palladio's stylistics and aesthetics. However, in spite of the intentions of the previous research to advance a rationale for the Olimpico's design sources and motives, no explanation exists which has established sufficient cause for the Olimpico as a whole.

The preceding review provokes several essential questions that should be answered in the course of this design source analysis; either implicitly or explicitly most of the previous studies have attempted to address some of these questions.

1. How accurately does the Teatro Olimpico conform to Vitruvius' prescriptive description of a Roman theatre? What was Palladio's apparent attitude toward strict allegiance to Vitruvius?

2. What influences can be observed in the Olimpico from Palladio's study of Roman theatre archaeology? Did Palladio, as an architect, discriminate between Vitruvius and archaeology?

3. Is there a retrievable explanation for some of the Olimpico's unique features? For example, is a rationale available for the semielliptical *cavea* and orchestra?

4. What were the effects of compromising practical limitations on the theatre's design? Was Palladio in control of the practicalities or did they control him?
5. Besides practical compromises, were there any design motive compromises? For example, was the Olimpico's scenic illusionism a design compromise or was it an organic part of the design? If there were design compromises, did Palladio or a "foreign mind" initiate them? Can non-Palladian features be identified in the executed Olimpico? Did Scamozzi and Ingegneri introduce design adjustments so that the theatre would be more functional, as one critic has suggested? Can we say that the so-called *cavea*-stage spatial "disproportion" was really a considered design problem?
6. What features in the Olimpico are stylistically Palladian? What is the nature of Palladio's organic aesthetic? How are stylistics and aesthetics measured and compared?

Evidence

Because of the importance of some of the primary documents relevant to the Olimpico, a short section will be devoted here to their inherent problems.

Six quadrangular achromatic frescos or "grisaille" are often cited as sources confirming the nature of Palladio's pre-Olimpico theatre designs and as sources illustrating the theatrical use of the Olimpico. These frescos are found along the ceiling cornice in the Olimpico atrium and were executed in about 1596 by an unknown artist. The six frescos (figures 4 through 9) represent the following:

1. The Olympic games stadium; part of the Olimpic Academy motto is inscribed—*Hoc Opus* [*Hic Labor Est*].
2. The academy production of Alessandro Piccolomini's *Amor cost[ante]* in 1561 in the Vicenza Basilica. The theatre was designed by Palladio. The date on the fresco is in error (M.D.LII) since the academy was not founded until 1555 and *Amor costante* was not produced until 1561. Hilron [Hieronymus] Scl[edo] is noted as being the *pr[incipe]* or president of the academy at the time.
3. The academy production of Gian Giorgio Trissino's *Sofonisba* in 1562 in the Vicenza Basilica. The theatre was designed by Palladio. The *pr[incipe]* was Valerio [Ch]ier[icato] V.F.
4. The academy production of Orsato Giustiniani's translation of *Edip[p]o* in 1584 [sic; old dating system, 1585] in the Teatro Olimpico. The *pr[incipe]* was Leo[nardo] Valm[arana].

5. The academy reception of the Japanese envoys, Iaponensivm Legatis, in the Olimpico, 1585. The pr[*incipe*] was Ang[elo] Calid[ogno].
6. The academy *torneo* (joust) in 1588. The pr[*incipe*] was Io[vanni] Bapt[ista] Ghel[lini].[105]

The authority of these frescos as accurate representations of the events depicted has not been questioned by some writers. Magagnato writes, "We can safely assume that it [the *Sofonisba* fresco] was based on some record contemporary with the performance."[106]If the contemporary account was that by Chiapin, as recorded in fragmentary form in Zigiotti,[107] the artist has been imaginative. Dalla Pozza accepts the frescos, arguing that they could not be the product of the artist's imagination since the academy "wanted to have these episodes painted to keep their remembrance through history; and the absence of any reference to reality would have been offensive."[108] Puppi, because of inconsistencies with the Chiapin report, says he cannot trust the frescos,[109] yet he uses them as unquestioned evidence in a later part of his work.[110] To illustrate the frescos' problems as authoritative evidence, compare the *L'Amor costante* and *Sofonisba frons-scenae*. While the entablature over the paired first order columns of the *L'Amor costante frons-scenae* juts out over each capital, the entablature on the *Sofonisba frons-scenae* juts out over each pair of capitals. Note, too, that the *Sofonisba* arch is confined within the first order while the *L'Amor costante* arch breaks into the second order. One would assume that we have illustrated here two different *frons-scenae*. Yet Magagnato and Puppi believe that the theatre used for the *L'Amor costante* was the same one used for the *Sofonisba*. Puppi believes that only the scenery was changed since *L'Amor costante* was a pastoral and *Sofonisba* was a tragedy.[111] Magrini argues that the basilica hall was too often used for city affairs to be monopolized by a temporary theatre for over a year. He thinks the *L'Amor costante* theatre was taken down and a new one erected for *Sofonisba*.[112] If the *L'Amor costante* used a classical *frons-scenae,* as all sources seem to indicate or believe, then why is only one opening apparent in the illustrated *frons-scenae*? Inconsistencies appear in the *Edippo* and "Japanese" frescos, too. The *versurae* or right-angled wall abutting the *frons-scenae* is shown to have a column between the niche and the door opening. No such column exists. In the "Japanese" fresco the orchestra area abuts precisely to the transverse wall. As is apparent in figure 49, the *cavea* overlaps the transverse wall. We are reminded of the above imprecision in the representation of the Olimpico in view of Dalla Pozza's claim that the artist would not have invented his representations. And yet these inconsistencies and others (for example, the *torneo frons-scenae* shows angled pediments over the *frons-scenae* niches when in reality the pediments alternate—angled and segmented) bring into question the artist's accuracy, especially since the Olimpico frescos are less than 100 feet from the real thing.

The frescos are not a useful source of independent evidence. The frescos important to this study, the *L'Amor costante* and the *Sofonisba,* require corroborating evidence before they can be used. The *L'Amor costante* has no corroborating evidence and the *Sofonisba* fresco may be based on the Chiapin description rather than be independent of the report.

Mention has already been made of the Chiapin description and its consistent use as corroborating evidence for the *Sofonisba* production. What writers do not warn the reader, except to admit that the document is fragmentary, is that it is found in an eighteenth century manuscript which is essentially a copy of sixteenth century academy records. Zigiotti, an academy secretary who died in 1763,[113] compiled the manuscript. As Zigiotti notes, this manuscript is the "most authentic *summary*" of the academy's activities in the sixteenth and early seventeenth centuries.[114] It has been derived from original academy minutes, deliberations of the academy council, and secretary's reports of events. In addition, the first part of the manuscript is not only an abstract of the academy's activities from 1555 to 1600, but is supplemented with accounts by various authors, not necessarily contemporary to the events. The manuscript includes the following sections:

1. Pages 1-78: Compilation of activities from 1555 to 1600 derived from the MSS "A," "D," "E" (marked "A"), "F," and "G" of the academy minutes. These entries are paraphrases and abstracts and include eighteenth century interpolations. Many of the entries are from non-academy sources—for example, Vicenza historians of the sixteenth through eighteenth centuries. There are marginal notations that cite the academy minute MS and page numbers.

2. Pages 78-80, 87-93, 133-35, 137-40, 199-200: Lists of academy members, officers, visitors, productions, and lectures drawn from the academy minutes and other sources.

3. Pages 81-88: Academy minutes from 1600-1642 abstracted from MSS "A," "E," "G," and "I."

4. Pages 101-31: Constitutional "statuti" of the academy including original constitution and subsequent resolutions and decisions, 1555-69. Number voting pro and con is recorded.

5. Pages 148a-64: academy transactions form 1579-82 especially concerning the Teatro. Copy of Zigiotti is drawn from Libro "D," once possessed by Pietro Castelli; Libro "D" was drawn from the Vigna MS entitled *Documenti antichi spettanti a Vicenza.* The Zigiotti copy does not represent the whole of Libro "D."

6. Pages 164-81: Academy transactions from 1582-86 especially concerning the Teatro. Libro "E," erroneously marked "A," is drawn from the Vigna MS. The whole of Libro "E" is not reproduced.
7. Pages 181-87, 189: Academy transactions from 1591-96. Libro "F" is not wholly reproduced.
8. Pages 193-97: Academy transactions from 1596-1600. Libro "G" is not wholly reproduced.
9. Pages 6, 94-100, 132, 136, 141-48, 188, 190-92, and 198 are blank.

The manuscript does not represent all of the activities or minutes of the academy; Zigiotti admits his selection was based on those activities which "give the most dignity and representation to the academy."[115] The manuscript is biased both by commission and by omission.

The Zigiotti manuscript is extremely important especially since the original MSS are no longer available and it remains the only extant record of the bulk of the academy's early existence. Yet the contents are potentially misleading or erroneous because of the cuts made, the selectivity of Zigiotti, the number of removes from the original, and expected copying errors. For example, the present Zigiotti MS was copied from the original in 1826 by Academician Leonardo Trissino.

As far as accuracy of reporting is concerned there are some tests. Published works contemporary to the events do corroborate the dating of the event and some details, although Zigiotti is generally more specific. Some transactions, because they involved the Vicenza City Council, are corroborated by the city archives; we must remember, however, that such corroboration only complements the Zigiotti and does not necessarily reflect an equal image of the same event. My use of the Zigiotti manuscript has been limited to only those entries that can be corroborated in contemporary archives and publications or are marginally noted in the manuscript to refer to original academy records (e.g., Books "A," "D," "E," "F," "G," and "I"). Interpolations by Zigiotti are identifiable by the pronoun person used. On the whole the manuscript's contents are quite accurate.

While not always primary documents, the iconographic history of the Olimpico is due a word. Mention has already been made of the London Studio. There are two early seventeenth century elevations of the *frons-scenae* (figures 54 and 55). With the exception of these drawings and the atrium frescos, there are no other contemporary illustrations. Until the publication of Montenari's work (1733), no ground plan of the theatre was available. Bertotti Scamozzi's publication in 1796 supplied us with considerably more accurate plans of the Olimpico, although even they have inaccuracies. Compare, for example, the ground plan (figure 44) with his section (figure 3) which represents a *cavea* with fifteen seating levels and not the executed thirteen. A minor part of this study is concerned with the evaluation of the extant iconography and the recording of an accurate survey of the theatre. Since the publications of Montenari and Bertotti Scamozzi, their drawings have been republished regularly and with complete faith.

Methodology

In 1959 Giangiorgio Zorzi's *I disegni delle antichità di Andrea Palladio*[116] made available a descriptive catalogue with reproductions of the majority of Palladio's autographic drawings of Latin antiquities. These drawings are mainly held by the Royal Institute of British Architects (London), although Zorzi has also reproduced drawings held by the Vicenza Civic Museum, the Bertoliana Library (Vicenza), and the Uffizi (Florence). The availability of these drawings affords a more thorough analysis of Palladio as humanist-archaeologist; inferences are now possible about his classical learning, his methods of examination and reconstruction, and his precision in those reconstructions. One wonders, for example, how much of the reconstructions were sheer Palladian invention.

In any causal analysis, the assumption is that a direct positive or negative influence can be demonstrated from one event to another. To test such hypothetical sources as Vitruvian interpretation and archaeological knowledge, a system of comparative overlays must be used. Basic to the use of a comparative overlay method is the awareness that we must discriminate between what the Italian Renaissance and Palladio perceived as fact as opposed to what modern archaeology perceives as fact. Only then can we talk with some awareness about the concepts of antiquity held by Palladio and his contemporaries. This is not to say that modern archaeological results will be ignored; they serve the useful purpose of supplying tests for humanist accuracy and bias, on the assumption that modern methods are more objective and scientific.

The other publication, Rudolf Wittkower's *Architectural Principles,* first appeared in 1949 and was substantially revised by Wittkower in 1962.[117] While the book's chief purpose is to illuminate Italian Renaissance architectural principles, of importance to this study is Wittkower's selection of Alberti and Palladio as the most consistent theorists and practitioners of these principles. The importance of Wittkower's book is that it persuasively establishes a Renaissance architectural aesthetic from the writings of Renaissance architectural theorists and from their practice. To quote Wittkower,

> The conviction that architecture is a science and that each part of a building, inside as well as outside, has to be integrated into one and the same system of mathematical ratios, may be called the basic axiom of Renaissance architects.[118]

The integration to which he refers is the operation of an organic aesthetic, the principle by which a building and all its parts (including decoration) were mathematically organized. At the base of this mathematical organization was a system of architectural aesthetics that was founded in Platonic metaphysics,[119] Pythagorean mathematics, and musical harmony. Out of these philosophies grew the proportional harmony of quantities. Wittkower thinks "it is not going too far to regard commensurability of measure as the nodal point of Renaissance aesthetics."[120] With Wittkower's publication, Renaissance architectural criticism gains new insights. No longer is mechanistic and impressionistic criticism satisfactory. While art critics have assumed the presence of organic principles in Renaissance architecture, they have not, in any detailed sense, demonstrated the presence in the Olimpico or in other Palladian practice. Wittkower's *Principles* now allows such an analysis.

2

Palladio's Archaeological and Architectural Learning

Andrea Palladio was born in 1508 at the peak of the Renaissance. Although geographically far removed from the center of humanism in Rome and its resultant art and architecture,[1] Palladio's architectural practice in Vicenza was at first strongly influenced by the classical architecture of Rome. Gradually he broke away from Roman classicism, not by an explicit disavowal of classical vocabulary but by the application of a functional and decorative theory and style that was consciously adapted to the public, ecclesiastical, and domestic architectural needs of Vicenza specifically and the Veneto generally; he executed forty-four separate architectural works.

This chapter will examine Palladio's architectural education and experience, theory and practice, in search of the foundations for Palladio's design of the Teatro Olimpico. Of necessity the discussion and analysis will be limited to the education and experience that is potentially related to his 1579-80 design of the Olimpico. My purpose is not to narrate an architectural career; it is to explore the potential influences on Palladio's final architectural design.

There are two distinct facets of Palladio's career which appear to have served as source material for his design of the Olimpico. The first part of this chapter will examine Palladio's study of Vitruvius and ancient ruins with specific reference to the ancient Roman theatre. The second part will examine Palladio as an architectural theorist and practitioner. The aim will be to outline Palladio's aesthetic and stylistic development insofar as they might potentially affect the application of his knowledge of the ancient Roman theatre to the Olimpico.

Palladio, or Andrea di Pietro, was born in Padua on November 30, 1508, the son of Pietro della Gondola.[2] Of the period between his birth and his association in 1537 with Gian Giorgio Trissino we know very little. Summarizing his early life, Ackerman says that Palladio

was apprenticed at thirteen to a stonecarver in Padua, but in 1524 he broke his contract, fled to nearby Vicenza and settled there. For the next fourteen years he worked as an apprentice and assistant to the carvers Giovanni and Girolamo called da Pedemuro, who did most of

Vicenza's monuments and decorative sculpture of this period in an up to date style derived from the architecture of Michele Sanmichele of Verona. At thirty, Andrea must have been the presumptive heir to this modest enterprise, when he had the good luck to be called to the outskirts of town to work on a new loggia and other additions that the Count Giangiorgio Trissino had designed for his Villa Cricoli. This loggia was the first actual building in Vicenza composed in the classical style of the Roman Renaissance.[3]

The work at Cricoli was a turning point in Palladio's life. Trissino's patronage of Palladio, who was not an aristocrat, allowed his participation in the activities of the Trissino Academy at Cricoli.[4] Since Palladio was nearly thirty years old and without extensive formal education, Ackerman speculates that Trissino recognized the limitation of trying to turn Palladio into a well-rounded humanist but saw advantages in developing his mathematical and architectural talents into an Academy specialty.[5] It was Trissino who bestowed the name of Palladio on him in tribute to Pallas Athena, goddess of wisdom. At Cricoli, Palladio advanced from stonemason to trainee in architecture. Here he probably read his first Vitruvius; Trissino, among his other endeavors, left a fragment of a book on architecture, *Dell'architettura* (ca. 1537-38), in which he noted that "Vitruvius is very badly understood" ("Vitruvio e malissimo inteso").[6] In the same fragments, Trissino demonstrated a knowledge of the *De re aedificatoria* of Leone Baptista Alberti.

Trissino was absent from Cricoli between 1538-40 and made his temporary residence in Padua near his friend Alvise Cornaro. Palladio's visits with Trissino in Padua, his birthplace, must have introduced him to another viewpoint toward architecture which was opposed to Trissino's strict classicism and allegiance to Vitruvius. Cornaro, really only an amateur architect, challenged Palladio with the need to build efficient practical housing. He argued that Vitruvius and his classical models least of all allowed simple functional solutions.[7] Besides the Cornaro functionalism, Palladio was influenced by the classicism of Jacop Sansovino and Sebastiano Serlio.[8] In 1536 and 1539, respectively, these architects were brought to Vicenza to suggest solutions for saving the then crumbling Civic Basilica (Palazzo della Ragione). Sansovino and Serlio's projected solutions were rejected by the city fathers (along with solutions by Sanmichele and Giulio Romano in ca. 1541), and in 1545 Palladio's solution was accepted. His solution has a striking similarity to Sansovino's Library of San Marco (Venice, 1536) and Serlio's double ordered and arcaded palace design published in his *Fourth Book* in 1537.[9] The basilica, while certainly not the first of Palladio's designs, was at least the most public and, perhaps, the most impressive of the time.[10] Before construction began on the basilica in 1549, Palladio was engaged in the design of seven villas to the north and south of Vicenza and the Casa Civena and Palazzo Thiene in Vicenza.[11]

Before his first trip to Rome in 1541, Palladio's experiences of architecture in the Roman Renaissance manner were limited. The Trissino Villa at Cricoli, the Loggia Cornaro in Padua, and the Sansovino Library in Venice represent the only buildings in this style in the Veneto. Serlio's *Fourth Book* (1537) and *Third Book* (1540)[12] must have left their impression on Palladio with their representations of classical orders and measured ancient buildings. His education started with Vitruvius through the narrow-visioned Trissino presentation; his vocabulary was strictly Vitruvian.

Palladio's Italian travels yielded his first experiences with ancient ruins, particularly Roman theatres. Those experiences were culminated in the publication of Daniel Barbaro's translation and commentary on Vitruvius in 1556;[13] Palladio was instrumental in the interpretation and illustration of the text, particularly with regard to the ancient theatre. Palladio came to understand Vitruvius not through Trissino, but through Barbaro and his Italian excursions.

Depending on whether we accept the contemporary biography by Gualdo, we can document either four or five trips by Palladio to Rome. His first three certain trips were with Trissino: summer 1541,[14] September 1545 to February 1546,[15] and May through July 1547.[16] During the 1545-46 trip, Palladio and Trissino used the Adriatic route,[17] travelling along the eastern coast of Italy through such cities as Ravenna, Rimini, and Ancona. To get from Vicenza to Ravenna, they would have passed through Padua, Ferrara, and, conceivably, Bologna. As evidenced by his drawings of antiquities, we know that Palladio's route from Ancona to Rome included Gubbio, Assisi, Trevi, and Spoleto.[18] While in Rome in 1547 Palladio visited antiquities in Tivoli, Palestrina, Porto (di Ostia), and Albano.[19] In November and December 1549, Gualdo says that Palladio was in Rome consulting on the construction of St. Peters. Palladio's arrival was ill-timed since Pope Paul III (1534-49) died on November 10 and work on St. Peters was discontinued.[20] If Palladio were in Rome in 1549 he certainly had occasion to work with Michelangelo, though aside from Gualdo we have no supporting documents for this. Palladio's final recorded trip to Rome was in 1554, at which time he published his *L'antichità di Roma.*[21] This tiny guidebook described Roman ruins and their history; it replaced the much outdated *Mirabilia Urbis Romae.*[22]

The fruits of Palladio's travels were numerous.[23] In each city he carefully copied and measured countless ancient ruins. In the preface to his *Quattro libri* (1570), Palladio spoke of his intention to publish his "books of antiquity."[24] While Palladio's "books" never appeared, the majority of his measured drawings made their way to England (many probably given to Inigo Jones by Scamozzi, 1614-15).[25] Lord Burlington built upon this collection in the early eighteenth century and published those drawings related to the

Roman baths *(thermae)* in his *Fabbriche antichi disegnate da Andrea Palladio* in 1730.[26] Palladio used some of his own drawings in the *Fourth Book* of the *Quattro libri* on ancient Roman temples,[27] and the *Quattro libri* reproduced (with some changes) a design of the ancient basilica at Fano that had originally appeared in Barbaro's Vitruvius.[28] With the publication of Barbaro's edition of Vitruvius, many of the vagaries of previous editions were removed. Barbaro and Palladio's work was enlightened by careful analysis of Vitruvius and a fund of knowledge about ancient ruins. The 1556 edition yields, above all, an extremely perceptive concept of the ancient Roman theatre.

The Ancient Roman Theatre

Palladio's first readings of Vitruvius in 1537-38 at Cricoli were no doubt tempered by the edition Trissino had available.[29] Palladio probably read from one of the early sixteenth century editions whose foundations were in the first illustrated Latin edition by Fra Jocondus (Venice, 1511) or in the first illustrated Italian edition by Cesariano (Como, 1521).[30] In any case Palladio's readings were no doubt affected by the interpretive illustrations in the editions. Without the illustrations, Palladio's understanding of Vitruvius would have suffered from the text's notable ambiguity. Before Palladio's first trip to Rome in 1541, his only experience with a Roman theatre ruin was the Berga theatre in Vicenza which had suffered considerable deterioration. Figure 10 illustrates that theatre in the only nearly contemporary extant drawing (1590).

To speculate on Palladio's concept of the Roman theatre in 1538-40 would be fruitless because we do not know what edition or editions of Vitruvius Palladio had read. Nor do we know whether Palladio had studied Alberti that early. Alberti's book VIII, chapter vii, contains a lengthy description of the Roman theatre which is in many ways comparable in ambiguity to Vitruvius.[31] To discover Palladio's concept of the ancient theatre we must first examine what is essentially Palladio's final theoretical statement on the nature of the Roman theatre.[32] Only after examining the features of that statement in Barbaro's edition of Vitruvius can we begin to speculate on the published and archaeological sources that informed Palladio's perceptions.

Barbaro's edition in 1556 contained the most faithful translation[33] and informed commentaries of the times. Palladio's contribution to the edition is appreciatively confirmed by Barbaro.

For the designs of important illustrations I used the works of Messer Andrea Palladio, architect of Vicenza, who of all those whom I have known personally or by hearsay, has according to the judgement of excellent men best understood the true architecture, having not only grasped its beautiful and subtle principles, but also practiced it, whether in his most delicate and exquisite drawings of plans, elevations and sections, or in the execution and erection of many and superb buildings both in his own country and elsewhere; works which vie with the ancients, enlighten his contemporaries, and will arouse the admiration of those who come after us. And with regard to Vitruvius, the building of Theatres, Temples, Basilicas, and those things which have the most beautiful and most hidden reasons for their proportions have all been explained and interpreted by him, with ready skill of mind and hand; it is he who has selected the most beautiful styles of the ancients from all over Italy and has made measurements of all their works in existence.[34]

Book V of Vitruvius is concerned with public utilitarian buildings. Of its twelve chapters, seven are devoted to theatre construction and related subjects. Of particular importance to this study are those Barbaro-Palladio interpretations of Vitruvius which serve as pointers to Palladio's use of Vitruvius as a design source. Beyond that function, an understanding of Palladio's concept of a Vitruvian Roman theatre will better inform our understanding of Palladio's archaeological perceptions. Thus Palladio's probable discriminations between the two sources can be identified.

Book V, chapter vi, begins with one of the most vexing of Vitruvius' statements. The interpretation of this section determines the features of a major portion of the Roman theatre—the depth of the stage and its relationship to the *cavea* in terms of both juxtaposed widths and depth. In English the section reads:

> The plan of the theatre itself is to be constructed as follows. Having fixed upon the principal center, draw a line of circumference equivalent to what is to be the perimeter at the bottom, and in it inscribe four equilateral triangles at equal distances apart and touching the boundary line of the circle.[35]

Barbaro's probable Latin source reads:

> Ipsius autem theatri conformatio sic est facie[n]da, uti quam magna futura est perimetrosimi, centro medio collocato circumagatur linea rotundationis, in eaq[ue]; qua Huor scribantur trigona paribus lateribus intervallis qual extremam lineam circinationis, tangant.[36]

The problematic phrase is "uti quam magna futura est perimetrosimi, centro medio collocato circumagatur linea rotundationis." Standing alone, the second part means that a line (circle) is circumscribed around a middle center *(centro medio). Centro medio* can also mean a radius center, but the interpretation is not changed by this alternative. The first part of the section refers to the size of the "perimetros" and implies that this size is determined by whatever dimensions the builder elects to use. Put together, the parts of the passage mean that a circle is circumscribed about a given area of flexible size.

The question remains, is the "linea rotundationis" the circle of the orchestra or the circle of the whole theatre? The modern interpretation, since the Perrault (1673) editions,[37] has been to inscribe the equilateral triangles in the circle of the orchestra. We can see this stance operating in the English translation quoted above by Morgan's words "perimeter at the bottom." The Granger edition is even so bold as to interpolate "orchestra" into the translation.[38] The modern interpretation is probably correct on two counts. First, extant Roman ruins favor this interpretation and, second, Vitruvius uses the twelve points of the four equilateral triangles to indicate the placement of certain features in the theatre (V.vi.3; "eqi dirigant ascensus scalasque"). If the triangles were inscribed in the outer circle, seven of the points would extend beyond the location of the feature they were supposed to designate.

Barbaro saw it differently. He inscribed the triangles in a circle that encompassed the whole of the theatre structure. The resultant theatre, as illustrated in Barbaro and drawn by Palladio (figure 47) yields certain unique features. Given that the front *(proscaenii)* of the stage (It. *pulpito,* Lat. *pulpitum*) passes through the center of the orchestra, the triangle face parallel to the "scena" locates the front of the *scenae* (It. *fatta la fronte della scena,* Lat. *ibi finiatur scenae frons*), and the *frons-scenae* length is twice the diameter of the orchestra (the orchestra diameter is used as a modular measure throughout chapter vi).[39] Barbaro's Roman theatre plan takes on the following modular dimensions: orchestra diameter = 1d.; *frons-scenae* length = 2d.; *cavea* radius = 1d.; stage depth = 1/2d. In the modern interpretation, the triangle inscription in the orchestra circle yields a stage depth of 1/4d. and a *cavea* radius of ca. 1 1/2d.

To compare the two interpretations (figures 11 and 12), Barbaro has executed a stage depth which is twice what Vitruvius meant it to be. Furthermore, because the orchestra diameter and *frons-scenae* length are fixed by Vitruvius, Barbaro's *cavea* fully confronts the stage length, yielding an awkward relationship between the ends of the stage and the extreme right and left levels of the *cavea.*

Barbaro's initial error is compounded when he interprets the arrangement of the stage (V.vi.3). Referring to the twelve triangle points or angles Vitruvius writes:

The angles at the bottom, which give the directions for the flights of steps, will be seven in number; the other five angles will determine the arrangement of the scene: thus, the angle in the middle ought to have the "royal door" opposite it; the angles to the right and left will designate the position of the doors for guest chambers; and the two outermost angles will point to the passages in the wings.[40]

Because the Barbaro stage fully fronts the whole of the *cavea* and because the triangle points extend beyond the plane of the *frons-scenae,* Barbaro's location of the royal door *(valva regias)*, the guest chambers *(hospitalia)*, and the wing passages *(versurae)* is only approximate. All five points of designation are placed along the *frons-scenae* plane, whereas Vitruvius implies that the *versurae* are directions to the right and left of the *frons-scenae* plane and are at right angles to that plane. Barbaro's translation recognizes the right-angle aspect of the *versurae:* "the final two designate the way where they turn," ("gli ultimi due reguarderanno le vie dove si volta").[41] But since the right-angle surface is also the exterior wall of the theatre, Barbaro has no place to locate the *versurae* except on the *frons-scenae* plane. In the Barbaro commentary that follows this passage, he admits that Vitruvius is unclear about where the *versurae* are to be located. (Vitruvius never refers to *versurae* as a door or opening, only as a direction; reconstructions of ruins have led us to believe that the *versurae* were structural surfaces, at right angles to the *frons-scenae*, pierced by openings).[42] Barbaro's plan yields all five features on the surface of the *frons-scenae;* the wall joining the *frons-scenae* plane to the *cavea* plane is not decorated with columnation (figures 49 and 51).[43]

Barbaro's next interpretive problem involves the physical relationship of the orchestra to the beginning of the *cavea* at its extreme right and left lower points (next to the stage front). At these points vaulted entrances were to be cut through the *cavea* allowing entrance into the orchestra area (V.vi.5). These entrances are derivative of the Greek *paradoi.* Vitruvius instructs that the height of the vault should be one-sixth of the orchestra diameter. Thus, at each side entrance, the *cavea* would be elevated over the entrance by one-sixth of the orchestra diameter (1/6d.). Barbaro interprets this passage to mean that the whole of the *cavea* is elevated above the orchestra by one-sixth the orchestra's diameter (figure 13). He does not even translate the section that involves the vaulted passages produced by the cut-back process.[44] Barbaro was influenced by Alberti in this interpretation, as acknowledged in his subsequent commentary; he does deviate from Alberti's instructions that the *cavea* should be raised above the orchestra level by one-ninth of the orchestra diameter in large theatres and no less than seven feet in small theatres. Alberti does not discuss the vaulted orchestra entrances.[45] We get further indication of Barbaro's confusion on the erection of the orchestra entrances when he glosses over the Vitruvius reference to *tribunali* (V.vi.7); the *tribunali* were elevated viewing positions for government officials and were located over the orchestra entrances.[46] Palladio's conception of the *cavea* exterior is illustrated in figure 14.

In the Renaissance one of the most difficult Vitruvian passages was the interpretation of the *periaktoi* placement. A *periaktos,* by Vitruvius' description, was a revolving machine used for revealing one of three surfaces; the surfaces were decorated with the three types of generic scenery. Vitruvius says, the doors on the right and left are for strangers *(hospitalia)*. Next on either side *(secundum autem spatia)* are the spaces prepared for scenery. These are called *periaktoi* in Greek (revolving wings).[47]

Barbaro's translation of *secundum* (literally "after") put the *periaktoi* "behind" rather than "beyond" or to the left and right of the *hospitalia*.[48] The result (figures 45 and 47) is the location of scenic surfaces behind the *frons-scenae* openings.[49] It is curious that Barbaro has substantially eliminated the three major *frons-scenae* openings as functional entrances.[50]

One of the clearest of Vitruvius' passages is that describing the nature of the *frons-scenae*. Barbaro's translation of the section does not deviate from the original and his commentary is mostly redundant. I quote the passage only because it relates to the tabular summary that follows (figure 45).

The height of the pedestal of the back wall above the level of the stage, along with the cornice and moulding, is to be one twelfth of the diameter of the orchestra. Above the pedestal, the columns with capitals and bases are to be of a height equal to one quarter of the diameter; the architrave and ornaments, one fifth part of their height. The parapet above, with its base and cornice, is to be one half of the lower parapet (or pedestal). Above the parapet are to be columns one fourth less in height than the lower ones; the architrave and ornaments a fifth of those columns. If there is to be a third order, the top parapet is to be half of the middle one. The top columns are to be one quarter less in height than the middle; the architraves with the cornices are also to have one fifth of the height of those columns.[51]

According to the passage, the *frons-scenae* is a two or three ordered surface of classical vocabulary. Vitruvius does not detail the type of column or the nature of the intercolumnation, and he gives no impression that the *frons-scenae* is anything but rectilinear. Yet we see in the Palladio drawings a curvilinear surface. Barbaro comments on the niched openings on the *frons-scenae* surface (figures 45 and 47).[52] As Barbaro acknowledges, this feature of the *frons-scenae* was derived from the Berga theatre ruin in Vicenza which Palladio and he examined.[53]

Chapter vi is completed with a brief description of the three types of generic scenery[54] and Vitruvius' classic disclaimer about the architect's right to diverge from the rules he has set down. Vitruvius is clear that while some features do not change in size according to the size of the theatre (e.g., seat dimensions) and others are flexible in size and proportion according to the modular system, the architect still has the right, within taste, to make changes due to practicalities and material limitations.[55] Palladio will apply this disclaimer in the Olimpico design.

One last aspect of the Barbaro-Vitruvius serves to illustrate the need to discriminate in a study of the Olimpico's design sources between Barbaro's Vitruvius and Palladio's archaeological learning. Barbaro, in the absence of an archaeological ruin, unwittingly misrepresents the Greek theatre (V.vii.1-

2). The Greek theatre's stage and orchestra are different from the Roman stage and orchestra in physical nature. Generated from three squares inscribed in the orchestra circle (recall Barbaro's misinterpretation on the matter of triangle inscription in the Roman theatre, V.vi.1), the Greek orchestra is deeper and the stage is narrower than the Roman orchestra and stage.[56] In describing the generation of the Greek orchestra's shape, Vitruvius speaks of three centers for striking the arcs that form the orchestra (figure 15); over half of the orchestra's curve is struck from the orchestra center. The remaining curve between D (on the Palladio drawing) and the stage front and between E and the stage front is struck from the ends of the orchestra diameter (D-E). This means that the curve from D to the stage front (C-B) is struck from center E (radius = orchestra diameter) and the curve from E to the stage front is struck from center D (V.vii.1). No such curves appear on the Barbaro-Palladio Greek theatre plan; the drawing has *meaningless* arcs from centers D and E which curve from C to the orchestra center and B to the orchestra center. The meaningless arcs are the product of the dutiful translation from Latin editions that inverted the side of the stage front (left or right along C-B) that the arc should intersect.[57] The point is important in that it accurately illustrates the naive blindness potentially inherent in Renaissance humanism.

Tabular Summary of the Barbaro-Palladio Ancient Roman Theatre

To better understand the physical nature of the Roman theatre as Barbaro and Palladio conceived it, the reader is directed to tables 1 and 2. Since many of Vitruvius' instructions refer to the modular dimension of the orchestra diameter, the measurements in the following tables are multiples or fractions of that modular dimension (orchestra diameter = 1d.). The dimensions have been derived from the Barbaro translation of the text and Palladio's drawings.[58] Table 1 concerns the plan of the theatre (figure 47); table 2 concerns the elevation of the theatre (figures 13, 14, and figure 45).[59] Along with the modular d-quantity column in the tables, a column that converts the d-quantities into meters is included. The use of 1d. = 49 meters in this column is arbitrarily based on the Berga theatre in Vicenza. As has already been noted, Barbaro's commentary (V.vii) cites this theatre as confirmation for the edition's interpretations and drawings. Looking somewhat ahead to the discussion of that theatre ruin as drawn by Palladio, we will discover that the orchestra diameter in the Berga theatre equals 141 feet Vicentine (one Vicentine foot = .347 meters) or approximately 49 meters (48.92 meters). The inclusion, then, of this second tabular column will allow both a real reference unto itself and a later comparative reference to the Berga theatre.

Palladio's rendering of the *frons-scenae* also includes non-Vitruvian interpolations. Noteworthy are the niched statues of feminine figures, the apparently programmatic bas-reliefs, the Corinthian capitals of the first order and the composite capitals of the second order, the frieze of festoons between the capitals, and the broken (thrusting and receding) second order entablature. While none of these features are discussed by Vitruvius, they all can be seen in decorative architecture of Imperial Rome.

The impression one gets from the Barbaro-Palladio rendering of Vitruvius, in comparison to previous editions, is that the Barbaro-Palladio conception is more credible. Certainly a large part of this credibility is the product of their archaeological research. Twentieth century archaeology has confirmed that credibility. Barbaro does repeat, for example, the error of inscribing the equilateral triangles in the *cavea* circle, which Jocundus first illustrates and Cesariano improves upon (figures 16 and 17). However, Barbaro seems so much more informed in his incorporation of accurate details (compare, for example, the fantasy of Cesariano's theatre, figure 18) that it becomes pointless to indulge in an estimate of the early editions' influence on Barbaro or Palladio.[60] In a similar sense, Alberti's discussion of the ancient Roman theatre as a Palladian design source is superseded by Barbaro.[61]

The importance of Palladio's archaeological research lies not only in that it supplied Palladio and Barbaro with interpretive information in their edition of Vitruvius, but that it supplied Palladio with a variety of real alternatives not described or illustrated in the ideal Vitruvius. Archaeological study in the Renaissance was not new to Palladio although in comparison to the quantity of archaeological drawings left by other Renaissance humanist-archaeologists, Palladio's work was larger in quantity and broader in geography.

On the whole, while Renaissance architects were familiar with the archaeological sketchbooks of others, their own reconstructions of ruins were independently produced. For example, three studies of the Marcellus theatre *cavea* in Rome by Baldassare Peruzzi (before 1536), Antonio da Sangallo the Younger (before 1546), and P. Ligorio (1558) illustrate the radically different interpretations given to Roman ruins (figures 19, 20, and 21).[62] The Peruzzi and Sangallo *caveas* have forty-three and forty-one seats respectively. Yet, Peruzzi illustrates only three exterior orders while Sangallo shows four. While the Peruzzi acoustical parapet above the top seat of the *cavea* appears to be the last interior surface of the *cavea,* the Sangallo drawing shows a fenestrated acoustical parapet surmounted by two ranks of arched loggias. Each drawing has its own interpretation of the passageways under the *cavea* as well. The Ligorio *cavea* (figure 21) is distinctly different from the earlier two in its illustration of two ranks of *cavea* seats separated by an intervening fenestrated parapet. The first rank of the *cavea* in the Ligorio drawing has what appears to be another parapet; the small niches in the parapet may be a conjectural placement of Vitruvius' spaces for acoustical vases (V.v.1-8).

    In comparison with the plan of the Marcellus published by Serlio[63] (figure 22), the stage and *frons-scenae* illustrated by Ligorio demonstrate other dissimilar comprehensions. Ligorio's apparently elongated orchestra and comparatively shallow stage is a radical departure from Serlio's nearly equivalent orchestra radius and stage depth (assuming the stage front passes through the orchestra's center). Ligorio shows what appears to be a *versurae* and *frons-scenae* on several planes while Serlio illustrates no apparent *versurae* and a *frons-scenae* on one plane. Serlio's *frons-scenae* has only one entrance (marked C) and the intercolumnation is without width variation; Serlio believes that the Marcellus theatre generally follows Vitruvius and blames divergence on the workmen. The measurements he cites (orchestra diameter = 194 *piede antico Romano; cavea* diameter = 417 *piede*) are essentially equivalent to a *cavea* radius of 1d., and the apparent stage depth equals 1/2d.[64] Serlio's apparent stage depth is equivalent to the Barbaro-Palladio conclusions and might have served as a source for the Barbaro-Palladio misinterpretation.

    Like Peruzzi, Sangallo, Ligorio, and Serlio, the frequently peculiar features in Palladio's drawings of theatre archaeology imply that Palladio regarded his own drawings as independently credible statements of fact. Palladio's drawings of the theatres in Vicenza, Verona, and Pola serve as explicit statements about his concept of the Roman theatre.[65] Because our overriding interest is to identify the sources and influences that affected Palladio's design of the Olimpico, this discussion of archaeological studies will look only to those matters which either uniquely inform the Barbaro-Vitruvius or are different from the Barbaro-Vitruvius findings.

    When Barbaro credits Palladio's assistance in the interpretation of Vitruvius' theatre description, he also admits to having looked to the Berga theatre in Vicenza to confirm their interpretation of the *frons-scenae*.

> In the plan of the Latin theatre, we have made three doors and in each one a revolving triangle ["triangolo versatile" = *periaktoi*] in order to provide the middle facade with perspectives, and we have also connected the stage with the theatre [*cavea*] in a different way as one can see in the plan [figure 47]; I don't deny, however, that there are other methods of arrangement of this [stage to *cavea*] and also designing the stage; but with careful thinking on this matter, of which we have no example in antiquity, I consulted together with Palladio and we judged this form to be very suitable; and besides we have been helped by the ruins of an ancient theatre which is in Vicenza among the orchards and houses of some gentlemen, where one can notice three niches in the scene in the place in which we have set the doors, and the niche in the middle is big and beautiful.[66]

Barbaro's commentary concerns two peculiar features of the Roman theatre that Palladio has drawn. First, there is "no example in antiquity" of the stage-*cavea* relationship. In other words, Barbaro does not know of any Roman theatre where the stage fully fronts the diameter of the *cavea*. Second, Barbaro has derived the curvilinear *frons-scenae* from the Berga ruin. What Barbaro is not admitting is that with the exception of the increase in stage depth from the Berga (figure 46) to the Roman plan (figure 47) and the presence of post-*scenae* rooms and portico, the Barbaro-Palladio Roman plan *is* the Berga theatre. However, the Palladio Berga plan is not merely transferred to the Vitruvius edition; there is a preliminary study of the Roman theatre (figure 49) in Palladio's hand[67] that has definite affinities to the Berga and the published Roman plan in Barbaro. Table 3 illustrates these similarities with regard to measurable features. The dimensions are Vicentine.

There are close similarities between the plans of the three theatre designs. The Roman study conforms precisely to the Vitruvius plan in the *cavea* radius, the *frons-scenae* length, and the stage depth. The Berga theatre plan approximates the correct *cavea* radius and *frons-scenae* length. The Berga theatre's stage depth is not 1/2d., but is ca. 2/11d. If Palladio inscribed Vitruvius' (V.vi.1) equilateral triangles in the Berga *cavea* circle, he obviously found the *frons-scenae* in the "wrong" place. If Palladio had any hint of the alternate triangle inscription method, he would have found the *frons-scenae* in a more "accurate" location. The Vitruvius 1/2d. stage depth appears to be the result of Palladio refusing to adjust to the Berga's "peculiar" stage depth. In both the Roman study and the Berga plan, the *cavea* and portico depths deviate from the Vitruvian prescription as represented in Palladio's drawing (figure 47).

In terms of *elevation,* Palladio seems to have been confronted with several design alternatives, some of which appear in the Vitruvius drawings (figures 13, 14, and 45). Palladio is obviously unsure of the Berga theatre's *cavea* elevation. The left-hand drawing has a continuous rake of seats while the right-hand drawing shows a cross-aisle and raised second section; while Vitruvius describes cross-aisles (V.iii.4), the represented parapet behind the cross-aisle is too high to accord with Vitruvius' acoustical considerations (V.iii.4). Palladio seems to settle on the left-hand section (in the Berga rendering); its proportions largely carry over to the Roman study. Along the side of the upper right-hand *cavea* section in the Roman study (figure 49) Palladio writes, in reference to the elevation of the *cavea* over the orchestra, "this height is the sixth part of the diameter of the orchestra" ("questo e alto la sesta parte del diametro dela orchestra"). This instruction comes from the Barbaro-Vitruvius (V.vi). We can see this proportion consistently applied in the Berga (left-hand rendering), the Roman study, and the Vitruvius rendering. However, Palladio's management of the height of the *cavea* seats and the portico is divergent from one drawing to the next. In the Roman study he reduces the *cavea* rake, yielding equal *cavea* and portico heights, but in the Vitruvius *cavea* section the *cavea* and portico heights are now not by any means equivalent. On the assumption that it would be more pleasing visually if the highest level of the *cavea* had the same elevation as the cornice of the first *frons-scenae* order (this is not a Vitruvian instruction, although Vitruvius does say that the elevation of the portico top and the *frons-scenae* top should be equal, V.vi.4), we can observe Palladio approximating this in the Roman study. He abandons this relationship in the Vitruvius rendering. He also abandons the acoustical parapet in the Vitruvius rendering; it is visible in the Berga and Roman study elevations. Clearly Palladio's Vitruvian *cavea* is the product of experimentation and modification. Speculation about the motives behind the changes is difficult. Palladio was certainly rendering the *cavea* by intuition and imagination, as is obvious in the alternate *cavea* sketches on the Berga drawing. The number of *cavea* seats is different, as is the arrangement of the *cavea* internal corridors and stairways and the *cavea* rake. In comparison to the earlier *cavea* porticos, the portico in the Vitruvian rendering is imposing (figure 13). The reason behind Palladio's rejection of the earlier *cavea* and portico designs is not retrievable. There is no Vitruvian stipulation concerning the construction details of the *cavea* and portico; Palladio was left to his own resources. Palladio probably arrived at his solution by surveying innumerable extant temple porticos for a source.

Just as there were alternate solutions to the *cavea* and portico before the final Vitruvian drawing, Palladio experimented with *frons-scenae* and stage arrangements that were unlike the Berga arrangement. The following deviations are found in the Roman study (figure 49): a stage depth of 1/2d., a *frons-scenae* length of 2d., and a double ordered *frons-scenae* colonnade of freestanding columns with unvarying intercolumnation. With this alternate in mind, we are reminded of Barbaro's statement that Palladio and he had alternatives but elected the Berga plan. What they seem to have rejected was the Roman study *frons-scenae*. They rejected it partly because, like the theatre, it had or lacked features that did not totally agree with their interpretation of Vitruvius. For example, the Roman study contains no apparent *frons-scenae* entrances. According to the Barbaro-Palladio placement of the *versurae*, there is no evidence of such openings in the Berga or the Roman study. If Barbaro had respected Vitruvius' implication (V.vi.8) that the *versurae* was a direction at right angles to the *frons-scenae*, he would have identified the Berga and Roman study *versurae* as merely passageways. Palladio's Vitruvius drawing invents the *versurae* openings.[68]

In elevation (figure 49) he represents a double ordered Corinthian colonnade fronted only partly by the *pulpito*. Within the lower pedestal Palladio writes, "this height should be the twelfth part of the diameter of the orchestra" ("questo sie alto la duodecima parte del diametro dela orchestra"). Palladio has misread his Vitruvius; the total height from orchestra level to pedestal cornice is P. 10, which is one-twelfth of P. 120 (1d.). But Vitruvius means to measure from stage level to the top of the pedestal; Palladio's pedestal is short by a half. In the same drawing Palladio accurately notes that the first order columns have a length of "one-fourth part of the diameter of the orchestra" ("queste coloni [sic] sono longe la quarta part del diametro de la orchestra"). And he marks the second order columns as P. 22 1/2 high. There Palladio rigorously applies Vitruvius (see table 2) in rendering the columns. As has already been noted, Palladio has mistakenly drawn the first order pedestal short by a half. The second order entablature is also short by 0.5′ Vicentine. Otherwise, the *frons-scenae* on the Roman study is precisely Vitruvian.

The source for this tight, freestanding colonnade is most probably a Palladian drawing of a ruin called Setezone in Rome (figure 23). Palladio thought this ruin was a *frons-scenae;* he wrote at the top of the drawing, "this is the impediment of the Setezone which I believe is a scene of a theatre" ("questo e [sic; è] lo impiedi de la setezone le quale credo era una sena de un teatro").[69] Unlike the Roman study, the Setezone has three Corinthian orders and the pedestal and entablature heights do not conform to Vitruvius. Like the Roman study, the column lengths conform to Vitruvius' instructions.

This discussion of the Berga theatre, the Roman study, and the Palladio-Vitruvius renderings has argued for their interrelatedness. Especially in terms of planometrics, the three designs are quite interdependent. In comparison with Palladio's Verona and Pola theatre drawings, to be examined shortly, the Berga, Roman study, and Vitruvius are in a distinct class. While no attempt has been made to order chronologically the designs in this class, by nature of the plan and elevation synthesis from alternatives to finite solutions, we can be relatively safe in assuming that the Berga and Roman study drawings predate the Vitruvius (1556). The following conclusions are suggested:

1. The Palladio-Vitruvius renderings are the product of a fusion of sources: Vitruvian readings and interpretations (or misinterpretations), theatre archaeology, and general archaeology.
2. The Berga theatre drawing and Roman study are essentially subsumed by the Vitruvius rendering.
3. The Berga theatre drawing remains unique in its stage depth, acoustical parapet, and curvilinear *frons-scenae.*
4. The Roman study remains unique in its *frons-scenae* rendering.
5. Palladio was aware of discrepancies between Vitruvius and ruins; he understood the fact of alternate solutions.
6. Palladio's knowledge of and respect for Vitruvian *frons-scenae* instructions are confirmed by the nearly precise Roman study *frons-scenae.*[70]
7. When Vitruvius did not stipulate a feature, Palladio felt free to use general archaeological resources.

8. When Palladio does guess about a feature, the feature's application seems more informed than the earlier fantastic Vitruvian illustrations.

The planometric divergence from Vitruvius of what Palladio saw in Verona and Pola serves further to substantiate the conclusion that Palladio knew alternatives to Vitruvius' ideas. What Palladio drew (figures 50 through 53) further documents a variety of special features, some seen earlier in the Vitruvius class of drawings and others wholly new and particularly relevant to his eventual design of the Olimpico.

The Verona and Pola theatres have several similar features, only a few of which have been seen in the Berga (see table 4).[71] Concerning the *cavea* in the two theatre drawings, we first note their truncated curves. Both *cavea* and orchestra curves are generated from atypical centers; unlike the Berga center, which generated a full half circle, the Verona *cavea* center is on the *frons-scenae* line and the Pola *cavea* center is on the stage front line (which is not the same as the *cavea* front edge). The results yield *cavea* of less than half circles. As drawn, Palladio shows *cavea* rakes in both theatres that fall below Vitruvius' minimum stipulation (V.vi.3). And there is no acoustical parapet indicated in either theatre drawing. Similar to the Berga drawing and Roman study, we note a raised *cavea* (over the orchestra level) and relatively equal heights for the *cavea* and *cavea* portico in both the Verona and Pola theatres. Unlike the Vitruvius class of drawings, the Verona and Pola theatres have unorthodox *frons-scenae* lengths and clearly identified *versurae* openings at right angles to the *frons-scenae* plane (figures 51 and 53). If Palladio were familiar with this placement of the *versurae* when preparing the Barbaro edition, he obviously did not convince Barbaro of the proper *versurae* placement.

In the Verona *cavea* portico's design we can note for the first time in Palladio's recorded experience an arched *cavea* portico and not a post and lintel portico.[72] Also evident is that the *frons-scenae* cornices do not match up with the *cavea* top level or the *cavea* portico cornice. The Verona stage has other peculiar features: the stage is physically ambiguous; there is a delineated *pulpitum* but no stage front; the central portal is recessed in a large central niche and the *frons-scenae* has three orders like the Setezone drawing.

The Pola rendering has other peculiar stage features: there is a clear indication of what would be termed *paradoi* (orchestra entrances) between the *cavea* front line and the stage building proper, and the *frons-scenae* is rectilinear (unlike the Berga) and uses pairs of freestanding columns to frame the *frons-scenae* openings. Most important are the piers which jut out from the *versurae* at the forward edge of the stage, in effect vertically framing the *frons-scenae* behind the piers. (I hesitate to call these piers proscenium walls for obvious reasons, but the analogy exists.)

Palladio recognized the differences between actual antiquities and the Virtruvian model. This point must be emphasized. The extant ruins and Vitruvius were not synonymous. Chapter 4 will confirm Palladio's use of archaeology and Vitruvius as independent design sources.

Vocabulary, Stylistics, and Aesthetics

Besides Vitruvius and theatre archaeology as obvious sources for his design of the Olimpico, Palladio's individuality as an architect must be accounted for. The assumption here is twofold: Vitruvius' very broad and generalized descriptions of particular features of a Roman theatre and Palladio's obvious awareness of archaeological alternatives (many undetailed or highly interpretive) lead us to expect that Palladio would have to go beyond Vitruvius and theatre archaeology to other sources; and regardless of the detail found in Vitruvius and theatre archaeology, we must presume, until shown otherwise, that Palladio designed both imitatively and interpretively.

Somewhat arbitrary categories will be used in this section—vocabulary, stylistics, and aesthetics; all are generally classified as style. Implicit in the use of a style term such as the Renaissance or, even more specifically, the Italian Renaissance, is an essentialism that claims identifiable peculiarity or uniqueness. As Meyer Shapiro notes, this essentialism is founded on "the assumptions that every style is peculiar to a period of a culture and that in a given culture or epoch of culture there is only one style or a limited range of styles."[73] Specifically:

> Style is, above all, a system of forms with a quality and a meaningful expression through which the personality of the artist and the broad outlook of a group are visible. It is also a vehicle of expression within the group, communicating and mixing certain values of religious, social, and moral life through the emotional suggestiveness of forms. It is, besides, a common ground against which innovations and the individuality of particular works may be measured.[74]

The Italian Renaissance has already been briefly explored in terms of the humanistic impulse to know and imitate the ancients. As an artistic phenomenon it implies that in a given time and place certain visible formal features can be identified, explained, and evaluated. It further implies a group style, which allows us to thrust a Michelangelo, a Raphael, a Bramante, and a Palladio together and say something concrete about their style. The limits of stylistic essentialism are obvious. As the scope of the group, time, or geography expands, the description and analysis become more general.

Our concern is with Palladio and his style as it affects our understanding of the motives that produced the Olimpico. At least partly to avoid the pitfalls of stylistic essentialism, I have erected three categories within style—

vocabulary, stylistics, aesthetics—which will allow us to become progressively more intimate with those things specifically Palladian and more divorced from those things generally of the Renaissance. Only then can we begin to outline the kinds of artistic expressions that Palladio might apply in the design of the Olimpico. By vocabulary I mean those architectural motifs or features that are largely derivative from classical archaeology, Vitruvian description, and their adaptations in the hands of their imitators. By stylistics I mean Palladio's manner of composing and arranging this vocabulary. By aesthetics I mean the philosophical system that guides Palladio's compositions and arrangements.

Unlike Palladio's limited known experiences with theatre archaeology, his experiences with archaeological ruins, regardless of building type, were numerous. In one sense, then, when Palladio engaged in the design of the Olimpico his resources for classical vocabulary and motifs were innumerable; he was only limited by what he had experienced or imagined in the reconstruction of ancient facades and by his own personal preferences in the handling of facades and their features. The assumption behind this viewpoint is that, since the Olimpico was Palladio's final architectural work with definite archaeological foundations, we cannot begin to understand all of the possible resources which Palladio tapped without analysis of his artistic vocabulary. On the other hand, if we look ahead to the actual design of the Olimpico, two things become readily apparent.

First, the exterior of the Olimpico is totally unlike any previous Palladian building. There is no single featured side to the building nor is there an implied single viewing surface or approach to the building. Built of brick and originally stuccoed, without any decorative surface, the exterior of the Olimpico is extraordinarily unattractive. The post-Palladian additions of the atrium and odeo to the north and the perspective scenery structure to the east of the original building, as well as the fact that a large portion of the south wall abutted another building, yield the exterior appearance of a building that has been cobbled together. Rooflines are arbitrary in rhythm with no sense of symmetry, and window and entrance placement are absolutely functional with no regard for symmetry or balance. No adequate explanation exists for the exterior appearance of the theatre. Conceivably finances and property limits were factors. If Palladio had intended some exterior decoration, which is likely, that design was never executed.

Second, the interior of the theatre has only two parts that refer to what would be called classical motifs: the *frons-scenae* and the *cavea* portico. In terms of sources for the designed *cavea* portico, we have precedents for direct imitation in the Vitruvius rendering and the Pola theatre drawing. As for the *frons-scenae,* we have ample precedent for a triple ordered colonnade, niched statues, and programmatic bas-reliefs in the Vitruvius and the Verona theatre drawings. Yet, only on the most generalized basis can it be argued that the Olimpico's classical motifs are all derived from Vitruvius and theatre archaeology. The Olimpico *frons-scenae* (figure 24), for example, contains details without apparent reference in Vitruvius or theatre archaeology. While there were niched statues in the Palladio rendering of the Vitruvius *frons-scenae,* the Olimpico has niches framed with formal pedimented *aediculae.* The Olimpico *frons-scenae* has a Tuscan third order attic of decidedly clear deviation from the precepts of classical architecture. There are dentils along the first order cornice; they are absent from the second and third order cornices. The use of dentils in only the first order is a motif that Palladio never used in his previous architecture; it is most probably a post-Palladian addition to the *frons-scenae,* judging from the absence of dentils in the Palladian autographic Studio rendering of the Olimpico (figure 48). Several other features can be listed that are without precedent in theatrical archaeology or Vitruvius: the consistently broken entablatures on all three orders, the central arch that breaks into the second order, the superposed *aediculae* pedestal on top of the major order's pedestal, or the Michelangelesque reclining figures over the central arch and the first order *aediculae* pediments. Not one of these detailed features has a theatrical precedent, yet each one is permitted within Vitruvius' general description and Palladio's Vitruvian rendering, and each one has a precedent in previous Palladian architectural motifs (with the exception of the dentil peculiarity).

Turning, then, to the earlier assumption that we must fully survey Palladio's architectural career, most of the motifs can be accounted for in general archaeology and/or Palladian architecture. The pedimented *aediculae* can be found in the Pantheon in Rome, a building which Palladio drew and even reproduced in his *Quattro libri;* Palladio used pedimented *aediculae* on the interior and exterior surfaces of many of his ecclesiastical buildings (San Giorgio Maggiore, Venice, 1565; Il Redentore, Venice, 1576-77; Chapel at Maser, 1579-80). A Tuscan third order attic is observable in the Palazzo Valmarana (Vicenza, 1565-66) and Palazzo Barbarano (Vicenza, pre-1570) facades, as well as the Arch of Constantine, Rome. Broken entablatures are the rule rather than the exception with Palladio and have their foundation in most Imperial Roman architecture. The central arch breaking into the second order can be seen in both Roman (middle chapel, Pantheon; Diocletian's Palace, at Split; Arch of Velabro, Rome) and Renaissance architecture (Brunelleschi's Pazzi Chapel, 1430-33; Alberti's San Sebastiano, Mantua, ca. 1460; Palladio, side of Loggia del Capitaniato, 1571). The reclining figures were used by Palladio in four Vicentine palaces (Chiericati, 1550; Iseppo Porto, pre-1552; Barbarano, pre-1570; Loggia del Capitaniato, 1571). No single period in Palladio's architectural career is favored in the Olimpico's applied motif.

Taken as a whole, the *frons-scenae* is broadly Vitruvian; taken as parts, the *frons-scenae* features are Palladian or, more accurately, a vocabulary drawn from that rich pool called Roman classicism. Since the aim of this study is to identify Palladio's design sources for the Olimpico with the end of substantiating the sources and motives that produced this theatre, our search for applied vocabulary is important insofar as it will reveal sources not specifically described or allowed by Vitruvius. But, as the preceding brief review of some of the Olimpico *frons-scenae* features has revealed, within Palladio's frame of reference the *frons-scenae* is at the same time both Vitruvian and extra-Vitruvian. And those extra-Vitruvian elements from classical vocabulary are so typical of pre-Palladian architecture that their use in the Olimpico merely confirms the obvious—they were part of Palladio's vocabulary, too. As will be seen in the detailed analysis of the Olimpico's *frons-scenae* and *cavea* portico in chapter 4, the motifs are derived from classical and Renaissance sources. Their execution is strictly Palladian.[75]

While the separate elements in the Olimpico's applied vocabulary are not surprising nor without Palladian or classical reference, what is surprising is the totally un-Palladian handling of the *frons-scenae* facade and *cavea* portico. To understand this apparent anomaly we must briefly examine Palladio's facade and colonnade stylistics. The type of building front that has the greatest potential similarity to a *frons-scenae* is the palazzo. In his maturity Palladio produced palaces with two striking features. Vocabulary was applied in what Ackerman calls Palladio's "stripped style of antiquity":[76] the orders and ornament were used but their application was functionally and not decoratively based. Secondly, a palazzo facade had either a strong verticalism or a strong horizontalism, never both. The strength and simplicity in Palladio's facade vocabulary seems largely based on his early archaeological reconstruction of facades of Roman *thermae* and the functionalism inherent in Alvise Cornaro's advice. Palladio's earliest palace designs are unsystematic collections of classical elements, probably the product of his naive copying from the period's sketchbooks and his archaeological renderings. His first realized palace designs postdate his trip to Rome in 1541 where he was obviously influenced by the Casa Raphael designed by Bramante and Raphael (figure 25). Returning to Vicenza, he completed the Casa Civena (1540-46) and built the Palazzo Thiene (1545-50) and the Palazzo Iseppo-Porto (1550-1552). Like the Casa Raphael, each of these buildings has a rusticated basement in the form of a real or suggested arched arcade and a single story above of alternately engaged columns or pilasters and pedimented windows. The strong horizontal string course and first story pedestal emphasize the horizontal, an effect that Palladio used when the viewing point for a facade was lateral, due to narrow streets, rather than frontal.

When Palladio was not restricted by the lateral viewpoint, his palace facades abandoned the Casa Raphael basement plus first story for two alternatives. In the case of the Palazzo Chiericati (1550) and the completed Palazzo Barbarano (pre-1570), he applied a strongly articulated order to each of the two stories. In the case of the Palazzo Valmarana (1565-66), Loggia del Capitaniato (1570-71) and Palazzo Porto-Breganza (1570's), and the initial design for the Palazzo Barbarano (pre-1570), Palladio used a single order superimposed over the first and second story plus an attic. In each of these last four designs, he emphasized the vertical and de-emphasized the lateral stories; all use a strongly articulated order of either engaged pilasters or columns. The bold outlines and features of Palladio's later facades are traditionally classical. Yet on discovering that underneath this single order facade are several stories, it becomes clear that Palladio was going against the traditional decorum of Vitruvian and Roman classicism of an order for each story. Equally important is the unclassical treatment of the surfaces between the columns of the major order. The Palazzo Valmarana is a good example (figure 26). Minor orders are applied for each story, and the windows are framed by even smaller orders; entablatures demark the stories but they are denied their existence by the major order. Only the end windows are pedimented, calling attention to the absence of the major order pilasters at the ends of the facade. These and the curiosities in the Loggia del Capitaniato (1570-71) have led critics to identify a "mannerism" in Palladio's late facades.[77] But, as Ackerman warns, the term is only applicable if by mannerist is meant the specific vocabulary application since there is nothing consistently unique from one late Palladian building to another except the strong superimposed single order.[78]

In terms of the total arrangement of the *frons-scenae* facade we are led to expect that Palladio would have applied a single order. Such a stylistic arrangement in 1579 would be directly contradictory to Vitruvius' two and three order description (V.vi.6). Clearly Palladio abandoned his late facade treatments for a more decorous treatment of the Olimpico *frons-scenae*. He returned to the articulated colonnade of the Palazzo Chiericati and the interspersed pedimented windows (in this case decorative *aediculae*) of the early palazzo designs.

Palladio's treatment of the Olimpico *cavea* portico seems largely to have been guided by his archaeological experiences with reconstructed curving colonnades. Examples of these reconstructed curving colonnades are the Temple of Fortune at Palestrina and the Temple of Hercules at Tivoli. Palladio used this archaeological motif in his villas, especially the Villa Badoer at Fratta Polesine (1554-63) and the Villa Trissino at Meledo (ca. 1568-69). The rules of colonnade design are found in Vitruvius' discussion of temples (III.iii.2-5). Palladio repeats these rules in his *Quattro libri* (IV, 4.).

Ancient temple colonnades were fully functional in that they supported the entablature which supported the temple roof. Therefore, the rules of colonnade construction were determined by the amount of spacing or intercolumnation allowable according to functionalism and actual and psychological statics.[79] The colonnade spacing must allow persons to pass between the columns easily, must in fact be spaced closely enough to support the actual weight of the entablature and roof, and yet must not be too wide apart since they must also appear to be able to support the weight of the entablature and roof. Palladio favored the *eustyle* (space equivalent to 2 1/4-2 1/2 shaft diameters) intercolumnation as the type which most fully satisfied each requirement. And he applied the *eustyle* in the curving colonnades in the Villas Badoer and Trissino even though these colonnades were not functional beyond their being independent covered porticos to outlying villa buildings. We would expect, then, that the *cavea* portico would be in the *eustyle* if only for psychological reasons; it is in fact *diastyle* (space equivalent to three column diameters), a treatment expressly warned against in the *Quattro libri* and not found in Palladio's drawings of antiquity, which include the Verona and Pola *cavea* portico colonnades.

As has been observed in the preceding discussions of Palladian vocabulary and stylistics (with particular references to expected applications in the Olimpico), the expected facade and colonnade motifs are largely related to classical orders and motifs. There are, of course, only superficial and decorative parts of the building. We come now to an investigation of Palladio's aesthetics, that philosophical system which is uniquely Palladian and that serves as a consistent unifier of Palladio's mature architecture. James Ackerman summarizes the essence of Palladio's design principles. Palladio, he says,

> sought in Roman architecture ways of organizing and of integrating complexes of spaces and masses, especially in patterns grouped about a central axis composed of major spaces. But these lessons were simply a stimulus for the formulation of principles not manifest in ancient designs, which may be defined as follows:
> 1. Hierarchy, or the systematic build-up from dependent parts to a focal core.
> 2. The integration of proportionality, in three dimensions, of part to part and part to whole.
> 3. The co-ordination of exterior and interior design organization on the facades and by consistency in the proportional system.[80]

A part of the third conclusion is not applicable here since the Olimpico has no systematically or decoratively designed exterior surface. What remains is an organic system where the major parts of any given structure are integrally related to other parts and to the whole and where nonintegral parts would detract from the whole. This theory is at one and the same time easily applicable and not applicable to the construction of an ancient Roman theatre. As has already been thoroughly discussed, a modular system of theatre architecture was propounded by Vitruvius. We have seen how the orchestra diameter as a module (1d.) was applied by Barbaro and Palladio (sometimes mistakenly) in the design of the Roman theatre's planometrics as well as the theatre's *frons-scenae* elevation. What is problematic about expecting an organic system of proportion in Palladian theatre architecture is that unlike Palladio's other mature architectural designs which document this system,[81] the Olimpico is a one-space building (excluding the scenic perspective space). In the face of Ackerman's conclusions, largely based on Rudolf Wittkower's monumental analysis of Renaissance principles of architecture, while the *frons-scenae* of the Olimpico is a focal surface (not a "focal core") and the plan of the theatre has axiometric orientation, there are no distinct spaces that allow a spatiometric comparison.

If the Teatro Olimpico conformed in both plan and elevation to Vitruvian modular instructions (according to the Barbaro-Palladio conception), there would be little point in examining Palladio's much more encompassing aesthetic since in principle Vitruvius would subsume it. However, the presence of an elliptical orchestra and *cavea* in the Olimpico forces the search for a system beyond the Vitruvian modular system. Here, as with the other parts of this Palladian stylistic analysis, only generalized conclusions will be outlined,[82] saving the detailed scrutiny for chapter 4.

Schooled by Trissino in the best humanistic manner, Palladio was introduced to a system of architectural aesthetics that was founded in Platonic metaphysics (see especially *Timaeus* 35B-36B), Pythagorean mathematics, and musical harmony. On the assumption that profitable endeavors seek to discover truths, Renaissance architects found that a mathematical foundation allowed the artist to get closer to the sphere of "certain truths."[83] In an organic aesthetic, the following statements by Barbaro and Palladio are not surprising: "The whole secret of art consists in *proportionalita,*"[84] and, "In all fabrics it is requisite that their parts should correspond together, and have such proportions, that there may be none whereby the whole cannot be measured, and likewise all the other parts."[85] *Proportionalita,* as the ratio of two or more quantities, was an overriding aesthetic principle in Palladio's designs.

The principle of *proportionalita* has its roots in the cosmological relationship of man to the universe. Quite familiar is the Vitruvian concept of human cosmological symmetry (III.i.1-4) where the figure of a man is drawn in a circle or a square (*homo ad circulum; homo ad quadratum*); popularized by the early editions of Vitruvius, the human figure, in relation to these ideal geometric shapes, is "the common measure, the harmony—of everything in the world."[86] The idea is fundamental to Plato when he describes the world sphere, the macrocosm of the human body:

And for shape he gave it that which is fitting and akin to its nature. For the living creature that was to embrace all living creatures within itself, the fitting shape would be the figure that comprehends in itself all the figures there are; accordingly, he turned its shape rounded and spherical, equidistant everyway from center to extremity—a figure the most perfect and uniform of all; for he judged uniformity to be immeasurably better than its opposite.[87]

With man as the center of the universe and man's navel literally at the center of himself, man became divided in half and his head was ideally a sixth of his whole body. Each half of man was then three parts, a fitting symbolic reference to the Pythagorean symbolism of three.[88] We are reminded here of Vitruvius' frequent analogy of the human body to the column shaft (IV.i.6ff.), as well as his discussions of the uniformity of proportions in building parts (III.i) and modular harmonics (I.ii.2).

Humanism's vast knowledge of the classics assisted the architect in his dilemma with Christian theology. Ideal church architecture was founded on the circular plan, and theology, architecture, and cosmic order were joined. "As man is the image of God and the proportions of his body are produced by divine will, so the proportions in architecture have to embrace and express the cosmic order."[89] Alberti was probably the first architect to employ and develop architectural harmonics. He was instrumental in relating physical harmony to musical harmony—"the numbers by means of which the agreement of sounds affects our ears with delight, are the very same which please our eyes and our minds;"[90] Pythagorean physical measurement of tones in space was his inspiration.[91] The musical analogy to church architecture first appears in Alberti; in plan, proportions of 1:1 (unison), 1:2 (diapson or octave), 2:3 (diapente or fifth), and 3:4 (a diatessaron or fourth) are recommended.[92] These musical and physical consonances, initially the Greek musical system with their composites (1:2:3, an octave plus a fifth; and 1:2:4, two octaves), can be found as early as Plato's discovery of "harmony in the squares and cubes of the double and triple proportions starting from unity." Plato's system produces "two geometrical progressions, 1, 2, 4, 8 and 1, 3, 9, 27. Traditionally represented in the shape of a *Lambda*

$$\begin{array}{cccc} & & 1 & & \\ & 2 & & 3 & \\ & 4 & & 9 & \\ 8 & & & & 27 \end{array}$$

the harmony of the world is expressed in the seven numbers 1, 2, 3, 4, 8, 9, 27."[93] The first four numbers are Pythagorean; the remainder are Platonic generations from them.

What were once simple arithmetic progressions in Alberti are now geometric progressions. To illustrate that architects designed in this fashion, we have only to quote from the first few lines of Francesco Giorgi's *Memorandum for S. Francesco dell Vigna* (Venice) concerning recommended changes to Sansovino's original design.

> April 1, 1535. In order to build the fabric of the church with those fitting and very harmonious proportions which one can do without altering anything that has been done, I should proceed in the following manner. I should like the width of the nave to be 9 paces (1 pace = 1.8 m.) which is the square of three, the first and divine number. The length of the nave, which will be 27, will have a triple proportion which makes a diapson and a diapent. And this mysterious harmony is such that when Plato in the *Timaeus* wished to describe the wonderful consonance of the parts and fabric of the world, he took this as the first foundation of his description, multiplying as far as necessary these same proportions and figures according to the fitting rules and consonances until he had included the whole world and each of its members and parts.[94]

This system remained largely restricted to ecclesiastical architecture until Andrea Palladio applied it throughout his lifetime. Palladio saw the beginnings of its domestic application in Trissino's Villa Cricoli (1536-37).[95] He was familiar with its foundations in Alberti (IX.v and vi), the Barbaro-Vitruvian commentary (III.preface; III.i; and V.iv), and Academician Silvio Belli's book *Della proportione e proportionalità*, printed in 1573.[96] He published a practical explanation of its application in the *First Book* of the *Quattro libri*, where he detailed the proper room ratios of width to length and height to width to length. The only incommensurable ratio he added to those already seen in Pythagorean and Platonic theory and Alberti and Giorgi's practice was the diagonal of the square ($\sqrt{2}$) producing the length of a rectangle where the width is equal to the square's side ($= 1$).[97]

The whole of the *Quattro libri* wherein Palladio discusses and renders most of his pre-1570 designs is a practical illustration of the application of this system. The examples that follow are representative of the kinds of harmonics Palladio designed into his buildings. The first example is quoted directly from Wittkower and concerns Palladio's early Villa Godi (1538-42; *QL,* II, 15, plate 48).

> Each of the eight small rooms—four at each side of the hall—measures 16×24 feet, i.e. width; length $= 1:1\ 1/2$ which is one of the seven shapes of rooms recommended by Palladio [*QL,* I, 22]. The ratio of width to length is 2:3 [a fifth or diapente]. The portico, has the same size of 16×24, while the hall behind it measures 24×36; its ratio—1:1 1/2 or 2:3—is therefore equal to that of the small rooms and the portico. The use of the same ratio throughout the building is apparent. But beyond this, the equation $16/24 = 24/36$ shows that rooms and hall are, one might say, proportionately firmly interlocked. The series underlying the plan as a whole is the progression 16, 24, 36, which we know from Alberti's analysis of the ratio 4:9 as 4:6:9 and which can be expressed in musical terms as a sequence of two diapente [4:6 or 2:3 is a fifth; 6:9 or 2:3 is a fifth].[98]

Palladio's Palazzo Valmarana (figure 26; see *QL,* II, 3, plate 12) serves as a good example of how Palladio linked the parts of a facade together. (The proportional relation of the facade to the palace's plan is not executed because of an extreme property reduction when the building was finally constructed.) The three bold elements of the design, the major intercolumnation (7' Vicentine), the minor order height (14' Vicentine), and the major order height (28' Vicentine) are proprotionally related by a pair of octaves 1:2:4 (7:14:28). Many more examples could be cited, each confirming Palladio's aesthetic of proportional harmony. From my earlier analysis of Palladio's vocabulary and stylistics I concluded that motifs were largely derived from classical or Renaissance sources and that Palladio's personal manner of executing them was not consistently bound by rules. In the case of Palladio's system of proportional harmonics, we have a consistent approach that is uniquely Palladian.

In conjunction with Palladio's concept of the Vitruvian Roman theatre and its modular system, we are led to expect that Palladio would apply some system of proportional harmony to the parts of the Olimpico. As I have already pointed out, the difference is that the applied harmonics cannot be spatiometric (except unto themselves) but must be restricted to the theatre in plan, the theatre in elevation, and the interrelatedness of the plan to the elevation. Such an analysis will require the correlation of surfaces to surfaces, as well as modular oriented classical motifs to themselves and to other surfaces.

This chapter has covered considerable ground. Its purpose was to identify and explain the hypothesized design influence sources of (1) the ancient Roman theatre according to Vitruvius, (2) the ancient Roman theatre according to archaeology, and (3) Palladio's vocabulary, stylistics, and aesthetics as they relate to an architect's design of a theatre. Some of the design sources have already been shown to have their application in the Olimpico.

Figures

Fig. 1 Montenari, elevation of Olimpico *cavea*.

Fig. 2 Bertotti Scamozzi, Olimpico section.

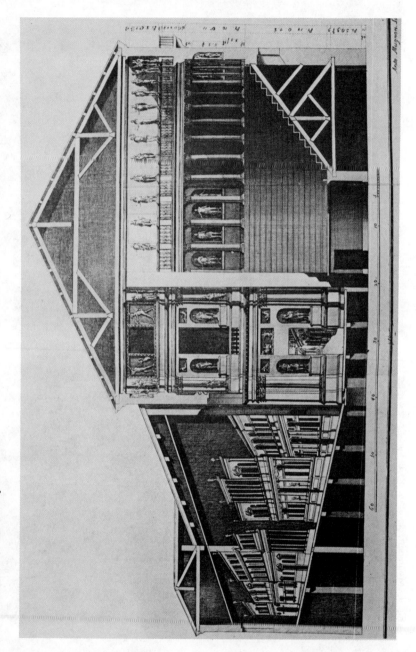

Fig. 3   Bertotti Scamozzi, schematic of Vitruvian method in Olimpico.

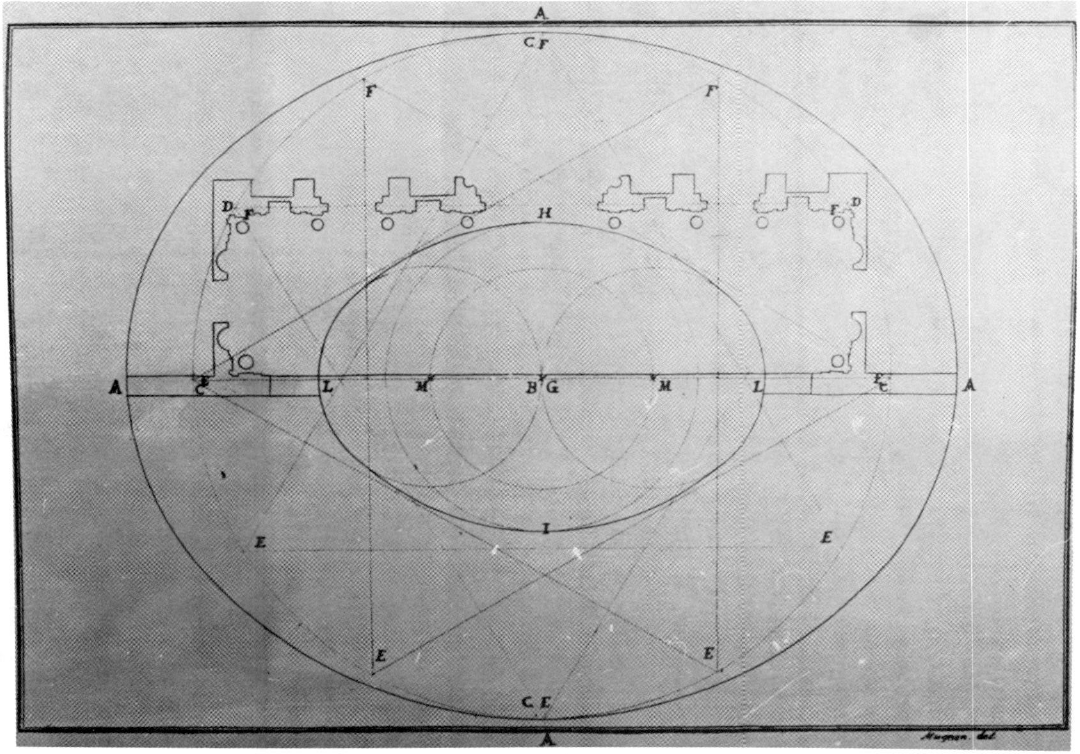

Fig. 4 Fresco, Olimpic Stadium (courtesy of the Centro
Internazionale di Studi di Architettura "Andrea Palladio,"
Vicenza).

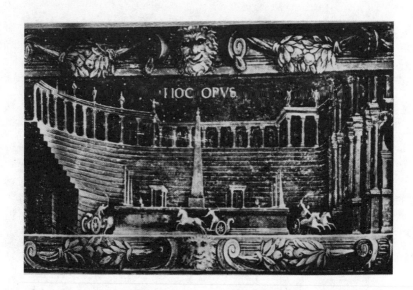

Fig. 5 Fresco, *L'Amor costante* (courtesy of the Centro
Internazionale di Studi di Architettura "Andrea Palladio,"
Vicenza).

Fig. 6   Fresco, *Sofonisba* (courtesy of the Centro Internazionale di
Studi di Architettura "Andrea Palladio," Vicenza).

Fig. 7   Fresco, *Edippo* (courtesy of the Centro Internazionale di
Studi di Architettura "Andrea Palladio," Vicenza).

Fig. 8 Fresco, Japanese envoy (courtesy of the Centro
Internazionale di Studi di Architettura "Andrea Palladio,"
Vicenza).

Fig. 9 Fresco, Torneo (courtesy of the Centro Internazionale di
Studi di Architettura "Andrea Palladio," Vicenza).

Fig. 10   Berga theatre (in Marzari, 1590).

Fig. 11   Schematic of Barbaro-Palladio Roman theatre.

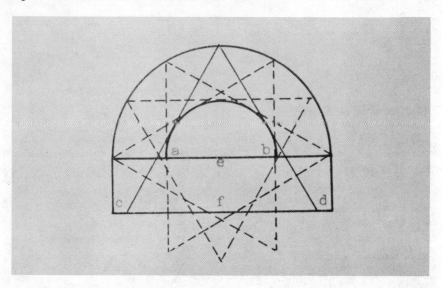

Fig. 12   Schematic of modern interpretation of Roman theatre.

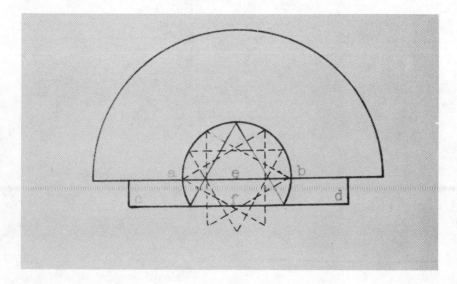

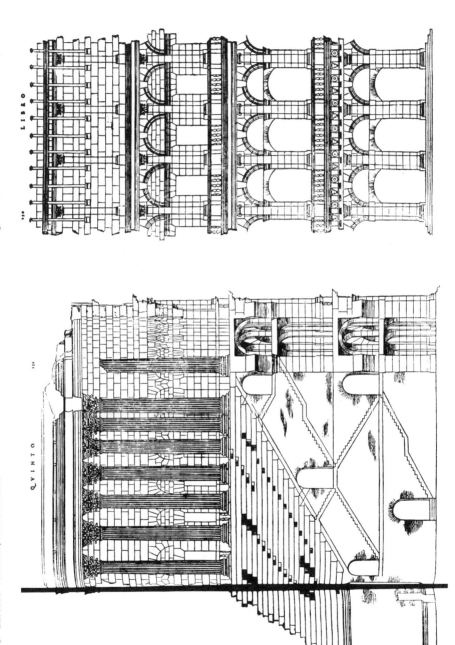

Fig. 14 Barbaro-Vitruvius, *cavea* exterior elevation.

Fig. 13 Barbaro-Vitruvius, *cavea* section.

Fig. 15 Barbaro-Vitruvius, plan of Greek theatre.

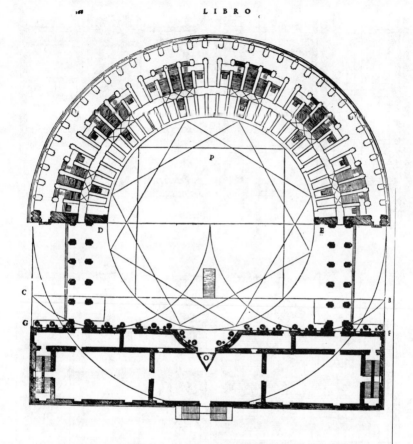

L'altezza di quel luogo non deue esser meno di dieci, & piu di 12. piedi: I gradi delle scale tra i cunei e le sedi all'incontro de gli anguli de i quadrati siano drizzati alla prima cinta, & da quella cinta tra mezzo di quelli siano drizzate an= cho le altre gradationi, & alla somma quante seranno altre tanto sempre siano ampliate.

L'altezza di quel luogo, cioe del Logeo, e pulpito, non deue esser meno de dieci piedi, ne piu di Dodici. Vit. alza il pulpito de Greci sette piedi piu del pulpito de Latini, perche essendo il pulpito de Latini piu uicino non douena hauer piu altezza, accioche quelli, che stauano nel= 70 l'Orchestra potesser uedere i gesti de i recitanti, ma i Greci che haueuano le lor scena piu rimota, poteuano alzar piu il pulpito loro, perche la distanza fa parer basse le cose alte, perche se uno na appresso una casa, non uede il colmo, ma piu, che egli s'allontana, piu la discopre, co= me la ragione della prospettiua ci dimostra.

Fig. 16 Jocondus-Vitruvius, plan of Roman theatre.

Fig. 17 Cesariano-Vitruvius, plan of Roman theatre.

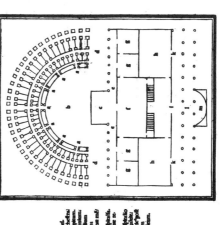

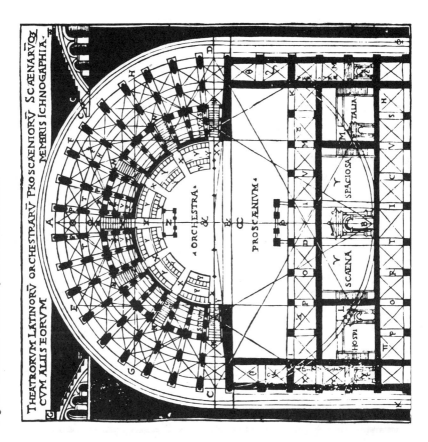

Fig. 18 Cesariano-Vitruvius, *cavea* exterior and interior.

Fig. 19 Peruzzi, Marcellus theatre (from Georgi Lukomski,
*I maestri della architettura classica da Vitruvio allo
Scamozzi*).

Fig. 20 Sangallo the Younger, Marcellus theatre (from Georgi
Lukomski, *I maestri della architettura classica da Vitruvio
allo Scamozzi*).

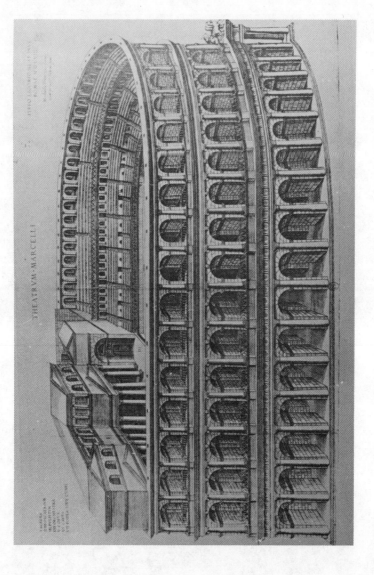

Fig. 21 Ligorio, Marcellus theatre (from Jean Jacquot, ed., *Le Lieu Théâtral á la Renaissance*).

Fig. 22 Serlio, plan of Marcellus theatre (Book III).

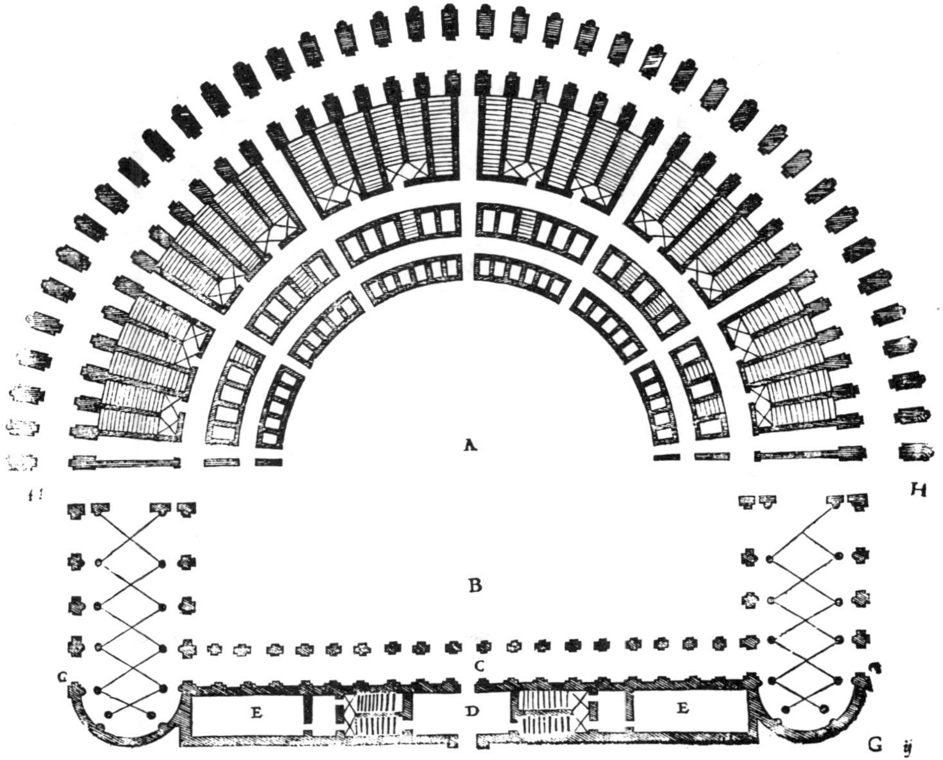

Fig. 23 Setezone "scena," Palladio autograph
(British Architectural Library, RIBA, London)

Fig. 24   Teatro Olimpico frons-scenae (courtesy of the Centro
Internazionale di Studi di Architettura "Andrea Palladio,"
Vicenza).

Fig. 25   Casa Raphael (from Rudolph Wittkower, *Architectural
Principles in the Age of Humanism*).

Fig. 26   Palazzo Valmarana (from Roberto Pane, *Andrea Palladio*).

Fig. 27 Conjectural reconstruction of *Sofonisba frons-scenae*.

Fig. 28 Vicentino, Henry III entry, Venice (from Rudolph Wittkower, *Architectural Principles in the Age of Humanism*).

Fig. 29 Artist unknown, Henry III entry, Venice (courtesy Museo Correr, Venice).

Fig. 30   Triumphal Arch of Septimus Severus, Rome (from
Rudolph Wittkower, *Architectural Principles in the Age of
Humanism*).

Fig. 31 Braun and Hogenberg map of Vicenza, c. 1540-1550 (from
Civitates Orbis Terrarum, World Publishing Co.).

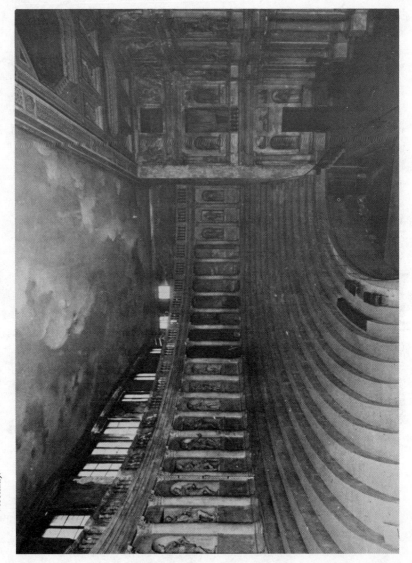

Fig. 32 Teatro Olimpico *cavea* (courtesy of the Centro Internazionale di Studi di Architettura "Andrea Palladio," Vicenza).

Fig. 33 Bertotti Scamozzi, *frons-scenae* elevation.

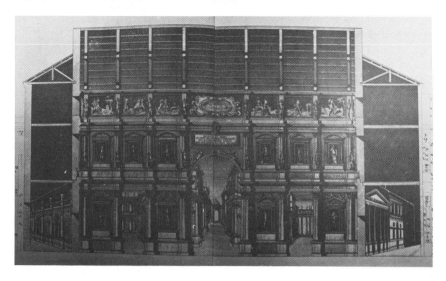

Fig. 34 Bertotti Scamozzi, *cavea* section.

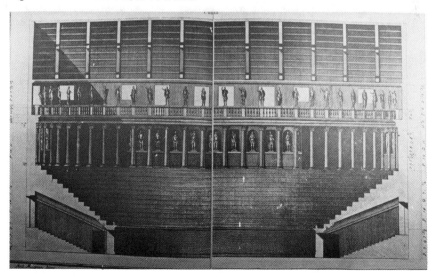

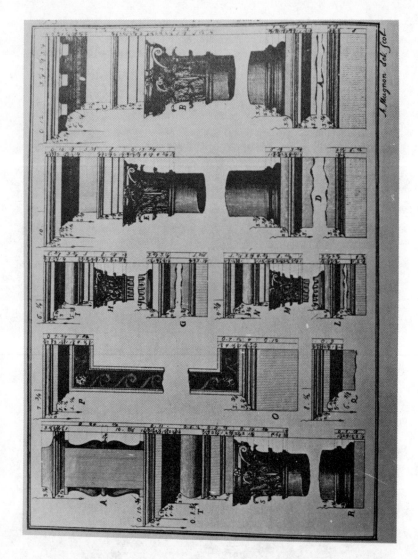

Fig. 35 Bertotti Scamozzi, order detail drawings.

Fig. 36 Montenari, Olimpico ground plan.

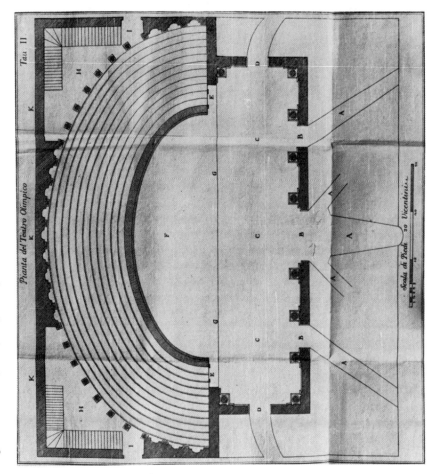

Pianta del Teatro Olimpico

Tau II

Fig. 37   Dumont, Olimpico ground plan.

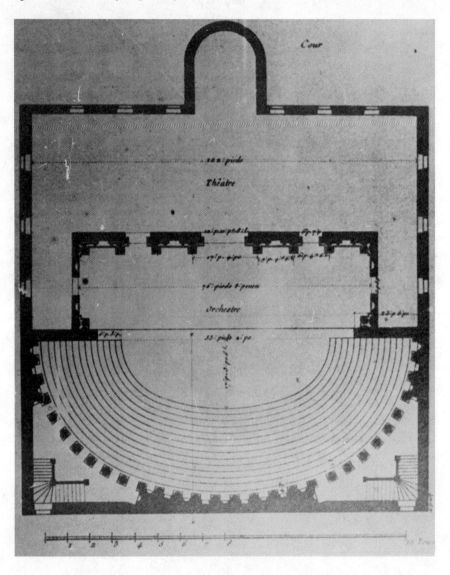

Fig. 38 Bennasuti, Olimpico ground plan.

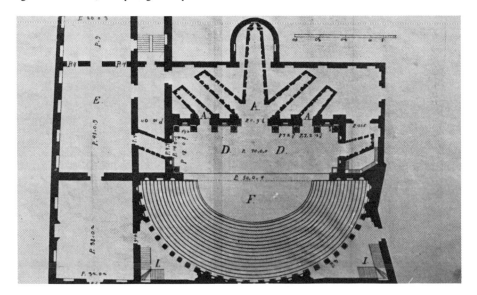

Fig. 39 Bennasuti, Olimpico *frons-scenae* elevation.

Fig. 40 Magrini, Olimpico *frons-scenae* elevation, *cavea* section and ground plan.

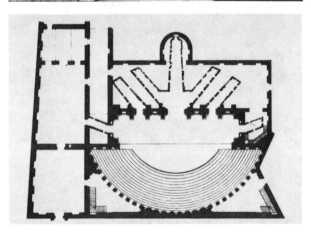

Fig. 41   Sonrel, Olimpico *frons-scenae* elevation.

Fig. 42   Sonrel, Olimpico ground plan.

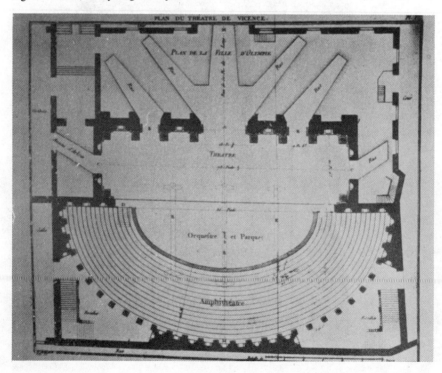

Fig. 43 Sonrel, Olimpico section.

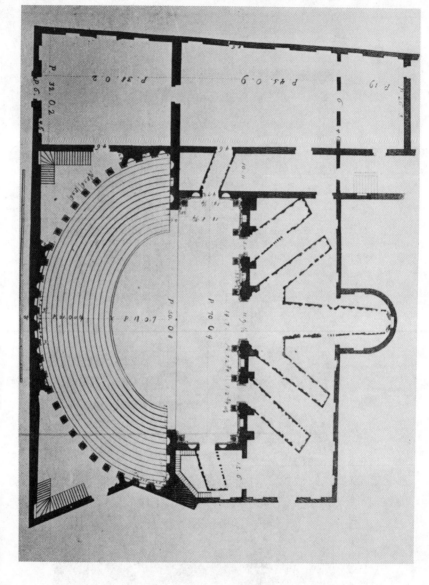

Fig. 44   Bertotti Scamozzi, Olimpico ground plan.

Fig. 45 Barbaro-Vitruvius, *frons-scenae* elevation.

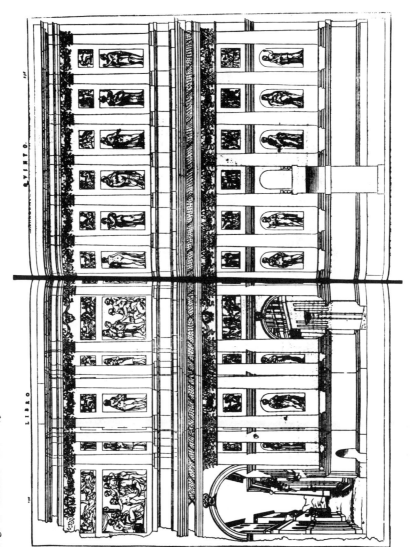

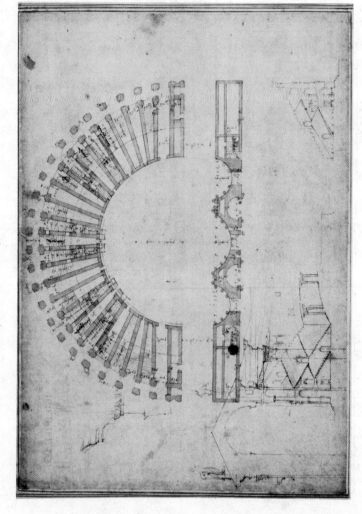

Fig. 46   Berga theatre plan and elevations, Palladio autograph
(British Architectural Library, RIBA, London)

Fig. 47 Barbaro-Vitruvius Roman theatre ground plan.

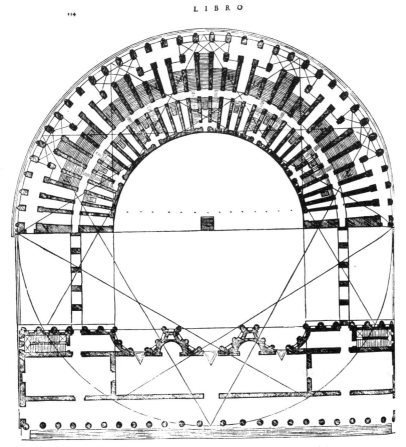

CAP. VII. DEL COPERTO DEL PORTICO
DEL THEATRO.

È Coperto di quel portico del Theatro che sta sopra l'ultimo ordine de i gradi superiori, si fa ad egual liuello dell'altezza della Scena; & la ragione è questa, perche la uoce crescendo egualmente peruenirà, & al sommo ordine de i gradi, & al tetto, perche se'l portico non serà eguale all'altezza della Scena, quanto men egli serà alto la uoce serà portata inanzi fin la doue ella prima peruenirà. Io ho detto, che questo portico era sopra i gradi, & come un corridore aperto uerso le piazze del Theatro, ma serrato di dietro faceua risuonar la uoce mirabilmente. Leon Battista lo chiama circonadlatione, & dice, che per restringere, & unir la uoce era fatto, & che sopra come per Cielo del Theatro, & per la uoce, & per l'ombra si tiraua una uela ornata di Stelle. Questo portico era fatto molto maestreuolmente, perche haueua sotto di se altri colonnati, & altri porticbi per sostenimento di quelli di sopra, ma aperti nella parte esteriore, & ne i grandissimi Theatri. Questi portichi si faceuano doppi, perche meglio al tempo delle pioggie le genti si potessero riparare. I colonnati di questi erà di opra soda, & ferma tratti i lineamenti da gli archi come dice Leone, che copiosamente di questi ne parla.

L'Orchestra

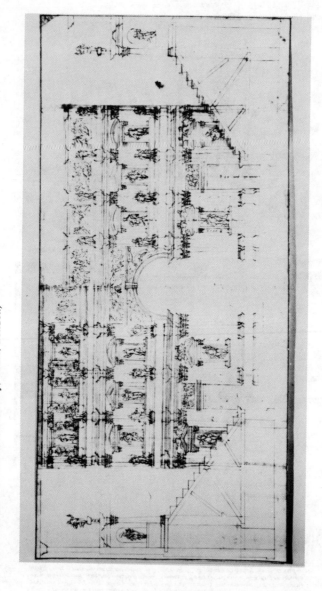

Fig. 48 "London Studio," Palladio Autograph
(British Architectural Library, RIBA, London)

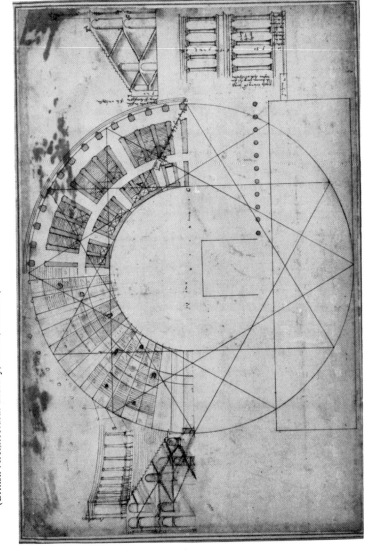

Fig. 49 Roman study of theatre, Palladio autograph
(British Architectural Library, RIBA, London)

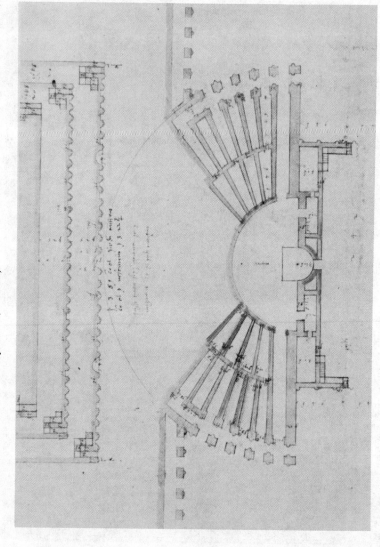

Fig. 50   Verona theatre plan, Palladio autograph
(British Architectural Library, RIBA, London)

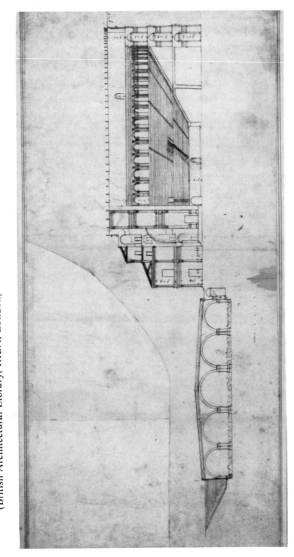

Fig. 51   Verona theatre section, Palladio autograph
(British Architectural Library, RIBA, London)

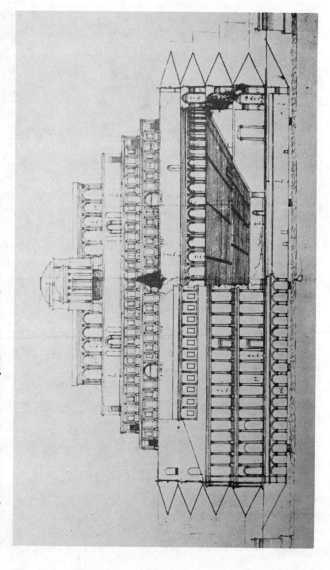

Fig. 52 Verona theatre section and elevation, Palladio autograph
(British Architectural Library, RIBA, London)

Fig. 53   Pola theatre ground plan and elevation, Palladio autograph
(British Architectural Library, RIBA, London)

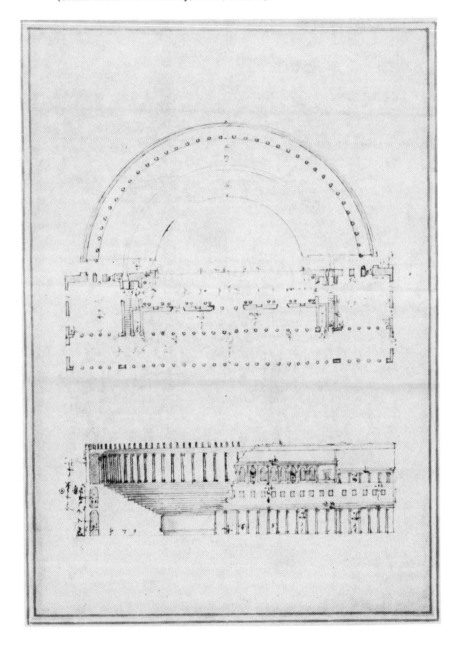

Fig. 54 Olimpico *frons-scenae* elevation, Albanese autograph
(British Architectural Library, RIBA, London)

Fig. 55 Olimpico drawings, Orefice, 1620 (courtesy of the Centro
Internazionale di Studi di Architettura "Andrea Palladio,"
Vicenza).

Fig. 56 Olimpico cavea (courtesy of the Centro Internazionale di
Studi di Architettura "Andrea Palladio," Vicenza).

3

Palladio's Theatrical Occupations

Palladio's design of the Teatro Olimpico did not occur in the vacuum of a purely academic enterprise. Certainly Palladio was knowledgeable of the ancient Roman theatre through his studies of Vitruvius and Alberti and his experience with the archaeological remains of theatrical structures. Along with Palladio's stylistics and aesthetics, these potential design sources have been discussed in the previous chapter. We come now to the actual theatrical activity in which Palladio engaged. The intent here is to describe, within evidential limits, the nature of Palladio's pre-Olimpico theatrical occupations. The assumption is that Palladio would look to these previous experiences as another source for the Olimpico design.

Palladio's membership in the Olimpic Academy (Academia Olimpica) provided the opportunities for theatrical activity. Chartered in 1555, the Olimpic Academy of Vicenza was typical of the many Italian city-state academies that had begun as early as the late fifteenth century. In purpose, academies existed as an outlet and shelter for humanistic intellectual activity; their end was the molding or well-rounding of a man into an "uomo universale." The frequent Papal suppression of academies sent many underground. Eventually some academies received Papal sanction (for example, the Rome Academy), but many academies remained secret and less open in their membership policies than these privileged academies. As Edward Conradi notes,

> It was supposed that with the establishment of privileged academies, the free secret academies would cease. The former, however, had not only literary men as members, but their membership included kings, princes, and nobles, scholars, poets, builders, sculptors, masons, and even men without qualifications. That such a society is not the means for men of high scientific ideals to accomplish their aims seems natural. So it came that besides the public academy, there continued to exist the free and secret academy.[1]

Before the Olimpic Academy, Vicentine academies existed in two forms. The earliest academy, the Academia dei Sociniani, flourished from 1536 until its dissolution in 1546. Its founder was Lelio Socino, scholar of ancient languages and literature and proponent of Lutheranism. Fulvio Pellegrino Morato of the Sociniani expounded an antitrinitarian philosophy. The heresy created considerable stir between Rome and Vicenza,[2] and Pope Paul III called for a council in Vicenza in 1538. The council was postponed until 1545, however, when it was convened at Trent.

Gian Giorgio Trissino's Academy at Cricoli has already been mentioned as the site of Palladio's early training as an architect and architectural humanist. Palladio was discovered by Trissino in 1536 or 1537 while the former was working as a stonemason on Trissino's villa at Cricoli. With the completion of the villa in 1538, Trissino created his learned Accademia Trissiana. Dogmatic in its classicism, Trissino's academy was "anachronistic" in its rejection of "any popular tendencies" toward adaptive classicism.[3] We might recall, for example, Trissino's *Poetica* (1529) with its philological arguments for an idealized Italian language rather than the *volgare,* or Trissino's Greek modelled *Sofonisba* (1515).

Trissino's Accademia di Vicenza[4] was attended by the young Vicentine aristocracy.

> Study, Arts and Virtue—these key-words embraced the programme of the Academy. Students lived at Cricoli and their work was regulated from day-break to night-fall. Trissino seems to have wished to blend the ideals of monastic life with the traditions of the Greek schools of philosphers. Strict moral conduct as well as physical cleanliness were peremptory demands. The study of Latin and Greek, guiding the student to an accomplished Italian style, was the medium through which he hoped to infuse civic virtues into the young generation.[5]

The academy's teachers were of high reputation. They included the philologists and philosphers Francesco Conternio, Bernardino Donati, and Bernardino di Melchiorre Bertolazzi (called Trebazio). The latter was a translator of Aristotle's *Ethics* and *Politics* and was cited for his erudition by Pope Paul III in 1547.[6]

As academies, the Sociniani and Trissino were like schools with faculties and student bodies; they were not societies of individuals gathered together serving at once as teachers and learners for the common humanistic good of the society.

The first such Vicentine humanistic society was the Academia Olimpica founded late in 1555[7] with twenty-one charter members. Included in the twenty-one were Giacomo Pagello, member of the Venetian Court (as a part of the Venetian republic Vicenza was ruled by Venetians who lived in Vicenza); Francesco Ghellini, philosopher; Agostino Rapa, writer of free verse; Alessandro Massaria, doctor of medicine and translator of classical dramas; Silvio Belli, Elio Belli, and Valerio Barbarano, doctors of medicine and mathematicians; and Andrea Palladio, architect.[8] The Olimpico charter members were varied in their professions but, at least initially, singular in purpose.

> The Olimpic Academicians have all one spirit and one wish: whence nothing is *marviglia* if all leads forth to a single end: and that is, that each one desires to learn all about science, and especially mathematics, which is the true ornament of all those who have the noble spirit and virtue.[9]

Their scientific rationalism is more than apparent in this opening paragraph of their statutes. The academy's membership grew rapidly. There were forty-five members on January 25, 1557.[10]

Brief mention is due another Vicentine academy which catered to the more prestigious families of Vicenza. The Accademia dei Costanti was formed in 1557.[11] A membership list found in the dedication to the dialogue *Del modo di tradurre*[12] yields an astounding collection of Vicentine civic and literary leaders. The family names of Piovene, Pigafetta, Gualdo, Porto, Valmarana, Barbarano, Thiene, Godi, Angarano, Chieregato (Chiericati), and Trissino confirm the aristocratically restrictive membership of the Costanti. With the Costanti's dissolution in 1568, the Olimpico's ranks were swelled with the names of older Vicenza families.[13] Noteworthy is that Palladio served, or would serve, as architect of Vicentine palazzi for six of the above families.

The Olimpic Academy was genuinely active in the pursuit of its stated purpose. For example, the academy was quick to authorize on March 30, 1556, a series of lectures on mathematics to be delivered by Academicians Elio and Silvio Belli.[14] On June 1 of the same year, Silvio Belli was authorized to give a lecture on Plato on June 8, 1556.[15] The Academy records show a continuous program of "discorsi, lezione e orazioni."[16]

While their initial intentions were avowedly scientific, an interest in literary studies was documented on December 23, 1556, in the form of a decision to "recite a comedy under the name of the Academy" to which each academician could bring three guests.[17] No immediate action was recorded; then on January 24, 1557, a statute established the function of dramatic performances as "principally for the learning of the academicians."[18] There followed a sequence of statutes regarding the production of a "comedia." Four academicians were elected to supervise the production, five academicians were elected to "make provisions and arrange the *scena* and those things relevant to that," five academicians were placed in charge of "the *vestimenti* and *habiti*," and another academician was made responsible for the music.[19] During the same meeting the members decided to be "proportionately" responsible for any production expenses, and the *principe* recommended the "salla di S. Marcello" as a place "to put the *scena* in order."[20] For some reason San Marcello was not used; instead; on January 30, 1557, it was decided that the production would take place in the court of Academician Elio Belli's home.[21] On February 23, 1557, we learn of four academicians being made responsible for allowing "no one to enter either the *scena* or the *apparato*" on the production day.[22] Girolamo da Schio was placed in charge of the whole production on February 26, 1557. On that same day, the mayor of Vicenza was assured that all "possible and necessary provisions" had been taken "in order that the comedy might be performed peacefully."[23] Sometime between February 26, 1557, and the end of the carnival (March 8), Academician Alossandro Massaria's Italian translation of Terence's *Andria* was performed "with great satisfaction and pleasure of all the audience."[24]

This sketchy chronology of the academy's first theatrical production tells us very little. For example, we are unable to tell what the nature of the *scena* and the *apparato* were, nor do we have any clue about the nature of the audience accommodations. We do know that lumber was purchased for the preparation of the performance, since the academy voted to pay that debt on February 24, 1558[25]—nearly a year after the production. The use of the terms *scena* and *apparato* allows a distinction between the stage proper (*scena*) and the mise-en-scène or scenery *(apparato)*.[26] Thus in some sense we can surmise that there was a specified playing area and some kind of scenery—apparently of wooden construction. We are unable to conjecture about the nature of the theatre as a whole since the location cannot be determined, much less about the physical nature of Elio Belli's residence. Lionello Puppi has suggested that the sculptor Lorenzo Rubini and the painter Giovanni Antonio Fasolo contributed to the preparation of the *scena* and *apparato*.[27] While "Gio. Antonio Fasolo" and "Lorenzo Schultore" were two of the five academicians elected to "arrange the *scena*," we can only guess that their professional talents were put to actual use.

Organizationally the academy was obviously concerned with the management and supervision of the production. If committee size means anything, the preparations and responsibility for the *scena* and the *vestimenti* were more important or complex than the music. The preparation schedule of little more than a month's duration is short in terms of twentieth century standards. However, we do not know who performed in the *Andria* or when the roles were cast.

Notably absent from the documents is any reference to Palladio's participation in the *Andria* production. Not until the academy's 1561 performance of Alessandro Piccolomini's *L'Amor costante* do we find Palladio engaged in play production. Between the *Andria* and *L'Amor costante,* the academy considered producing Machiavelli's *La Clizia* on November 22, 1557; the idea was not carried out. Sometime during 1560 they "recited" Alessandro Piccolomini's *L'Alessandro* in their "residence."[28] No details are available about the production.

Then on the December 1, 1560, the academy council decided to produce Piccolomini's *L'Amor costante* at the next carnival (late February 1561) and they appointed the *principe*, Valerio Barbarane [sic], and Andrea Palladio [sic] to be in charge of the arrangements for the production. On the same day they elected three other members to assist Barbarano and Palladio in the overall supervision.[29] In the face of continued complaints from the treasurer that some academicians were not paying for their share of the *Andria* debt, and in-council reminders that the academicians were obliged to assume a proportional financial responsibility for other productions,[30] the academy determined on December 27, 1560, to produce Gian Giorgio Trissino's tragedy, *Sofonisba*, after their production of *L'Amor costante*.[31] Two days later three academicians were elected to distribute the *Sofonisba* parts and three academicians were elected to supervise the intermezzi for the comedy and the tragedy.[32] On January 26, 1561, final arrangements were made for the comedy. Ten academicians were appointed to remain at the door ("alle porte"), apparently as greeters; ten members were appointed for the "introduction of the ladies" ("introdur delle donne"); four members were appointed for "the guarding of the *scena*" ("la guardia della scena"); and five members were appointed "to the door of the theatre" ("alle porte del Teatro").[33]

As with the production of *Andria* in 1557, we are unclear about the precise production date of *L'Amor costante*. Clearly the production was completed by February 26, 1561, because on that date the city hired someone to remove from the "palazo" (Palazzo della Regione, the Vicenza basilica) costumes and lumber used in the performance.[34] We do know that Palladio was responsible for the design of the theatre, that it was built of wood, and that it was "similar to that of the ancient Romans."[35] We know nothing of the nature of Palladio's first theatre beyond that it inspired comparison with the Roman theatre. Of its size we can only guess; the basilica hall, located on the second floor of the basilica, measures 25 × 55 meters. There is a monochrome of the theatre in the atrium of the Teatro Olimpico, but the discussion of this piece of evidence in chapter 1 has disallowed its use without more detailed corroboration. The scenic requirements are typically nonspecific for *L'Amor costante*. Presuming even illusionistic scenery, which we have been led to believe was not foremost in Palladio's mind, the most that can be conjectured is a city street in Pisa.[36] Of the intermezzi, we know that Academician Antonio Maria Angiolelli's *La lidia* was performed. *La lidia* was a madrigal performed by persons dressed as muses and nymphs.[37]

Meanwhile, on February 22, 1561, conceivably even before the performance of *L'Amor costante*, the academy made several decisions about the *Sofonisba* production. Four academicians were elected to "direct and regulate the chorus of the tragedy," to find persons to recite in the chorus, and to arrange for their costuming. The same four academicians who were in charge of the "scena nella comedia" were placed in charge of the "scena nella tragedia"—this included Andrea Palladio. They were responsible for the maintenance of the "palazzo della scena, et Teatro" and any alterations needed for the tragedy.[38] (The use of the term "palazzo della scena" suggests a formal *scena* structure akin to a Renaissance palazzo or noble in-town residence; we are reminded of Vitruvius' description of the *frons-scenae* as a royal palace, V.vi.3, as discusssed in chapter 2.)

Whatever the academy's intentions, their production of *Sofonisba* was not realized in 1561. On April 7, 1561, the academy council proposed to do *Sofonisba* in a private performance.[39] This proposal was prompted by a council discussion two days earlier about their comedy debts and the need for academicians to honor their financial responsibility.[40] On October 9, 1561, the academicians confirmed their desire to produce *Sofonisba*. The production took place during the carnival of 1562.[41] The theatre was in the basilica or Public Palace, as was the *L'Amore costante* theatre.[42] For the first time in the Academy's production history, we have a documented description of at least part of the *Sofonisba* theatre and a direct association of Palladio to the theatre's design.[43]

There is considerable debate over whether the same theatre was used for *L'Amor costante* and later *Sofonisba*. Magagnato, Puppi, and Zorzi believe the absence of documentation regarding the *Amor* theatre being torn down implies that the two productions used essentially the same seating accommodations and stage. Thus they argue that the description of the *Sofonisba* theatre can be used as descriptive evidence for the *L'Amor costante* theatre as well. Their argument cannot reconcile the differences between the *Sofonisba* and the *L'Amor costante frons-scenae* as documented by the Teatro Olimpico atrium monochromes.[44] Puppi argues that only the scenery was changed since *L'Amor costante* was a comedy and *Sofonisba* was a tragedy. Counter to the 'same theatre' theory, Antonio Magrini argues that the Vicenza basilica was used too frequently to permit a theatre to remain in the hall over a year's time.[45] Magrini points to the city archive document which concerns the removal of costumes and lumber from the basilica on February 26, 1561— *after* the *Amor* performance.[46] We are further confused by the proposal of the academy to do *Sofonisba* privately (April 7, 1561) and by the academy election of Palladio and others on February 22, 1561, to be in charge of any changes made to the *scena* and to have custody of the *palazzo della scena*.

Clearly, in February 1561 changes in the *Amor scena* were predicted. The proposal of a private *Sofonisba* performance and its proximity to the discussion of financial problems suggest that the proposal was based on reducing production expenses—a partly irrelevant consideration if the *Amor* theatre was still standing. Since more substantial evidence suggests that the two theatres were not wholly the same, and since we have no descriptions of the *Amor* theatre, we must accept any reconstruction of the *Sofonisba* theatre as a reflection of only the *Sofonisba* theatre.

Produced at the end of the carnival in 1562, *Sofonisba* was well attended not only by citizens of Vicenza but by many Italian and foreign visitors. Castellini says the visitors included ambassadors living in Venice and France and notes that only the rains kept the Duke of Ferrara from attending.[47] Marzari states that nobility from "Lombardia" attended.[48] In the play's prologue written by Andrea delle'Angiullara and transcribed in the Zigiotti manuscript, the writer emphasized the importance of the academy's first production of Trissino's play and the glory it brought to Vicenza, the birthplace of Trissino.[49] These sources, and others transcribed in Zigiotti, refer to the "superb theatre," the "tragic scene," "the beauty and pomp of the costumes," the "chorus," and the spectators' tearful pity at Sofonisba's death. One reporter mentions a cast of eighty.[50] This number is not surprising when we consider the probability that there were many nonspeaking attendants to the twelve speaking characters, as well as the chorus of fifteen women of Cirta.[51] We are reminded that Trissino modelled *Sofonisba* on Greek tragedies, especially those of Sophocles and Euripides, and that his conception of the chorus had them remain "on stage" during the whole performance. As a *coro stabile* they entered the stage after Sofonisba and Herminia's dialogue-prologue, and spoke the *parode*.[52] We do not know whether the chorus used the orchestra or the stage. If *Sofonisba* was staged like the academy's *Edippo* in 1585, then the chorus was on the stage, since ladies and dignitaries were seated in the Olimpico orchestra.[53]

Of the *scena* and *apparato* used for the *Sofonisba* we have an eyewitness account by the academy's secretary, Paolo Chiapin. The reader will note several textual ellipses; the original from which Zigiotti transcribed the description was deteriorated and fragmentary. Chiapin writes,

> ...through the right hand side door [*Porta* = opening] one could perceive the houses that accompanied the major perspective; through the left-hand side door one could see the country with many trees and through the other doors from the sides one could see other houses; all the things that could be seen through those doors were not complete but mostly in relief; through these doors as well as from the major perspective people came out and every door had two of the aforementioned columns on each side, considering also the fourth part that served as a column for both facades and had golden capitals, and bas-reliefs and pedestals. Between the columns there was a niche with statues in relief, fully round, made of bronze of human size; above the niche there was a painted picture of chiaroscuro in green color made of bronze, and this system was repeated on all sides of the square doors, that is to say, between the two columns there was a niche with a statue and a painted panel by Mister... there were sixteen paintings and sixteen statues... in the lower and in the upper parts. Above the panels ...a festoon that hung from one column to the next. In the upper parts the same order was maintained between the columns that supported... the frieze and

the architrave and they were composite... the place where, in the lower part there was the big door... above the columns there was a big painted picture in chiaroscuro made of gold with very excellent figures of human size made by Messer Gio. Batta [Zelotti] of Venice and by Messer Gio. Ant. Fasolo of the academy. Above the circle of the arch of the main door two victories were painted in the above mentioned color and manner and in the middle of the arch hung the enterprise of the academy, that of the Olympic games, with their motto, HOC OPUS, HIC LABOR EST; all that I mentioned concerns the order and arrangement of that wall.

The plane [floor] of the perspective was false in a pavement of beautiful squares with a certain surface, which became gradually smaller toward the narrowing point of the perspective, therefore taking the eye of the spectator very far, although in reality the distance was very short to the eye...[54]

The Chiapin description contains some important similarities to Vitruvius' description of the *frons-scenae* (V.vi.6) and Palladio's drawing of the Roman *frons-scenae* in the Barbaro edition of 1556 (figure 45). The *Sofonisba* production had a *frons-scenae* decorated with columns, pedestals, capitals, architraves, friezes, bas-reliefs, statues, niches, and painted panels. The surface of the *frons-scenae* was pierced by a central arched opening, openings flanking that central opening on the right and the left, plus (two?) other openings to the sides of the flanking openings. A pair of columns flanked each opening. Between each pair of columns was found a niche for a statue surmounted by a panel. In the second order of the *frons-scenae* the same arrangement was used with the exception that a large panel and the academy motto were placed over the central opening. To schematize the arrangement of the first order, the *frons-scenae* would "read" from left to center: opening (?), column, niche, column, column, niche, column, flanking opening, column, niche, column, column, niche, column, central arched opening—and then the reverse of the sequence. With eight pairs of columns, there would be, as Chiapin describes, eight statues and eight niches in each order, totalling sixteen for the whole *frons-scenae* surface. Figure 27 suggests a probable reconstruction. There are several "unknowns" in this schematized arrangement. The nature of the extreme openings is unclear and we are uncertain as to whether they were on the same plane as the *frons-scenae*. The probability exists that these openings were equivalent to Vitruvius' *versurae* (V.vi.4). As was noted in chapter 2, the Palladio-Barbaro placement of the *versurae* was on the same plane as the *frons-scenae*. According to this schematized arrangement, there were no apparent columns or other decoration on the left side of the left extreme opening or the right side of the right extreme opening; at least in Chiapin's description, this undescribed decoration did not participate in the sixteen statue-panel scheme. We do not know the treatment or size of the spaces between the pairs of columns on either order nor do we have any available measure of the other elements. Also absent is a description of the treatment of the *frons-scenae* surface on the second order above the flanking openings. Of major distinction from the 1556 Palladio-Barbaro plan is the apparent rectilinear handling of the *frons-scenae* plane as opposed to the curvilinear *frons-scenae.*

Chiapin's description of the "prospettiva" is informative. The scenery was located beyond the *frons-scenae* openings and "was not complete but for the most part in relief." The floor treatment, apparently beyond the *frons-scenae,* was feigned by foreshortening. Chiapin's use of the term "rilievo" is a certain clue to the three-dimensionality of the scenery, espeically when he implies real space in the foreshortened floor treatment. Acknowledging that the actors used the three central openings as entrances, we can be relatively certain that either the forepart of the "prospettiva" was in full scale or that there was a space between the back of the *frons-scenae* plane and the forepart of the "prospettiva."

Chiapin's notation of two different types of scenery is curious. He cites both "houses" and "country with many trees." In effect there were "houses" beyond all of the openings except the left *hospitalia* opening with its rural description. One would suspect that this was the designer's attempt to satisfy, the scenic requirements for *Sofonisba.* Except for the third episode which occurred in the camp of the Romans outside the city of Cirta, the whole action of the play took place before the palace of Syphace (Syphax) and Sofonisba, his wife. If in fact Palladio was making the left flanking opening symbolic of the Roman camp he twice deviated from tradition: first, the flanking doors were traditionally the *hospitalia* or guest chambers and second, the left *extreme* entrance traditionally designated the *way* to the country (Vitruvius, V.vi.8).

Frustratingly absent from Chiapin is a description of the physical nature of the auditorium. While we could conjecture that the *cavea* would not have been substantially different from the *Amor* theatre—which was described as "similar" to that of the ancient Romans"—the specific implication of Palladio's use of a semicircular *cavea* does not come to us until his 1565 theatre in Venice built in the Monastery of the Carità for the Compagnia della Calza.

Writing to Conte Vicenzo Arnaldi on Sunday, February 23, 1565, Palladio talked about the vaulting in an unidentified building and then wrote briefly about his Venetian theatre.

> I still believe that I will be in Vicenza unless something comes up to be done, because I have finished working on this damned [*benedetto*] theatre, in which I did penance for all the sins I have ever done or am yet to do. Next Tuesday they will present the tragedy, and if your lordship wants to see it I would suggest you come, because it is hoped that it will be something special.[55]

As reported by Vasari,

> Andrea Palladio, architect, made for the *signori* of the Compagnia della Calza, a half theatre of wood in the manner of a colosseum, in which a tragedy was recited; Federigo [Zucchero] made in the *apparato* twelve large *storie* of seven and a half feet, one for each verse, together with a vast number of items of Ircano, King of Jerusalem, according to the subject of the tragedy.[56]

Temanza reports that the theatre and the Monastery of the Carità were burned down in 1630.[57]

These brief reports of Palladio's Venetian theatre are enlightening. Although he apparently had trouble with the theatre structure, we do not know the cause of the problems. We learn from Vasari that the theatre was built of wood and had the appearance of a colosseum. His use of the term "half theatre" suggests reference to a theatre being half an amphitheatre—a definition not uncommon in, for example, Alberti and Barbaro.[58] The painter, Zucchero, prepared twelve programmatic scenes which corresponded to actions in the play. We do not know whether these scenes were part of a *frons-scenae* surface, as with the panels for *Sofonisba,* or whether they had a more scenic value and function. Vasari's typifying them as part of the *apparato* does not clarify their usage. Most important to this inquiry is the probability that the theatre's *cavea* was semicircular in shape—an expected shape in view of reports about Palladio's previous theatres and in view of his apparent fascination with the Roman theatre. As with the basilica theatres in Vicenza, the size of the Venice theatre is unknown beyond the fact that the only sizable space for a theatre was the Carità monastery court which measured approximately 21 × 27 meters.[59] This court was open to the sky.

The play that was produced by the Compagnia della Calza in Venice on February 25, 1565, was Olimpic Academician Conte de Monte's *Antigono.*[60] Conte de Monte was a professor of medicine and philosophy at the University of Padua.[61] His *Antigono* was a tragedy about the last days in the life of Antigonus I (second century B.C.) and his Jerusalem co-regent brother Aristobulus I, sons of King Ircano of Jerusalem. The Compagnia della Calza, an unknown company of actors, produced the play. Their name is suggestive of a *commedia* troupe, but their existence is undocumented with the exception of the Vasari citation.[62]

These theatres represented Palladio's designs until the academy elected to produce a play in 1579. Before examining the source of Palladio's inclination to design functioning theatres having an apparent kinship to Roman models, brief notice is due two additional academy productions and three paratheatrical designs by Palladio that predate 1579. On March 4, 1563, the academy produced Machiavelli's *La mandragola.* The performance was done "privately without apparatus."[63] Antonio Magrini claims Terence's *Eunuch,* vulgarized into Italian by Massaria, was produced by the academy in 1564 in the church of San Francesco Vecchio.[64] We have no contemporary documents in support of this assertion. As with the attempt in November 1557 to produce Machiavelli's *La Clizia,* the movement to produce the play privately in 1572 was never brought to fruition.[65]

Aside from Palladio's designs of the theatres for *L'Amor costante, Sofonisba,* and *Antigono,* he had occasion to design three paratheatrical apparatuses. Before the *Amor* theatre in 1558 the academy held a "celebration of the Olympic games in honor of Hercules."[66] At this celebration they inaugurated a stone statue of Hercules. Palladio's involvement was the *apparato*—the statue was placed "alla fronte della scena" in the court of their residence.[67] No other details are available about this event. In 1565, upon the entry of Cardinale Matteo Priuli, Magrini reports that Palladio designed the entry devices—"raising arches, statues, and pyramids along the street of the passages."[68] In 1574, Palladio prepared the triumphal arch and monumental loggia used for the Venice entry of Henry III of France.[69] The apparatus is recorded in two paintings (figures 28 and 29).[70] Both paintings show a triple arched triumphal arch backed by a loggia of colossal Corinthian columns. The similarity of this triumphal arch to the arch of Septimus Severus (Rome) is obvious (figure 30).

The relevance of these paratheatrical designs to Palladio's actual theatre designs is questionable. I have already noted in chapter 1 Magagnato's argument that the Palladio *frons-scenae* was a formal triumphal arch. This argument may be formally valid. At the same time it denies whatever functional significance Palladio placed in the *frons-scenae* and implies that Palladio would turn to his knowledge of the triumphal arch before he would turn to the more theatrical description by Vitruvius (V.vi.6).

Palladio's predisposition to the ancient Roman theatre as a design source for the Olimpico is not surprising. Chapter 2 was largely concerned with the depth of Palladio's knowledge of classical Roman ruins, specifically those of a theatrical nature. For a humanist, his diligent study of Vitruvius, Alberti, and others is not surprising; there is no doubt that his contribution to the Barbaro-Vitruvius (1556) made that edition the most accurate and authoritative of the time. In view of the Olimpic Academy's interest in the production of classical or classically modelled plays, we are not the least surprised when the academy's theatres are also classically modelled. What is surprising is the late dates attached to Palladio's active modelling of a functional theatre after the ancient Roman structure; by the time of the *L'Amor costante* theatre (1561), not to mention the later Teatro Olimpico (1580-85), the pendulum of current theatrical practice and convention in Italy had swung from Roman inspiration to a Renaissance concept of theatre architecture and stagecraft.

The most agreed upon dates for the beginning of Italian humanistic interest in theatre production are 1485-1486. Four loci are important: (1) the publication of Leone Baptista Alberti's *De re aedificatoria* (Florence, 1485),[73] (2) the appearance of the *editio princeps* of Vitruvius' *Architectura* by Sulpitius Verulanus (Rome, 1486), (3) the Rome performances by Pomponius Laetus, ca. 1485, and (4) the publication of the first illustrated Terence, the *Eunuchus* (Ulm, 1486).[74]

In book VIII, chapter vii, Alberti makes an important statement about the nature of the Roman theatre's *frons-scenae*; at the rear of the stage is a surface in imitation of houses (*demorum imitatione*) pierced with openings.[75] Alberti used Vitruvius as a source.[76]

In the dedicatory letter to the first edition of Vitruvius (1486), the editor (Sulpicius/Sulpitius Verulanus/Giovanni Sulpizio da Veroli) praises Cardinal Raffaele Riario's efforts (during the papacy of Innocent VIII) to erect, for the first time, a classical stage for an ancient tragedy (done by Pomponius Laetus) and for having shown him what the Roman *picturatae scenae faciem* ("painted scenic surface") was like at a performance of the Pomponiani.[77] The letter mentions three different performance sites: "a fair adorned stage, five feet high, for the tragedy in the forum," "a second performance in the Castle of St. Angelo," and "a third in Riario's house, where the audience sat under *umbracula*" and where the *picturatae scenae faciem* was viewed.[78]

Richard Krautheimer's convincing analysis of the Alberti-Vitruvius-Sulpitius documents establishes certain precepts. The Sulpitius letter was a "harangue" to get Riario to build a new theatre, not just a temporary one.[79] Cardinal Riario's connection to the courts of Urbino and Ferrara "through the marriage of his Rovere cousins to the princely houses of Ferrara and Urbino"[80] suggests Riario's knowledge of a Ferrara production of the *Menaechmi* on January 25, 1486. The scene for this production was described as five houses *(case)* with windows.[81] The five-foot-high raised stage is clearly derivative of Vitruvius and Alberti.[82] The *picturatae scenae faciem* is an interpretation of Alberti and Vitruvius' scenic surface and probably favors Alberti's *domorum imitationi*. Sulpitius explains that the *faciem* can be moved by rotating it or by moving it laterally ("versatilem et ductilem quando libuerit facies non difficulter"), thereby suggesting that the *faciem* was a flat surface.[83] And, finally, the Baltimore and Urbino panels which date around 1470 are "the first representations of the *scena tragica* and the *scena comica* of the Renaissance."[84] They were flat scenic surfaces, like backdrops, and were intimately connected to the type of scenery described by Sulpitius.[85]

There are many questions regarding Krautheimer's analysis. They concern the probability of the Baltimore and Urbino panels being representations of scenery, and the apparently "naive" Pomponiani executions of Alberti and Vitruvius' descriptions. Even if the panels are rejected as scenic representations, we must try to understand the apparent Sulpitius readings. The scenic surface was painted apparently to represent houses *(case)*. There is no sense of the formalized *frons-scenae* that our twentieth century hindsight allows.

Krautheimer's analysis does not seem so protracted in view of the woodcuts for the Ulm *Eunuchus* (1486), with their different backgrounds representing streets, houses and characters, or the more formalized curtained compartments or houses in the Lyons *Terence* (1493)[86] and the Venice *Terence* (1497).[87] We have already noted in chapter 1 the problematic nature of this Terence iconography in regard to Kernodle's arguments about the origin of the Olimpico *frons-scenae*. I argued that Kernodle was begging the question by calling the formalized compartments arcade screens. In view of Krautheimer's analysis, the illustrations are the artist's concept of a *frons-scenae* filtered and modified through successive interpretations of Alberti's *domorum imitationi* and the Ferrara-type five *case*. Two late fifteenth century examples support Krautheimer's argument for the early pictorial and domestic conception of what we now term the *frons-scenae*. In 1491, *Amphitrio* and *Menaechimi* were produced in Ferrara. For the *Menaechimi* a "prospect of four castles" was seen.[88] The perspective drawing of ca. 1495 (attributed to Bramante) is frequently cited as an example of a tragic scene.[89]

Before the close of the fifteenth century we can see the potential for two threads developing. In one thread, seen in the Ferrara "prospects," the *case* are more naturalized and less formalized; in the other thread, seen in the Terence compartment illustrations, the Vitruvius *frons-scenae* is more formalized. Of the formalized *frons-scenae*, there is little subsequent record of this type of scene until Palladio's activities.

After the 1491 Ferrara *Menaechmi*, the Bramante perspective, and the earlier Baltimore and Urbino panels, the pace of recorded perspective illusionistic stages increases. Only a few examples need to be reported. The often-cited description of the 1513 Urbino production of Bibienna's *La Calandria* is one example of perspective scenery. Castiglione's letter is lengthy; I quote here only a fraction.

> The scene was feigned of a very beautiful city, with streets, palaces, churches, towers, and each thing in relief, but the effect being completed by admirable paintings in scientific perspective. Among the other things there was an eight-sided temple in half relief.[90]

The same play was produced in Rome in 1514. The scenery was designed by Baldassare Peruzzi and Vasari praised his work for being very contemporary.[91]

Without the publication of Sebastiano Serlio's *Il primo (secondo) libro d'architetture* in Paris (1545) and Venice (1551, 1560, 1566, and 1584),[92] his familiar 1539 Vicenza theatre design would have joined the list of poorly documented Italian Renaissance theatres. There is little point in dwelling on the importance of Serlio's generic perspective scenery, his semicircular *cavea* similar to the ancients', and his raised and raked perspective stage.[93]

While Serlio's causal association with subsequent theatrical and scenic designs is not directly documentable, the preponderance of evidence confirms that Italian theatre was devoted to perspective illusionistic scenery and its functional counterpart, the proscenium arch. The Vasari and Bountalenti theatres at the Medici court (1565 and 1585),[94] the Vincenzo Scamozzi theatre at Sabbioneta (1590), and the Aleotti theatres in Ferrara (1606) and Parma (1618-19) confirm the maturation of the Peruzzi-Serlio type of scenery and theatre.

Between the Alberti-Vitruvius-Sulpitius theatre interpretations in 1485-86 and the Serlio Vicenza theatre in 1539, the concept of the "teatro rinascimentale" was formulated. What at first were, most likely, *serious* attempts at capturing the nature of the classic theatre's stage soon became staging methods in their own right. Their genesis was in Alberti and misinterpretations of Vitruvius; they became deviantly independent when progressing archaeological sophistication clarified the Vitruvian *frons-scenae*. Capitalizing on his archaeological sophistication, Palladio retrieved Vitruvius and the classical stage.

In effect, Palladio could have designed his pre-Olimpico theatres in total ignorance of the surrounding theatrical practice because his interests were counter to that practice. Vitruvius and archaeological knowledge were his prime sources. And with the exception of the *apparato* in *rilievo* for the *Sofonisba,* Palladio made little use of the theatre of illusionistic stagecraft. This is not to say that Palladio, determined to design a theatre in the Roman manner, was ignorant of the theatrical practice of the times. In the *Sofonisba* theatre, Palladio seems to have participated in a design compromise; he mixed a formal *frons-scenae* with illusionistic scenery. In the Olimpico the same compromise will be documented at the *beginning* of the design procedure and executed much after Palladio's death.

4

The Teatro Olimpico Design

After the academy's production of *Sofonisba* (1562) and the privately recited *La mandragola* (1563), sixteen years passed before the academy renewed its theatrical inclinations. Apparently spurred by the urging of the mayor and civic capitano to produce publicly a "Rappresentazioni si Tragiche,"[1] the academy decided on August 10, 1579, to produce a pastoral at the March 1580 carnival. As a preamble to that decision, the academy council explained that their "silentio" from public theatrical performances was because "it was difficult to outdo the grandeur of [*Sofonisba*]."[2] The council stipulated that four academicians should be elected to seek out a new pastoral, the production should be held in the academy residence, and expenses should be kept down in accordance with the academy's dignity. The four academicians were elected by September and the minutes show that Academician Fabio Pace made available his own pastoral, *Eugenio*.[3] Then on November 15, 1579, the academy council reported that it could not produce a play at the coming carnival "because of legitimate obstacles."[4] Regardless of the "legitimate obstacles," on January 3, 1580, the majority of the academicians confirmed their desire to produce a play at the carnival.[5] Nine days later, two academicians were elected as supervisors of the "construction for the performance of the pastoral" and three members were put in charge of the intermezzi.[6] By February 15, 1580, the academy had found a place to build a theatre for this and other performances and decided to ask the city council for permission to use this property. Their decision refers to a theatre designed "according to the model made by [their] coacademician Palladio, and the design already made of the perspective."[7] The academy petitioned the city on February 22, 1580.

Request of the Olimpic Academicians, very illustrious Deputies, very distinguished Council.

Since the Olimpic Academy has several times striven to make itself and the country illustrious by praiseworthy actions, it would not have fallen into apathy if it hadn't remained until now without a place suitable for public performance. Now, having been proposed to newly represent a Pastoral and considering that in the parts of the old prison of this magnificent community one would find a very large place half covered and half exposed, located near the fountain of the Angeli, uninhabited and not used for either public or private service, from this situation the Academy could profit not only at the moment but also in the future. By this request, we ask the very Illustrious Deputies to lend the Academy this particular place, provided that there is the approval of this magnificent commune, in each case that it is needed. We also ask to grant the Academy the freedom to adjust the place to their needs. On the other hand the Academy offers to return the place without the claim that they will be able to improve it. But certainly the place will not only be improved and embellished, but it will be used for good performances. You will give this Academy a continuous stimulus that will inspire honorable public deeds to its own credit, with glorification of this town, and with the satisfaction of the very Illustrious Deputies to whose benevolent attention the Academy addresses itself.[8]

On the same day the city council appended the following five stipulations.

1.   The petition is good for ten years after which the Academy must re-petition and get two-thirds of the Council's majority vote. The Council has the right to take back the property with a simple majority.
2.   The Academy and its successors will get no reimbursement of their investment if they discontinue use of the property.
3.   The Academy is not allowed to dismantle their construction on the property, especially timber and iron that reinforces the building and the roof.
4.   If cannibalizing occurs, the roof must be alternately reinforced, according to methods espoused by an expert's opinion.
5.   To protect the City Council three academicians and their successors are made legally responsible for the property and these agreements.[9]

The academy accepted the stipulations on February 24, 1580,[10] and the city council approved the agreement on February 25, 1580, with an official vote of eighty-one for and fourteen against.[11] The fifth stipulation, or suretyship, was confirmed on March 15, 1580.[12] Presumably, construction began on the theatre sometime in late February or early March.

Although a pastoral was not performed at the March carnival, as late as February 28, 1580, three academicians were elected to seek out performers and three academicians were made responsible for the "vestimenti."[13] On March 23, 1580, Luigi Grotto, the actor from Adria, was contacted to perform in the yet-to-be-named pastoral.[14] No new performance date was recorded.

To encourage voluntary contributions from the academicians, the academy council decided on May 23, 1580, that the statues on the *frons-scenae* should be changed from the original design of feminine figures to statues of academicians. Each statue was to have the academician's family name, motto, and coat of arms on its supporting pedestal.[15]

Palladio died on August 19, 1580. The records of November 7, 1580, claim "the construction of our theatre is now almost completed and with a little amount of money in a short while it will be covered with a roof."[16]

Construction continued through April 1581; on the April 1 the academy council decided that "each academician is obliged to come for a day and be responsible for those things related to the construction proceeding well and to the fullest advantage of the academy as possible."[17] On the same day, the council decided to place the Vicenza coat of arms over the *frons-scenae* central opening.[18] The plan to have academy members act as construction supervisors was apparently unsuccessful; on April 18, 1581, Andrea Palladio's son, Silla (an academy member since October 4, 1579), was hired to act as construction supervisor.[19]

Financial problems seemed to delay the successful completion of the Olimpico. No available record accounts for the academicians' voluntary contributions. They apparently did not meet the financial needs, since on April 16, 1581, the academy council petitioned the city council for assistance. The petition was granted. The assistance was in the form of receiving Vicenza citizenship taxes from twelve prominent and voluntarily nominated citizens.[20]

On April 26, 1581, the academy requested more land from the city. The request concerned the property containing the house of the "superstite" and the payment of rent to the "superstite" for his displacement; the academy wanted the land to build their "residence room and in order to extend [the building] for the perspective."[21] The land was located to the east and north of the original building and also on the old prison property; the perspectives, the odeo, and the artrium had not been begun on this date. Only the structure containing the *cavea* and stage had been built. The city council did not act on the request. On June 3, 1581, the academy considered whether to call the theatre the "Accademia," the "Ercole Olimpico," or the "Teatro Olimpico."[22] They renewed their request for the "superstite's" house on August 17, 1581, this time ignoring the possibility of tearing it down. Rather, the record says that they had such "little time to be able to build one [a house] to our satisfaction," that they decided to ask the city council for permission to rent for thirty-six ducats the "superstite's" house as an Academy residence.[23] Here we learn that the "superstite" was named Antonio Tavola; the academy residence was not only a meeting place but also housed the custodian and the salaried musicians.[24] There is no record of the city acting on this request.

On August 28, 1581, the academy held a banquet in their theatre.[25] Sometime after October 28, 1581, Angelo Ingegneri (an academy member since April 22, 1580) proposed that the academy produce his pastoral, *Limonata*. Academician Fabio Pace (the member who suggested his own pastoral for production in 1579) objected because he thought the inaugural script should be by a Vicentine author.[26] Two things become apparent: the theatre was apparently enclosed in August and the academy had yet to select a play. Thus, in reference to the academy's request for land for the perspectives in April 1581, either their use of the term "prospettive" refers to a stock kind of pastoral setting or it refers to the *space* for perspective scenery, not implying any particular generic type of scenery for any particular play. The latter seems more probable in view of the indecision about the play choice.

The academy was still without additional property. On January 11, 1582, the council elected three academicians to personally petition the city for the much needed land. As before, they agreed to pay Antonio Tavola thirty-six ducats per year for his displacement. Here, however, they wanted the property; they have obviously decided to go ahead with the building program and not be satisfied with merely using the Tavola house as their residence.[77] The city council granted the request on January 28, 1582, setting down stipulations concerning the manner of paying the "superstite."[28] With the property to the north and east of the original structure, the academy proceeded to complete its building. I assume that Silla Palladio was still acting as construction supervisor.

The academy's attentions turned to a sequence of decisions about the theatre's interior appearance, particularly the statuary. It elected to mount a relief of the Olympic Stadium on the *frons-scenae* third order on February 5, 1582.[29] Disagreement between academicians about how the statuary ought to look led to a lengthy decision on April 1, 1582. No changes were indicated in the transaction which would affect the *frons-scenae* proper.[30] The academy was not sure about whose statues would be placed on the *frons-scenae*. On April 24, 1582, they decided to put Palladio's statue on the third order at the corner of the *frons-scenae* and the audience right *versurae,* next to the statue of Francesco Floriano.[31] Since the initial list of February 5, 1582,[32] Palladio and Floriano had been added and Lugo and Michieli were removed. Palladio's statue never made its place there; instead, it was located over the *cavea* portico and was not erected until after 1751.[33]

The academy minutes claim on July 29, 1582, that "our theatre is leading, as each can see, to a good end of its completion."[34] A musical concert was held in the theatre on September 2, 1582, in honor of the visit of the Duke of Mantua, Signor Giuglielmo Gonzaga.[35] Still no play had been selected nor a date set for the inauguration of the Olimpico.

Then, on January 2, 1583, Academician Livio Pagello's tragedy, *Eraclea,* was proposed for production.[36] In a quandary about what kind of play to produce, the academy deliberated on February 7, 1583.[37] Twelve days later they decided to do a "tragic pastoral" and recommended Fabio Pace's *Eugenio* "for production during the festival of Pentecost in the coming year, 1584." Pace's pastoral was voted down (fifteen for, seventeen against); an alternate vote on a tragedy was twenty for and twelve against.[38] Some academy council members called for a revote on February 21, this time proposing to do a tragedy at Pentecost 1584, followed by Pace's pastoral sometime later. The proposal was passed thirty-one to thirteen.[39] Two days later Pace wrote a bitter letter to coacademician Giulio Pogiana.[40] Still the academy had no inaugural play, but one thing was clear: the play would not be Pace's *Eugenio.*

On May 8, 1583, the academy council renewed its search for a tragedy and decided to place an inscription over the *frons-scenae* central arch.[41] The inscription read OLIMPICORUM ACCADEMIA THEATRUM HOC. ANN. M. D. LXXXIII PALLADIO ARCHITECTO. Sometime after the February 21 vote and before the council's confirmation on April 19, 1583, that they would produce a tragedy,[42] several other plays were suggested for production. They were Academician Muzio Manfredi's *Semiramide*, Torquato Tasso's *L'Aminta*, Academician Alessandro Massaria's *L'Alessandro,* Maffio Venier's *L'Idalba,* Luigi Valmarana's *La Placidia*, Girolamo Vida's *L'Alessio,* and Antonio Loschi's *L'Achille.* Antonio Riccoboni, professor of letters at Padua, Sperone Speroni, and Academician Guerini (Giambaptista Guarini) were asked to find a play. Apparently dissatisfied with the above list, they turned to Fabio Pace and asked him to prepare a translation of Sophocles' *Oedipus.* Understandably, he refused.[43] They then turned to Orsato Giustiniani of Venice for a translation of *Oedipus.* His actual agreement to prepare the *Edippo* is not recorded until March 1584,[44] although by this time the translation had been completed. Meanwhile, in August of 1583, on the occasion of an oration in the Teatro Olimpico, "musicians were placed in the perspective" and a 100-seat rostrum was erected on stage.[45] Judging from the use of the term "prospettive" in the 1581 transactions and the probability that the *Edippo* had not been selected by August 1583, the presence of musicians "in the perspective" merely means that they were located in that area behind (to the east of) the *frons-scenae* and no scenery had been erected there at the time. In November 1583, the "construction on the building ended except for the statues,"[46] and Academician Angelo Ingegneri demonstrated an interest in doing the lighting for the production.[47] On the first day of 1584, the academy ate dinner "in the new room of the theatre,"[48] meaning that the atrium and/or odeo were completed.

Interest grew in the *Edippo* production after March 1584, as indicated by Guarini's recommending Giambatista Verati as an actor, Antonio Pasi's (engineer for the Duke of Ferrara) coming to prepare the lighting, Filippo Monti's agreeing to be the chorus leader ("principale ne Chori"), and Montagna of Ferrara's sending a discourse on lighting to the academy.[49] On May 6, 1584, numerous preparatory activities were put into motion.[50] Six academicians (including Fabio Pace, who renounced the appointment) were appointed to "find actors" and supervise the preparation of the vocal and instrumental music for the intermezzi and chorus. Six others were elected to prepare the "*proscenio,* and *scena* of relief, and the painting of the *prospettive.*" They were also responsible for the preparation of the orchestra for seating, the ceiling covering, the invention and placement of the lighting, the "scoprir della scena" (curtain), as well as keeping people away from the stage. The direction of the musicians, the chorus, and their housing and payment fell to six additional academicians, and six others were placed in charge of costuming. Twelve members were elected to guard the entrances to the stage and theatre during the performance, and twelve members were elected to introduce the men and twelve others to introduce the ladies at the performance. At the same time, the academy minutes record that Vicenzo Scamozzi was preparing the perspectives for the *Edippo* production.[51]

Still the statues remained incomplete; on May 9, 1584, a contract between the academy and the sculptors Ruggero Bascapi and Domenico Fontana was made for their completion. They were to complete the statues, cut the inscriptions, and prepare the bas-reliefs on the *frons-scenae*.[52] They apparently completed their work since the contemporary drawing of the Olimpico by Gio. Battista Albanese (figure 54) shows a finished *frons-scenae*.

Luigi Grotto was contacted on June 4, 1584, to play Tiresia,[53] and the wife of Giambattista Verati was recommended for the role of Jocasta.[54] That the perspective scenery was probably completed in the middle of November is confirmed by an academy directive that prohibited anyone from seeing it.[55] Eight actors were auditioned in November.[56] They included Grotto as Tiresia, Nicolo Rossi[57] as Edippo, Verati's wife as Jocasta, and Verati, Zabarell, Melchior Giulandini, Girolamo Mercuriale, and Christoforo Ferrari.

Final decisions were made by the academy on February 9, 1585, for the seating of city officials, their wives, important female visitors, and academy members and their wives in the orchestra. They also ruled that no masked men or women would be allowed in the theatre for the performance.[58]

Edippo was finally performed on March 3, 1585, and was repeated on March 5 with Giambattista Verati playing Edippo.[59]

The reasons behind the nearly seven year delay between the inception of the idea in 1579 to produce a play and the 1585 inauguration of the Olimpico are imbedded in this chronology. Certainly finances were a contributing factor. But more likely the apparent internal dissension, mismanagement, and lack of direction, as well as the gulf between the academy's intentions and actions, must bear most of the blame for the delay. We turn now to the two building and design phases for the theatre.

The extended construction period, the academy's indecision about an inaugural play choice, and the 1585 date for the use of the theatre imply only one long construction period. Yet, the property that Palladio had to work with in comparison to the property gained in January, 1582 argues for two distinct building phases. And the differences between the extant preliminary design and the executed theatre argue for two distinct design phases.

The initial property grant was for land located "in the parts of the old prison" which were "half covered and half exposed, near the fountain of the Angeli." The old prison was located on the eastern edge of the old town, to the west of the Bridge of Piero over the Bacchiglione River. The most contemporaneous map of Vicenza, ca. 1540-50 (figure 31), marks the "Prigon Vachio" (old prison, Prigioni vecchie) as number 25. The building in the northern end of the prison yard was apparently not the only building in that yard.[60] Another building was documented by the academy's desire to lay claim to the "superstite's" house in the transactions of April 26, 1581, and August 17, 1581, and in its final grant of January 28, 1582. In these transactions they wanted property to build the academy meeting rooms (located to the north of the original academy property) and the perspectives (to the east of the original property), without which property neither structure could be built because of the "building in the old prison."[61] Until the acquisition of this additional property to the north and east, the original Olimpico property (figure 48) was encroached upon by a building to the north (replaced by the atrium and the odeo), a building to the east (replaced by the perspectives), a public road to the west, and another building to the south. The west road is confirmed by the three original entrances to the theatre along the theatre's western face. The southern building left its mark through the large notch in the southern face of the Olimpico *cavea,* where even today the remaining double wall of that building can be seen.

The shape of the original property was nearly rectangular and contained the *cavea,* the stage, and the *frons-scenae.* On the exterior of the theatre can be seen the joint where the structure containing the perspectives was added and the joint where the atrium and odeo were added. The length of the original western wall is 40.25 meters. The distance from the outside of the western wall to the joint where the perspectives were added is 22.50 meters. Because of the south wall notch, the maximum unencumbered north-south length (including wall thickness) is 34.40 meters. Into this nearly rectangular space Palladio was asked to build a theatre.

There is no record of what the academy expected of Palladio for his design of the Olimpico. There were no instructions or specifications recorded. Apparently the academy was guided by its past productions of classically modelled plays. Judging from the academy's August 10, 1579, justification for their "silentio" since their production of *Sofonisba,* the academy must have regarded that endeavor as a model and something hard to match. Without records to the contrary, it is assumed that, as architect, Palladio turned to these earlier experiences as models. No doubt Palladio made several preliminary designs, but only one of these drawings is extant. The drawing is known as the London Studio. A comparison of the drawing with the executed theatre reveals two things. (Compare figure 48 with figure 56.) The decorative motifs in the London Studio are very similar to the Olimpico. However, the physical size of the features in the London Studio are different from the completed Olimpico. Immediately apparent in the London Studio are the two alternate solutions to the height of the *frons-scenae*. Less apparent in the London Studio are the differences between the left and right halves: different *frons-scenae* length, *cavea* portico order heights, and portico depths. None of these features are physically duplicated in the completed theatre. Tables 5 through 8 list basic measurements derivable from the drawing (in Vicentine feet) and their counterparts in the present Teatro Olimpico in meters and converted Vicentine feet.

Apparently Palladio was commissioned to design the Olimpico before he knew the precise limits of the initial property grant of February 22, 1580, because the London Studio could not have fit on that site. The scale on the drawing (confirmed by the Palladian handwriting in the audience right *hospitalia* opening which reads "height in full 43 1/2 feet" ["alto in tuto piedi 43 1/2"]) gives the maximum length of the London Studio as 117.5' Vicentine. This distance is measured between the exterior walls of the *cavea* portico. Even if Palladio *did not have to* design around the south-wall notch, the maximum property length measured only 116'-0" Vicentine. When the academy's desire for the property in the old prison was recorded on February 15, 1580, they referred to a model and perspective design already prepared by Palladio: it is likely that Palladio redrafted his designs to account for the then definite property limits. The model and perspective designs must have been a product of that redesign. Neither the plans nor the model is extant. Some form of plans did exist since Palladio's son, Silla, was awarded academy funds and use of the drawings on January 27, 1581, for a posthumous publication.[62] The publication never appeared.

The London Studio does not seem to have been designed with regard for compromising property limits. On that assumption, a design source analysis should reveal an understanding of Palladio's idealized conception of the Teatro Olimpico. The analysis which follows will also serve as a comparative foundation for the design sources present in the executed theatre.

On a very generalized basis the London Studio has the earmarks of a Vitruvian Roman theatre. It has a classically decorated *frons-scenae* of three orders, the central portal and the *hospitalia* openings as described by Vitruvius, the *cavea* raised over the orchestra level (according to the Barbaro-Palladio misinterpretation), a raked *cavea,* and a *cavea* portico. We can even speculate that Palladio relocated the *versurae* at right angles to the *frons-scenae* according to his archaeological experiences and counter to the Barbaro interpretation. But the similarities between the London Studio and Vitruvius are deceiving. Under close scrutiny we will see Vitruvius deviated from to the point of negation. What Palladio seems to be doing is adapting the strict

Vitruvian instructions to his own liking, sampling very minutely from archaeology, and producing his own concept of an archaeologically *acceptable* Roman theatre that, like other theatre ruins he examined, is quite un-Vitruvian.

The following discussion of the presence of effective design sources in the London Studio is based on the analysis of design sources in chapter 2. Of necessity, the analysis will make frequent reference to tables 1 and 2. Comparisons to the London Studio features refer to tables 5 through 8. To simplify the reader's understanding of the analysis, data will be abstracted from the above mentioned tables and repeated in the body of the text. Generally I will cite the modular specifications of Vitruvius (the Vitruvian "canon"), the expected dimension based on Vitruvian canon, and the executed dimension scaled from the London Studio. Two expected and executed dimensions are given, one for the right half of the London Studio and one for the left, based on the different orchestra diameters of the Studio (53.5' left, 54.0' right). The same procedure will be followed for the analysis of the executed Teatro Olimpico.

Drafting and scaling errors will be differentiated from deliberate deviations from the norm by a 2% error tolerance. When a design feature deviates more than 2% from the norm, that deviation will be considered to be deliberate. In the normative system of architecture which Palladio espoused, deviations from the norm were generally the product of practical limitations. Ideally Palladio followed a mathematical system which was based on a retrievable norm, usually in the form of a module. The differences between one norm and another are minute in their distinctions, yet Palladio did discriminate between norms.[63]

The planometrics of the London Studio have both Vitruvian and non-Vitruvian features. The Barbaro-Palladio Vitruvian *frons-scenae* length, *cavea* outside radius, and *cavea* and portico depth compare with the London Studio as follows (measurements are in d-quantities and Vicentine feet):

| | Barbaro-Palladio Vitruvius | | | London Studio | |
| | | Expected | | Executed | |
	Canon	Left	Right	Left	Right
Orchestra diameter	1d.	53.5	54.0	53.5	54.0
Frons-scenae length	2d.	107.0	108.0	79.0	78.0
Cavea outside radius	1d.	53.5	54.0	58.5	58.25
Cavea + portico depth	1/2d.	26.7	27.0	32.5	31.5

The executed London Studio *frons-scenae* length and *cavea* and portico depth do not conform to Vitruvian canon. The executed *frons-scenae* length is only 1

1/2d. and not the Vitruvian 2d.; the *cavea* and portico depth is nearly 3/5d. rather than the expected 1/2d.

Nor do the London Studio *cavea* elevation, the *cavea* height, or the portico height (to the ceiling) conform to Vitruvian description as derived from Palladio's drawings. The dimensions are in Vicentine.

	Canon	Expected		Executed	
		Left	Right	Left	Right
Orchestra diameter	1d.	53.5	54.0	53.5	54.0
Cavea elevation	330/1920d.	9.19	9.28	8.25	8.25
Cavea height	390/1920d.	10.86	10.96	15.25	15.0
Portico height	630/1920d.	17.55	17.71	28.0	23.5

The executed *cavea* elevations are less than 90% of the expected canonical dimension. The deviation is more than 10%. The *cavea* and portico heights in the London Studio are even more radical in their divergence from Vitruvian canon. If Palladio had intended the portico height to be measured to the top of the portico statuary (22.5' left, 21.5' right), while these heights more closely approximate the canonical height, Palladio at the same time has broken Vitruvius' instruction that the portico height should never be less than the *frons-scenae* height (V.vi.4). The *cavea* portico is post and lintel in design, like the Vitruvius drawing (figure 13).

With regard to the relation of the top of the *cavea* to the first order *frons-scenae* cornice, Palladio has achieved an alignment much as he approximated in the Roman Study (figure 49 and table 3); this relationship was ignored in the Vitruvian renderings. Yet Palladio appears quite unconcerned with aligning the portico cornice with the *frons-scenae* second order cornice. In the London Studio it would have been no difficult matter for Palladio to have eliminated the balustrade under the portico statues. In doing so he could have retained the designed statue height and increased the portico order so that the entablature and cornice would align with the second order cornice.

Palladio's execution of the London Studio *frons-scenae* is equally without reference to Vitruvian instruction. Represented in tabular form, according to the x/1920d. common denominator (table 2), the executed *frons-scenae* design deviated from the expected canon. (Again the dimensions are in Vicentine feet.)

| | Expected | | Executed | |
	Left	Right	Left	Right
First order				
pedestal height	4.46	4.50	4.00	4.00
column height	13.37	13.50	14.25	14.25
entablature height	2.67	2.70	3.00	3.00
Second order				
pedestal height	2.33	2.25	2.75	2.75
column height	10.03	10.12	10.50	10.25
entablature height	2.01	2.02	2.25	2.25
Third order				
pedestal height	1.11	1.12	2.00	0.88
column height	7.52	7.59	8.50	6.25
entablature height	1.50	1.52	2.50	1.00

Only in the case of the second order column height is there any sense of a feature approximating Vitruvian canon. In most cases the executed London Studio dimensions contain increases that deviate by 10%. The first order pedestal heights and the third order right Studio feature heights exhibit peculiar exceptions; these features contain decreases of 10% under the Vitruvian expectation.

As a design source for the London Studio *frons-scenae* and *cavea* portico, the Barbaro-Palladio Vitruvius canon must be rejected. The question remains whether there are other sources which better explain Palladio's design of the London Studio classical orders. We have been led to expect that Palladian vocabulary followed a consistent application of systematically designed classical orders. His early designs followed the rigors of classical decorum more closely than his late designs, which applied a purely Palladian system. Therefore we could expect Palladio to execute the orders (having rejected Vitruvius) in a classically derived structure according to the decorum espoused in his *Quattro libri* (1570). The *First Book* of the *Quattro libri* contains specifications for the proper construction of classical orders. For example, in a Corinthian order (which is the applied order in the London Studio *cavea* portico, the *frons-scenae* and the *aediculae*), the parts of the order are generated from the diameter of the column shaft at its base (one module). Thus, with a shaft diameter of one unit, the column height is nine and one-half units, the pedestal height is one-fourth of the column height and the entablature height is one-fifth of the column height.[64]

Comparing the expected portico order, as derived from the *Quattro libri,* with the executed London Studio order, it does not appear that Palladio followed the *Quattro libri*. (The dimensions are in Vicentine.)

	Expected	Executed	
		Left	Right
Column module	1.25	1.25	1.25
Column height	11.87	12.25	11.25
Entablature height	2.37	2.50	2.50

Rather, what Palladio appears to have done was to turn to his current (post-1560) stylistic attitude toward the Corinthian order. Chapter 2 traced Palladio's late-style favoring of a 1.10 ratio of module to column height (as opposed to the 1:9.5 ratio). And it was observed that this new Corinthian order ratio was indicative of Palladio's breakaway from strict classical decorum. According to the 1:10 ratio, we get the following Vicentine comparisons:

	Expected	Executed	
		Left	Right
Column module	1.25	1.25	1.25
Column height	12.25	12.50	11.25
Entablature height	2.45	2.50	2.50

Admittedly the 1:10 ratio is not consistently applied throughout the Studio's portico order although the Studio's left portico order might as well be called a precise execution. The left Studio entablature height has a deviation of less than 2%.

Palladio's execution of the London Studio *frons-scenae* also exhibits the application of his current stylistic Corinthian order. However, in comparison to the portico order's execution, there is less consistent rigor in evidence. The following compares the 1:9.5 expectation and the 1:10 expectation with the left and right executions (table 7 contains the complete dimensions in Vicentine feet).

	Expected		Executed	
	1:9.5	1:10	Left	Right
First order module	1.25	1.25	1.25	1.25
pedestal height	2.97	3.12	4.00	4.00
column height	11.85	12.50	14.25	14.25
entablature height	2.37	2.50	3.00	3.00
Second order module	1.00	1.00	1.00	1.00
pedestal height	2.37	2.50	2.75	2.75
column height	9.50	10.00	10.50	10.25
entablature height	1.90	2.00	2.25	2.25

Third order module	.85	.85	.85	1.75
pedestal height	2.02	2.10	2.00	.85
column height	8.07	8.50	8.50	6.25
entablature height	1.61	1.70	2.50	1.00

The London Studio *frons-scenae* first order has radical divergence from the expected proportions. The second order only approximates the 1:10 ratio, as does the left Studio third order. Because the right Studio third order uses a Tuscan pilaster, it should follow the *Quattro libri* rules where the pedestal and entablature heights are one module and the column height is seven modules.[65] Therefore, the order should read: module = 1.75, pedestal height = 1.75, column height = 12.25, and entablature height = 1.75. Comparatively, Palladio seems to be following no system in his execution of the right Studio third order. On the whole, the executed dimensions contain deviations of between 5% and 10%. This amount of deviation seems deliberate.

The London Studio's *frons-scenae* design sources are varied. Palladio has not drawn from Barbaro and his translation of Vitruvius or from his own *Quattro libri* stipulation with any kind of rigor or consistency. Palladio is clearly experimenting with different proportions on the same facade that only approximate his stylistic posture. The proportion's follow no retrievable system at all (as seen, for example, in the peculiar first order column height which exceeds his recent stylistic ratio by 15%). As far as applied design sources are concerned, Palladio seems to rank his own stylistics above Vitruvius as a source. Yet for some unknown reason he has even deliberately deviated from that system.

The *frons-scenae aediculae* reveal additional insights into Palladio's application of design sources. As has already been noted, what were once simple niched statues on the Palladio-Vitruvius *frons-scenae* (figure 45) become in the London Studio elaborate decorative *aediculae* or tabernacles. Their classical function was to display statuary and is typified by their presence between the chapels in the Pantheon; their Renaissance application was largely ecclesiastical—for statuary, altars, urns, or sarcophagi (tombs). Palladio's familiarity with *aediculae* most probably was based on his studies in Rome and especially his drawings of the Pantheon. As a classical vocabulary motif, Palladio applied *aediculae* in three of his church designs. Why Palladio elected to use *aediculae* on the London Studio *frons-scenae* is unknown, especially when he did not encase the *cavea* portico niches with *aediculae* on the same drawing. The most likely reason is that Palladio recognized the *frons-scenae's* decorative potential and looked to the *aediculae* as a useful source; the reason is logical but speculative.

Stylistically the *aediculae* in the London Studio (table 8) have affinities to the Pantheon *aediculae* and Palladio's *aediculae* used on his Venice San

Giorgio Maggiore (1560-62) exterior.[66] Each repeats the relative proportions of *aediculae* intercolumnation to *aediculae* total height (essentially an arithmetic progression of 1:2:3), although recognizably their features have their own individual measurements relative to the size and features of the facade onto which they have been applied. The Corinthian orders that make up the *aediculae* are not designed according to the *Quattro libri* canon or Palladio's 1:10 Corinthian ratio. Tabulated below are the 1:9.5 and 1:10 expectations for the *aediculae* order compared with the London Studio execution. (There is no difference between the left and right Studio executions; the dimensions are in Vicentine.)

	Expected		Executed
	1:9.5	1:10	
Right order module	0.75	0.75	0.75
pedestal height	1.78	1.88	3.00
column height	7.12	7.5	6.50
entablature height	1.42	1.5	1.00
Second order module	0.75	0.75	0.75
pedestal height	1.78	1.88	2.00
column height	7.12	7.5	5.50
entablature height	1.42	1.5	1.00

Here there is no correspondence between the expected heights derived from either the 1:9.5 or the 1:10 ratios and the executed heights. While Palladio has clearly derived the motif from previously experienced and applied vocabulary, there is no systematic application of the orders within the motif.

Before examining how Palladio's aesthetic of harmonic proportion operates in the London Studio, we must briefly examine the presence or absence of the other source derivations in the London Studio features.

The *frons-scenae* openings (central portal, *hospitalia,* and *versurae*) have only one observable derivation from the Vitruvian canon as drawn by Palladio (figures 49 and 51) and tabulated in table 6. That single derivation is in the *hospitalia* opening height where according to the Vitruvius drawing the height should be 430/1920d. The opening height is only approximated since the height should be 12.1′ Vicentine (based on a 54.0′ orchestra diameter); it is only 11.0′ left and 10.5′ right. There is no Vitruvian precedent for the central portal breaking into the second order. However, Palladio had both ancient and Renaissance precedent for this execution of the central portal.

Application of features from Roman theatre archaeology to the London Studio is nil. (Refer to tables 3 and 4 for specifics.) The Verona and Pola *frons-scenae* lengths, which are 1d. and not 2d., are not seen in the London Studio.

There is no proportional carry-over of the *cavea* dimensions, portico levels, or the *frons-scenae* orders from the Verona theatre ruin. The London Studio *cavea* radius does reflect the 1d. dimension seen in the Berga and Pola ruins. However, this feature has already been observed in Vitruvian canon as well. It is likely that Palladio has relocated the *versurae* at right angles to the *frons-scenae* according to his Pola and Verona perceptions, and the possibility exists that Palladio saw in the Verona central portal niche the motif for extending the London Studio central portal into the *frons-scenae* second order. There are no idiosyncratic features in the ruins that are observable in the London Studio. If anything, Palladio's knowledge of Roman theatre ruins gave him precedent for deviating from Vitruvius. Admittedly, this conclusion does not serve to identify specific sources, but it does serve to negate the force of formulary Vitruvianism.

The stylistic source for the balustrade and statuary over the *cavea* portico can be found in some of Palladio's early designs: the Basilica (1549), the Monastery of the Carità (1561), and the Palazzo Iseppo-Porto (pre-1552).[67] Essentially the same relative proportions can be seen in these three designs as are seen in the London Studio (table 5). The statuary and balustrade motif is not documentable in Roman architecture although Palladio's drawings of ancient buildings often included the motif.

Thus far in this analysis of the London Studio, we have observed a consistent lack of allegiance to Vitruvian canon as conceived by Palladio and Barbaro. Nor can any specific features or proportions in Roman theatre ruins be conclusively identified as sources for its design. The London Studio vocabulary is classical as tempered by Palladio's Renaissance stylistics. The executed motifs (the *aediculae,* the portico balustrade and surmounting statuary, and the *frons-scenae* bas-reliefs) are directly derivative of Renaissance and Palladian stylistics and not Imperial Roman architecture. This is not to say that as a source the Renaissance motifs diminish the classical nature of the design; surely Palladio and his contemporaries regarded the motifs as classically valid. On the other hand, much of their execution appears to derive from Palladio's peculiar late stylistics.

After rejecting Vitruvian theatre construction canon and the planometric modularism inherent in Vitruvius' instructions, Palladio appears to turn to his own aesthetic of harmonic proportions as the means for integrating the London Studio into an organic whole.

Largely because of the overwhelming quantity of elements that *might* be related, Palladio's system appears more generally applied and is more loosely applied than was observed in the representative examples in chapter 2: the facade for the Palazzo Valmarana and the facade and plan relationship in the Villa Godi.

The most striking ratios in the London Studio are the harmonics between the length of the first order *aediculae* shafts (5.5'), their corresponding major order shaft (11.0'), and the orchestra diameter (when rounded to 55.0' from 53.5' left, 54.0' right).[68] Represented in the form of a musical analogy, the three quantities relate by the ratios of 1:2:10 or three octaves and a major third. In other words, the ratio 1:2 is an octave. The ratio 2:10 is more obscure; within the ratio 2:10 are two octaves (2:4:8) and a major third (8:10 or 4:5). The second order *aediculae* shaft (4.5') is more loosely related to the second order major shaft (8.25' left, 8.0' right) and the *frons-scenae* major intercolumnation (8.0'); the *aediculae* shaft relates to the other quantities by a 1:2 ratio or an octave.

The second order *aediculae* shaft (4.5') and the major intercolumnation (8.0') are loosely related to the height of the *cavea* (orchestra floor to top seat: 23.5' left, 23.25' right) and the height of the *cavea* portico (to the top of the statuary: 22.5' left, 21.5' right) by a proportion that yields an octave and a major tenth (1:2:5). This musical analogy is only possible when the *aediculae* shaft height is rounded off to 4.0', the major intercolumnation is defined as 8.0', and the *cavea* and portico heights are rounded off to 20.0'. It would be dangerous to seek out additional harmonics from the quantities enumerated in tables 5 through 8, for even with the above bold features many of their quantities require rounding off before they yield commensurable ratios.

In this analysis of what appears to have been an early design for the Teatro Olimpico we have been able to identify both general and specific design sources. Palladio seems to shun Vitruvian canon in favor of the liberties permitted by his knowledge of archaeological ruins. Counter to our expectations, Palladio applies his current vocabulary in preference to that of his earlier career or the idealized *Quattro libri*. Harmonically, there are some bold and loose ratios but nothing that compares with the precise system he followed in his domestic plans and facades (chapter 2).

The London Studio has general affinities to the description of the *Sofonisba* theatre design of 1562 and, of course, to the Barbaro-Palladio Vitruvius *frons-scenae* rendering. Palladio was designing a theatre after the Roman manner; however, in terms of Palladio's deviations from the Vitruvian instructions, the London Studio is a Renaissance mutation.

We turn now to the final design of the Olimpico—that process by which Palladio appears to have adapted the London Studio to the property limits of the city's land grant of February 22, 1580. At this juncture we gain a new problem in analysis; even though Palladio died in August 1580 and the records claim that the theatre was ready to be roofed in November of that year, we cannot be certain that the *cavea, cavea* portico, stage, or *frons-scenae* had even been started by the end of 1580. It was normal in Renaissance architectural practice to erect the shell of a building and to roof it before treating the interior features.[69] The original Olimpico structure was essentially a one story building and the *frons-scenae* orders served no static function. It is likely that the extended construction period (to as late as July 29, 1582, when the records note the building as nearly completed) involved the interior carpentry and masonry. Therefore, it bears noting that my subsequent references to the Olimpico as being executed according to Palladio's ideas form an assumption.

Two drawings of the Olimpico nearly contemporary to its completion are extant. The drawing by Giovanni Battista Albanese (figure 54) is held by the Royal Institute of British Architects; Albanese was a sculptor and architect contemporary to Palladio and active in Vicenza architecture in the early seventeenth century.[70] The drawing by Otavio Orefice (figure 55) is dated 1620 and is held by the National Museum of Stockholm. A comparison of these drawings with the London Studio (figure 48) reveals several vocabulary and decoration changes, many of which are documented in the academy records. Even before Palladio's death, the initially conceived feminine statues on the *frons-scenae* were changed to statues of academicians in accordance with the decision of May 23, 1580. Over the central portal, from the ceiling to just above the arch keystone, the following changes occurred: the decision to include the Olimpico Academy stadium emblem was made on February 5, 1582, the Vicenza city coat of arms was the product of an April 1, 1581, decision, and on May 8, 1583, the academy decided to erect the plaque which named Palladio as architect. The scenic perspectives in the Albanese and Orefice drawings are those built for the *Edippo* production. There are no perspectives in the London Studio.

A radical change in the *frons-scenae* vocabulary is documented in the Albanese and Orefice drawings. What were originally all Corinthian columns in the London Studio's first two orders are now engaged Corinthian pilasters. There are two exceptions. Both orders' forward columns remained columns, and the first order forward columns remained freestanding. The central portal and the *hospitalia* openings have been changed. The central portal in the London Studio was framed by freestanding columns; the arch is now imposted on the *frons-scenae* wall and the wall is treated as the edge of a Corinthian pilaster. The *hospitalia* openings in the London Studio were cut through the *frons-scenae* wall and dissociated from the flanking columns; now the opening is framed by pilasters and its height has been increased by the elimination of the lintel frieze and bas-reliefs. The *aediculae* orders were changed from Corinthian columns to Corinthian pilasters in the final design. These changes and others, some of which may be of definite post-Palladian invention, will be discussed in the analysis of the design sources for the completed Teatro Olimpico.

The following analysis is based on the most current and accurate survey of the theatre since its completion. The survey was sponsored by the Centro Internazionale di Studi d'Architettura Andrea Palladio (Vicenza) in 1965. Until the publication of drawings based on the 1965 survey, the most accurate set of drawings of the theatre was that published by Bertotti Scamozzi in 1796. I will use these drawings for visual reference only—many of their measurements and scales are not consistent or accurate.[71] The Olimpico has not changed substantially since its completion in 1585. Parts of the stage, orchestra, and cavea have been replanked in modern times. The scenery and statuary were disassembled and stored during World War II; the theatre proper suffered no direct bombing raids although the atrium and odeo were damaged and had to be rebuilt after the war.[72] With the increase in tourism, and the deterioration of the original stairway up to the rear of the cavea, new entrances were cut through the extreme lower ends of the cavea (figure 56). The current summer use of the Olimpico for theatrical productions necessitated the elevation of the orchestra floor so that it was only .65 meters below the stage floor. The theatre's ceiling went through several design changes in the eighteenth and nineteenth centuries; the importance of these changes will be reviewed shortly. Otherwise, the Olimpico remains as it was completed for the inaugural performance in 1585.

Palladio's adaptation of his design (the London Studio) to the property acquired in February 1580 involved the reduction of the *frons-scenae* length and the orchestra diameter and the essential elimination of the *cavea* portico. The actual *cavea* radius was retained from the London Studio to the final design. Tables 5 and 6 enumerate the changes which allowed Palladio to fit the *cavea,* stage, and *frons-scenae* onto a site measuring 22.50 meters (east-west) by 40.25 meters (north-south; unencumbered north-south length, 34.40 meters). What is unexpected about the final planometric design of the Olimpico is the semiovoid shape of the orchestra and *cavea* curves (figure 44). We recall the several explanations advanced by critics (as reviewed in chapter 1) for Palladio's use of the "elliptical" orchestra and the rationalization of this shape to conform to Vitruvian modular theatre planometrics. Montenari, for example, praised the solution to the property site problem but attempted no analysis of motives. Bertotti Scamozzi argued that the "elliptical" shape was forced by practical limitations and that the sum of the length of the resultant major axis and half the length of the minor axis nearly equalled the *frons-scenae* length. Lawrenson attributed the shape to truncated half-circle orchestras in Roman theatre ruins. There is no doubt that Palladio did in fact collapse the ideal Vitruvian Roman semicircular orchestra so that it would fit into the allotted space. The rationale for his design of this shape demands analysis. First of all, without any evidence to the contrary, we must assume that Palladio's original design used a semicircular orchestra. His experiences with Vitruvian theatre planometrics, the *L'Amor costante* (1561) theatre that was "similar to that of the ancient Romans," the Venice theatre in the Carità (1562)—"a half theatre of wood in the manner of a colosseum," and Palladio's probable knowledge of Serlio's 1539 Vicenza theatre all argue for a semicircular design.

To understand how Palladio apparently transformed a semicircular orchestra and *cavea* into a semiovoid orchestra and *cavea* requires an understanding of the collapsing process. To this day analysts and critics of the Teatro Olimpico have referred to the theatre's orchestra and *cavea* as semielliptical in shape. The precise measurements acquired in the 1965 theatre survey reveal that the executed curves are not semielliptical. From the survey measurements[73] the actual curve of the *cavea* can be drawn. Since the distance from the orchestra curve to the *cavea* curve is consistently 7.98 meters, the curve describing the orchestra can be extracted from the *cavea* curve. The two curves are duplicated into two enclosed ovals, the *cavea* oval encompassing the orchestra oval. Major and minor axes are then erected in the ovals. Presuming them to be ellipses, foci can be extracted for each oval.[74] The elliptical curves generated from these foci do not conform to the existing *cavea* and orchestra curves.[75] Although the executed curves are not elliptical, we cannot summarily say that Palladio did not know how to generate an ellipse. The geometrics of conics were a post-Euclidian Greek subject of inquiry and were known in the Renaissance.[76]

The possibility exists that Palladio merely drew a pair of similar curves, executing the *cavea* curve so that it took full advantage of the property site. This explanation may be satisfactory except for two important issues: we have been led to expect Palladio to be more systematic than this casual explanation affords, and the oval was not a popular geometric shape in the Renaissance.[77] Only one architectural theorist preceding or contemporary to Palladio took the time to discuss the generation of ovals; in Serlio's *First Book* he described four methods of drawing "ovali."[78] Palladio appears to have turned to Serlio's systems; curves produced by Serlio's first "ovali" method conform precisely to the Olimpico *cavea* and orchestra curves using the stage front as the major axis.[79]

Having discovered Palladio's probable geometric source, questions arise about the rationale for integrating these ovoid shapes into the Olimpico design. Did Palladio in fact manage to satisfy any of the modularism inherent in Vitruvius' theatre planometrics? Close scrutiny reveals a rationale for the total integration of the semiovoid orchestra and *cavea* according to Vitruvian planometrics. Admittedly the rationale that follows is speculative. Yet the rationale accounts for Palladio's peculiar concept of the Roman stage depth and manifests Palladio's aesthetic of harmonic proportion.

While the unencumbered maximum north-south length of Palladio's property site was 34.40 meters, the peculiar arrangement of the south wall notch allowed a maximum length of 35.00 meters. The stage front is located along this seemingly arbitrary axis. Drawing on Barbaro and Palladio's interpretation of Vitruvius and the near confirmation of the Berga theatre ruin, the 35.00 meter axis is divided in half, yielding a *cavea* radius (to the exterior face of the walls) of 17.50 meters (1d.) and a nearly equivalent orchestra diameter of 17.42 meters (1d.). From this major axis Palladio generated his ovoid shape. Notably, the ovoid cavea curve is tangent to the south wall notch (figure 44) and remains within the limits of the unencumbered north-south property length. From the second and shorter major axis, or orchestra diameter, the ovoid orchestra curve is erected producing a minor orchestra semiaxis, or "radius," of 6.22 meters. In conformity to the Barbaro-Palladio Vitruvius, the *frons-scenae* length equals twice the orchestra diameter and the stage depth equals half the orchestra diameter (canon, table 1). By doubling the minor orchestra semiaxis (6.22 meters), a second orchestra "diameter" (12.44 meters = $1d._1$) is established. When doubled this second orchestra "diameter" produces the *frons-scenae* length (25.05 meters = $2d._1$) and when halved generates the stage depth (6.52 meters = ca. $1/2d._1$). The validity of this rationale is further substantiated in Palladio's aesthetic of proportional harmonics. The ratio of the major orchestra diameter (1d.) to the *cavea* diameter (2d.) is an octave (1:2). The ratio of the stage depth (ca. $1/2d._1$) to the minor orchestra diameter ($1d._1$) to the *frons-scenae length* ($2d._1$) is a double octave (1:2:4). It appears to be no accident that the building designed acording to this system completely consumes all of the available property site.[81]

With the *frons-scenae* that this system produced, Palladio was forced to reduce the length of the London Studio *frons-scenae*. Palladio definitely favored the right half of the London Studio in its transferal to the Olimpico's execution. (Compare the right London Studio, figure 48, with the Albanese and Orefice drawings figures 54 and 55, as well as the relevant figures in table 7.) Palladio's reduction process is detailed in table 9. The distance between the *versurae* walls and the second forward column (from each direction) maintains the London Studio dimensions; the corner forward columns increased distance from the *versurae* surface reduces the extreme left and right *aediculae* space. Apparently Palladio reduced this initial *aediculae* space so that he could maintain a consistent *aediculae* spacing across the whole *frons-scenae* and still reduce the total *frons-scenae* length by 2.0 meters. By eliminating the freestanding central portal arch columns and engaging them to the *frons-scenae* wall as pilasters, Palladio manages to lose only .62 meters of central portal width from the initial London Studio design.

Palladio's reduction of the Olimpico *frons-scenae* length involved substantial changes. But the redesign of the right London Studio *cavea* to the executed Olimpico *cavea* involved only minor adjustments as indicated below. (The dimensions are in Vicentine and are derived from table 5.)

	Right London Studio	Olimpico Execution
Cavea elevation over orchestra	8.25	7.75
Cavea height	15.00	14.66
Portico height (to ceiling)	23.25	24.00

As with the London Studio, these executed *cavea* and portico dimensions have no relevance to the Vitruvian canon as derived from Palladio's drawings.

The *cavea* portico also fell victim to the practicality of designing for a restricted property site. The depth of the London Studio *cavea* portico has been virtually eliminated in the Teatro Olimpico. Because of the practical limitations of space, Palladio has elected to retain the portico by an optical device; the portico has no real depth except in the northwest and southwest corners of the building (figure 44). Palladio's optical device is effected by his management of the niched statues within the post and lintel colonnade and the surmounting balustrade and statuary. When the portico is "read" the eye sees a complex of volumes (figure 32). The windows which bound the majority of the portico behind the balustrade and statuary create the impression of much more space beyond the balustrade and statues than there really is. Below the balustrade, the eye expects an equivalent ostensible space. Rather, it is confronted by the solid boundaries of the colonnade niched statues. Yet, as each of these physically bound surfaces recedes into the northwest and southwest open spaces, they carry an additional niched statue; in effect, these carry-over niches imply more space. The brightness of the bounded surfaces also helps to imply more space or depth than is actually there, as does the treatment of the transverse walls that separate the *cavea* from the stage area. On the transverse walls Palladio has executed three-dimensional niched statues but has painted the colonnade, balustrade, and terminal statues. The interplay of real and implied space was not stylistically foreign to Palladio; he used the same optical device of an enclosed colonnade screen juxtaposed to an open colonnade screen to achieve an apparently larger choir in his two major ecclesiastical works, the San Giorgio Maggiore and the Il Redentore (Venice).

The planometric and horizontal relationship of the *cavea* and *cavea* portico to the *frons-scenae* and stage have been the source of much criticism. Roberto Pane's argument is that the junction of the two parts (*cavea* and stage) was so poorly handled that certainly Palladio had nothing to do with this aspect of the design.[82] The "invading idea," argues Pane, was indicated by the absence of horizontal continuity between the *cavea* portico cornice and the *frons-scenae* second order cornice. Pane's argument is uncritical when we recall that only once was Palladio concerned with this horizontalism and that was in the Roman Study (figure 49). Even the London Studio ignores this potential relationship, and the London Studio does not indicate the presence of transverse walls; the presence of the transverse walls in the Olimpico helps to hide this lack of continuity. The transverse wall itself has an archaeological source in the theatre ruin at Pola (figure 53). The use of transverse walls, or piers, in the Olimpico serves to deny a horizontal comparison of the *cavea* portico and the *frons-scenae*. Pane also argues that the portico niche style's similarity to the *versurae* niche style was further evidence of Palladio's intention to better relate the two surfaces. On close examination, the two niche styles are as different as they are similar: the *versurae* niches have their own pedestal and are surmounted by reliefs while the portico niches have no pedestal or surmounting reliefs. Conceivably Palladio saw in the similar but different niches the opportunity for a more integral transition from *cavea* to *frons-scenae*. The only objectionable and afunctional aspect of the Olimpico transverse walls is the poor sightlines they produce. In the London Studio more than half of the *cavea* depth was superimposed over the *frons-scenae* length (table 6). In the Olimpico less than a third of the *cavea* depth extends beyond the transverse wall; spectators in the extreme corners of the *cavea* cannot see more than a third to a half of the stage. The physical reason for the poor sightlines is explained by Palladio's demonstrated planometric allegiance to Vitruvius. By retaining the 1d. *cavea* radius but reducing the *frons-scenae* length, the sightlines were inevitable. Here is a design instance where theatrical functionalism succumbed to practicalities and canon.

In contrast to the London Study, which exhibited very few affinities to Vitruvian canon, the Teatro Olimpico's executed planometrics demonstrate a consistent attempt to respect Vitruvian instructions. At this juncture it would be reasonable to expect that the applied classical vocabulary in the Olimpico would, like its planometrics, look to Vitruvian canon. On the contrary, the following analysis of the *cavea* portico, the *frons-scenae* orders, and the *aediculae* reveals a nearly precise application of Palladio's current Corinthian stylistics.

According to the 1:10 Corinthian stylistic, the executed *cavea* portico compares well with the expectation. (Measurements are in meters.)

	Expected	Executed
Column module	.35	.35
Column height	3.50	3.99
Entablature height	.70	.79

If Palladio had looked to Vitruvian canon, the *cavea* portico would have the following dimensions (the major orchestra diameter equals 17.42 meters):

	Canon	Expected	Executed
Column diameter	50/1920d.	.45	.35
Column height	520/1920d.	4.72	3.99
Entablature height	90/1920d.	.82	.79

While neither the Palladian stylistic nor the Vitruvian canon are precisely executed, the *cavea* portico favors the Palladian stylistic system. As a motif, the post and lintel portico colonnade is derivative of the Palladio Vitruvian *cavea* (figure 13) and Palladio's use of colonnades in his villa architecture. Palladio's expected *eustylic* colonnade intercolumnation is not carried out in the Olimpico; the Olimpico colonnade intercolumnation is in the *diastyle* (intercolumnation equals three shaft diameters), an unacceptable inter-columnation according to the *Quattro libri* and Palladio's practice. Because the colonnade serves no static function, it might be speculated that Palladio increased the intercolumnation with the intention of improving the sightlines from behind the colonnade to the stage.

The affinities of the present *frons-scenae* to the right London Studio have already been mentioned. In the London Studio only a close approximation to Palladio's current stylistics was observed in the applied major orders and the *aediculae*. In the Olimpico *frons-scenae* orders, nearly all of the features follow Palladio's current stylistics. The deviations are less than 2%.[83] (Table 8 contains the complete *frons-scenae* measurements for the present theatre, as well as their Vicentine equivalents. The following measurements are in meters.)

	Expected	Executed
First order module	.43	.43
pedestal height	1.07	1.39
column height	4.25	4.28
entablature height	.86	.86
Second order module	.35	.35
pedestal height	.88	.88
column height	3.50	3.49
entablature height	.70	.70

Third order module	.40	.40
pedestal height	.40	.35
column height	2.80	2.15
entablature height	.40	.25

Like the London Studio, the Olimpico's first order pedestal and the third Tuscan order fail to follow the expected stylistic ratios. No retrievable systematized source offers an explanation for these deviations.

The *frons-scenae aediculae* vocabulary is also based on Palladio's 1:10 Corinthian stylistics. (Table 8 contains the complete *aediculae* measurements; the dimensions here are in meters.)

	Expected	Executed
First order *aediculae* module	.22	.22
column height	2.20	2.20
entablature height	.44	.53
Second order *aediculae* module	.20	.20
column height	2.00	1.95
entablature height	.40	.39

Other sources for the Olimpico *frons-scenae* features are Vitruvian canon and Palladio's own decorative stylistics. Palladio's use of pilasters in the present *frons-scenae* orders (except for the forward columns) is not unusual. Corinthian pilasters were applied by Palladio to the facades of the Palazzo Thiene (ca. 1545-50) and the Palazzo Valmarana (1565-66). The *frons-scenae* openings (central portal, *hospitalia*, and *versurae*) have peculiar dimensions. The executed openings allow no systematic comparison to Vitruvian expectations. (The canon is derived from tables 1 and 2; the execution is derived from table 6. Dimensions are in meters.)

	Canon	Expected	Executed
Orchestra diameter	1d.	17.42	17.42
Central portal width	150/1920d.	1.36	3.75
Central portal height	620/1920d.	5.29	8.32
Hospitalia width	105/1920d.	.95	1.74
Hospitalia height	420/1920d.	3.67	5.67
Versurae opening width	60/1920d.	.45	1.78
Versurae opening height	430/1920d.	3.81	3.68

The executed opening widths are two to three times larger than they should be according to Vitruvian canon. If Palladio had followed the proportions inherent in his Vitruvian drawings, none of his Olimpico openings would have been practical. For example, the .95 meter *hospitalia* opening is about 37″ (U.S.) wide and appreciably less than the London Studio. We recall Vitruvius' instruction (V.vi.7) that certain theatre features retain a relatively constant size regardless of the theatre's modular size. Recognizing that the Vitruvian drawing (figure 47) uses an orchestra diameter or module of 49.0 meters (tables 1 and 2), while the Olimpico orchestra diameter is 17.42 meters, it would not have been practical to reduce the openings proportionally. To gain functional stage opening widths Palladio appears to have applied Vitruvius' practical suggestion.

The heights of the stage openings are another problem. Palladio repeated the right London Studio *hospitalia* opening height in the Olimpico *versurae* opening height. The Olimpico *hospitalia* height has been enlarged by over a half of the London Studio model, which was 10.5 meters. The 1:2 ratio of width to height in the London Studio *hospitalia* opening (5.25′ compared to 10.5′ Vicentine) was increased to a ratio of 1:3 in the Olimpico. This height increase may have been executed to improve the sightlines into the *hospitalia* opening. The increase in the *hospitalia* opening may have been executed by Scamozzi, who was responsible for the design of the Olimpico radial perspectives.

The central portal breaks into the second order. The central portal in the Palladio-Barbaro Vitruvius did not break into the second order. This motif is unusual but not without precedent in Renaissance practice. Conceivably Palladio used the Verona theatre ruin's large central portal niche as a source for the order-breaking Olimpico arch.

Antecedents of the *frons-scenae* and *versurae* statuary and reliefs are found in Palladio's original design of the Roman theatre (figure 45), although they have been elaborated in the present design.

In contrast to Palladio's constrained ideal decorative sculpture (for example, the original design of the Palazzo Barbarano), the sculptors who executed the Barbarano, Loggia del Capitaniato, and Olimpico decorations have managed to destroy much of the strong linear qualities expected of Palladio.[84] Magagnato has argued that the Olimpico *frons-scenae* decoration has affinities to the Imperial Roman triumphal arch with its depiction of the labors and triumphs of Hercules in the bas-reliefs.[85] For example, such programmatic reliefs can be seen in the arch of Septimius Severus, Rome (figure 30).

Palladio's applied Vitruvian modular harmonics in the Olimpico plano-metrics are also integrated with the Olimpico *frons-scenae*. The major orchestra diameter is related to the *cavea* diameter in a ratio of 1:2 and the stage depth is related to the minor orchestra "diameter" and the *frons-scenae* length by a ratio of 1:2:4, a sequence of octaves. We can further note the following harmonics of elevation (in meters):

	Aediculae shafts	Major order shafts	Ratio
First order	1.75	3.49	1:2
Second order	1.50	3.01	1:2

The orchestra diameter, *cavea* diameter, and *frons-scenae* length are harmonically related to the *frons-scenae* elevation through the first order *aediculae* shaft as module (in meters):

	Quantity	Ratio Progression
First order *aediculae* shaft	1.75	1:
Orchestra diameter	17.42	10:
Frons-scenae length	25.05	14:
Cavea diameter	35.00	20

Musically the ratio analogy is obscure. The ratios of 1:10:14:20 must be broken down as follows: 1:10 is three octaves and a major third or 1:2:4:8:10. (1:2:4:8 equals three octaves and 8:10 or 4:5 is a major third.) The ratio 10:14:20 is an octave (10:20 or 1:2); the 14 reduced to 1.4 (e.g., 1:1.4:2) is the square root of 2. Palladio's aesthetic of harmonic proportion is evident in the Olimpico design. Palladio's success with harmonic proportion was made more complex by his use of the ovoid planometrics, but was simplified by his vocabulary stylistic ratio of 1:10.

With the exception of the scenic perspectives, the odeo, atrium, and present Olimpico ceiling, the Teatro Olimpico has all the earmarks of a Palladian design. Discounting the statue changes, the addition of the Olimpico Academy stadium and inscription, and the city's coat of arms, which do not affect the essential design of the theatre, I cannot agree with Pane and others that Palladio's death permitted the intrusion of un-Palladian features. In fact, even the perspectives cannot be defined as un-Palladian since Palladio used three-dimensional perspectives in the *Sofonisba* (1562) theatre and the academy records indicate the existence of some kind of Olimpico perspective designs on February 15, 1580.[86]

What is un-Palladian about the Olimpico perspectives is their arrangement and subject matter. The radial or multiple vanishing-point aspect of the perspectives cannot be documented in Palladio's earlier use of illusionistic scenery. Note, for example, the single vanishing point in Palladio's Vitruvian *frons-scenae* (figure 45). Palladio's death came far before the selection of *Edippo* or even a specific play type for the theatre's inauguration.

That Scamozzi was responsible for the actual Olimpico scenery has been the subject of a heated debate between Lionello Puppi and Giangiorgio Zorzi.[87] Puppi supports the traditional argument that Scamozzi was responsible. The academy documents Scamozzi's contribution twice (May 6, 1584, and February 28, 1585). Scamozzi claims the perspectives in his *Dell' idea della architettura universale* (1615).[88] The designs of the Olimpico scenery held by the Uffizi, Florence (Gabionetto dei Desegni, numbers 195, 196, 197, and 198), and the Chatsworth Library contain Scamozzi's handwriting.[89] Zorzi argues that Scamozzi was only involved with the Olimpico inaugural lighting and that the designs were by "Palladio and his assistants." This argument must assume that Palladio was clairvoyant since he died when the academy intended to produce a pastoral. Zorzi's evidence involves the interpretation of several Scamozzi documents which concern the theatre but *not* the scenery in particular. Zorzi claims that had Scamozzi designed the scenery, his letters would have contained references to it. Zorzi says the autographic Uffizi designs are the result of Scamozzi's use of them in the preparation of his unpublished work on perspective. The citations of Scamozzi in the academy minutes, Zorzi claims, are eighteenth century interpolations.[90] Zorzi commits a crucial omission when he does not mention Marzari's (1590) citation of Scamozzi as the perspective designer.[91] The perspective designs are clearly Scamozzi's.[92]

The odeo and atrium are post-Palladian additions. Vicenzo Scamozzi claims their design and completion (1584) in his *Architettura*.[93] The atrium contains the problematic monochromatic frescos painted by an unkown artist in 1595. The odeo contains wall murals of Roman mythology and plaques listing sixteenth and seventeenth century contributors to the Olimpico construction.[94]

The Olimpico ceiling is a design feature of questionable Palladian attribution. The present-day theatre has a plaster ceiling over the *cavea* and orchestra painted to imitate sky. The stage ceiling is divided into fifteen panels, which have been painted with allegorical subjects in what Ackerman calls Palladio's Palazzo Ducal style. Palladio did similar ceiling designs for the Doges Palace, Venice, "after the fires of 1574 and 1577."[95] The academy's post-Palladian handling of the ceiling for the inaugural production was to cover it with a cloth in imitation of the Roman theatre awning.[96] Marzari (1590) writes that the ceiling was completely stuccoed and painted ("scoperto tutto di stucco et a pittura").[97] The 1620 Orefice design (figure 59) shows a fifteen-panelled stage ceiling. Magrini reports ceiling repairs in 1647 and 1677 and says the stage ceiling was replanked into three painted compartments in 1734. In 1755 the academy decided to return the ceiling to Palladio's design, which they interpreted as covering the total ceiling in the Ducal style.[98] In 1811 and 1816 the academy sought to change the ceiling design back to Palladio's original intentions and in 1828 the whole ceiling, including the stage ceiling, was painted in "representation of an awning, sustained by ropes" ("rappresenta un velario sostinuto da funi").[99] This action was the result of a controversy between Conte Enea Arnaldi and Ottone Calderari in 1762. Arnaldi argued that the ceiling should be returned to the 1620 Orefice design since that was surely Palladio's intention.[100] Calderari argued that the whole ceiling should be covered with an awning in imitation of the ancients, since that was Palladio's intention.[101] In 1870 the stage ceiling was repanelled according to the Orefice design,[102] but the *cavea* ceiling was left with the painted awning. In view of the Orefice drawing and the academy's 1584 action, there is an immediate contradiction of design motives. If Palladio designed the ceiling over the stage as represented by Orefice, Palladio was certainly making a nonantique interpolation. If Palladio's intentions were those executed by the academy for the inaugural performance, then his source was archaeologically inspired. Palladio's contribution to the Doges Palace ceilings argues for the Orefice concept; from all that we have seen in the preceding design source analysis, this concept is more in line with Palladio's other nonantique interpolations.

From the original idea in 1579 to produce a play with minimal expense to the inaugural *Edippo* in 1585, the academy built an expensive theatre. Much like the academy's unexpected actions, Palladio produced a building that was in many ways counter to his apparent motive to imitate the Roman theatre.

Essentially the Olimpico design has its basic source in Vitruvius as interpreted by Palladio and Barbaro; the reference to this source is not unexpected in light of Palladio's classical studies and the interests of the academy. Vitruvius' influence is especially observable in the Olimpico general planometrics. However, beyond the general modular features of the design, Palladio shows no great respect for Vitruvian canon and turns to other sources. Theatre archaeology gave him precedent for deviating from Vitruvius, and the practical limitations of the original property site forced Palladio into an ingenious solution that complements the design's Vitruvian modularism. In effect Palladio designed his own archaeological interpretation of a Roman theatre. Palladio did not practice a classically decorous vocabulary; instead he applied his current stylistics. His vocabulary, while derivative of Roman classicism, was distinctly affected by Renaissance practice. He exhibited a conscious attempt at organically integrating the whole structure through his aesthetic of harmonic proportion. While we cannot say for certain what Palladio intended to do with the perspectives, Palladio's use of perspective illusionism in his *Sofonisba* production (according to the theatrical conventions of the times) is fundamental to the perspective idea that

Scamozzi executed. By the strictest of definitions, the Olimpico is only loosely Vitruvian. Palladio's refusal to bow to practical limitations and his late Renaissance interpolation of nonclassical vocabulary are equally important. The Olimpico is a Renaissance hybrid of Roman theatre archaeology.

Conclusions

A substantial quantity of previous scholarship attempts to present a rationale which explains the design of the Olimpico. That scholarship is inadequate largely because its assumptions either totally exclude significant influences from consideration or give the evidence such relative importance as to prevent a thorough design source analysis. Most theatre and art historians essentially concur in their conclusion that the Teatro Olimpico is a Roman imitation tempered by Renaissance culture. That conclusion is patent. What is objectionable are the methods by which the historians perceive the evidence and produce their conclusions.

The study is based on two assumptions: (1) the Olimpico was executed according to the ideas of Andrea Palladio, and (2) because those ideas were the product of a systematic architect, they could be retrieved as explanations for the major influences on his design. As such, the analysis places exclusive concentration on Palladio and on detailed comparisons of the Olimpico's design, feature by feature, with evidence drawn from Palladio's earlier work and thought.

Seven hypothetical design influences are examined. They are (1) Palladio's knowledge of Vitruvius, (2) his experiences with theatre archaeology, (3) his architectural stylistics and aesthetics, (4) his designs for theatres prior to the Olimpico, (5) his knowledge of the theatrical practice of the times, (6) his client's expectations, and (7) the practical limitations imposed on him. Each of these influences is shown to have a direct effect on the Olimpico's design and execution. Therefore, the following conclusions seem warranted.

Clearly the primary motive behind the design of the Olimpico was to build a theatre in imitation of the ancients. The Olimpic Academy, Palladio's architectural client, used this type of theatre in previous productions; Palladio's earlier theatre designs followed this archaeological motive. Palladio was very much aware of the evolution of the "teatro rinascimentale"; his motives were merely different. The theory advanced by Magagnato and Lawrenson that Palladio designed in conscious reaction against the "teatro rinascimentale" is, at best, hasty speculation. There is no contemporary

documentation of the attitude that physical imtimacy between the actor and
the audience was a necessary design consideration. Without documentation of
that attitude, Palladio's design motive appears to have been chiefly antiquarian.

The actual design of the Olimpico involves the unique synthesis of four
measurable influences: Vitruvian planometrics, theatre archaeology, Palladio's stylistics, and practical contingencies. By the strictest of definitions, the
Olimpico must be regarded as non-Vitruvian, but it is misleading to suggest
the Vitruvius was not an important influence in its design. It is probable that
had Palladio been granted a less restrictive site he would have designed a
theatre based on the modular planometrics of a Roman half-circle orchestra.
His previous theatre designs suggest the likelihood of a semicircular plan. In
spite of Palladio's practical limitations, he ingeniously manages to satisfy the
Vitruvian planometrics. According to the rationale advanced in this study,
Palladio's ovoid orchestra yields two modules which variously accounts for
the basic stage and *cavea* dimensions derived according to Vitruvius'
instructions as Palladio understood them. Furthermore, Palladio overcomes
the practical limitations and achieves a design that rationalizes Vitruvian
planometrics. Palladio's concept of the decorative features in a Roman
theatre is also derived from Vitruvius. The *frons-scenae* motifs (the orders, the
statuary, and the bas-reliefs) and the *cavea* portico are Vitruvian conceptions.
However, their execution is Palladian.

Palladio's study of Roman theatre ruins demonstrated to him that
Vitruvius presented an ideal that actual Roman theatres never met. Archaeological alternatives gave Palladio a rationale for the design of an ovoid plan
and, in the cases of the *frons-scenae* and portico, the systematic deviation
from Vitruvius. There is nothing unusual in Palladio's stylistic experimentation with archaeologically derived orders and motifs. The designs he produced
is his last twenty years show the Olimpico to be the last in a series of
experiments. The most apparent motive for this experimentation resides in his
aesthetic. In his final Olimpico design Palladio does not follow Vitruvius'
frons-scenae and *cavea* portico proportions as he had in the published
Vitruvian drawings and the Roman study. Instead he follows his current
stylistic attitude toward Corinthian orders, a decidedly Renaissance temper-
ing of the building. The use of his current stylistic allows a more effective
harmonic integration of the decor with the plan of the theatre.

Palladio's archaeological studies are confirmed as a specific design
source in only two instances. The Pola stage piers and the Verona and Pola
versurae appear in the Olimpico. In contrast to the awkward location of the
versurae in the Barbaro-Vitruvius, Palladio's studies of the Verona and Pola
theatre ruins appear to confirm their more accurate placement.

The influence of practical limitations is more than apparent. It forces Palladio into a strictly non-Vitruvian plan. It substantially eliminates the *cavea* portico, although Palladio's optical device of real and implied space produces what is best described as an ostensible portico. In an apparent effort to maintain the semblance of a Vitruvian *cavea* radius that is equivalent to the orchestra diameter, the extreme sections of the *cavea* are left with problematic sightlines. On the whole Palladio adjusts to the practicalities with ingenious solutions. No doubt in the absence of practical limits he would have designed a different theatre plan.

In view of Palladio's apparent motive to design a theatre in imitation of the Roman model, several design compromises are readily identified. The less than classically decorous vocabulary is a case in point. However, Palladio's stylistics are imitative mutations and not direct imitations of antiquity. Pane and Puppi argue that the disproportion of *cavea* and stage spaces and their poorly handled connection point to the presence of a "foreign mind" introducing design changes which were counter to Palladio's intentions. It seems, rather, that the *cavea*-stage transverse walls were necessitated by the peculiar shape of the theatre and that their so-called poorly handled connection was not considered a design fault by Palladio. Only in the Roman study did Palladio attempt to unify the vocabulary of the *cavea* portico to the *frons-scenae.* This unifying feature is not found in other archaeological studies of theatres by Palladio or the extant preliminary design of the Olimpico. While the volumes of the two spaces are disproportionate, Palladio unifies them through the harmonics of their plans and elevations.

The perspective scenery in the Olimpico was designed and executed by Vicenzo Scamozzi. The subject matter and radical arrangement of the scenery seem to be Scamozzi's invention. Still, Palladio uses three-dimensional perspectives and locates them behind the *frons-scenae* openings in his *Sofonisba* design. The Scamozzi designs, if not Palladio's intent, are at least not contrary to Palladio's ideas. This type of illusionistic scenery is derivative of Renaissance theatrical practice; its location behind the formal *frons-scenae* is the product of the Barbaro-Palladio misinterpretation of the *periaktoi* placement.

Puppi's argument that Scamozzi and Ingegneri adapted the *cavea*-stage transverse walls into a rudimentary proscenium arch is specious by its implication that the stage piers were extended from the transverse walls by someone else after Palladio's death. As has been noted, the stage piers have a precedent in the Pola theatre ruin as drawn by Palladio.

Dalla Pozza and Magagnato assert without testing that Palladio's stylistics are present in the Olimpico. The stylistic analysis in this study confirms the presence of Palladio's late stylistics in the *frons-scenae* vocabulary, the *frons-scenae aediculae,* and the *cavea* portico. Unlike previous studies such as Dalla Pozza's, which argues only from a visual comparison of Palladio's stylistics, this study has been able to discriminate unique stylistic tendencies through mathematical comparisons.

The comparative overlay method used in this study identifies the Olimpico's vocabulary and motif sources. It confirms the ingenuity of Palladio's allegiance to Vitruvius. Through the application of Palladio's architectural aesthetic as derived from Wittkower, the study demonstrates the organic design of the Olimpico.

The purpose of this study is not to evaluate the Olimpic Academy as a producing organization or the Teatro Olimpico as functional architecture. These are studies for the future. Although the study by Leo Schrade of the inaugural production of *Edippo* speculates about the Olimpico as a functional theatre, much more available evidence could be put to use. Most enigmatic is the theatre's nearly total disuse until the present century. A comparative study of the decline of academic theatre and the growth of court and popular theatre at the end of the sixteenth century might be revealing. Such a study would necessarily address itself especially to the Renaissance academic concept of ancient dramatic production.

The Teatro Olimpico is a theatrical curiosity. Injected into the history of the theatre architecture it is the belated terminus of the humanistic impulse. Generally the Olimpico design motive was to imitate the ancient Roman theatre. However, the widespread, application of Palladian architectural stylistics in the theatre suggests a Renaissance-controlled hierarchy of motives. The theatre is ingeniously Vitruvian and uniquely Palladian.

Tables

Table 1. Barbaro-Palladio Roman Theatre: The Plan*

	Module d-quantity	Meters, base 49 m.
Orchestra diameter	1 d.	49.0 m.
Cavea radius (includes portico)	1 d.	49.0 m.
Cavea depth (excludes portico)	720/1920 d. (3/8 d.)	18.0 m.
Portico depth	240/1920 d. (1/8 d.)	6.0 m.
Frons-scenae length	2 d.	98.0 m.
Stage depth	960/1920 d. (1/2 d.)	24.5 m.
Niche depth	240/1920 d. (1/8 d.)	6.0 m.
Central portal width	150/1920 d.	3.8 m.
Hospitalia width	105/1920 d.	2.7 m.
Versurae width	60/1920 d.	1.5 m.

*See figure 47.

Table 2. Barbaro-Palladio Roman Theatre: The Elevation*

	Module d-quantity	Meters, base 49 m.
Orchestra level to stage level	90/1920 d.	2.3 m.
Frons-scenae height	1248/1920 d.**	31.7 m.
First order height	736/1920 d.	18.6 m.
First order pedestal height	160/1920 d.	4.1 m.
First order column height	480/1920 d.	12.2 m.
First order entablature height	96/1920 d.	2.4 m.
Second order height	512/1920 d.	12.8 m.
Second order pedestal height	80/1920 d.	2.0 m.
Second order column height	360/1920 d.	9.2 m.
Second order entablature height	72/1920 d.	1.8 m.
Third order height	364/1920 d.	9.2 m.
Third order pedestal height	40/1920 d.	1.0 m.
Third order column height	270/1920 d.	6.8 m.
Third order entablature height	54/1920 d.	1.3 m.
Central portal height	620/1920 d.	15.5 m.
Hospitalia opening height	420/1920 d.	10.1 m.
Versurae opening height	430/1920 d.	10.6 m.
Orchestra level to *cavea* first level	330/1920 d.	8.4 m.
Cavea first level to top seat	390/1920 d.	9.9 m.
Top seat to portico terminal cornice	630/1920 d.	16.0 m.

*See figures 13 and 45.

**Total excludes third order total d-quantity. With a third order, the *frons-scenae* height would be 1612/1920 d.

Table 3. Comparison of Palladio's Berga Theatre and Roman Study with the Barbaro-Palladio Vitruvius

	Berga Theatre	Roman Study	Vitruvius
Orchestra diameter	Piede 140	Piede 120	1 d.
Cavea radius (includes portico)	135	124	1 d.
Cavea depth (excludes portico)	50	48	3/8 d.
Portico depth	15	16	1/8 d.
Frons-scenae length	268	240	2 d.
Stage depth	26-2	60	1/2 d.
Orchestra level to stage level	?	5	90/1920 d.
Frons-scenae height	?	73	1248/1920 d.
First order height	?	41	736/1920 d.
First order pedestal height	?	5	160/1920 d.
First order column height	?	30	480/1920 d.
First order entablature height	?	6	96/1920 d.
Second order height	?	32	512/1920 d.
Second order pedestal height	?	5	80/1920 d.
Second order column height	?	22-6	360/1920 d.
Second order entablature height	?	4	72/1920 d.
Cavea total height	87/53*	80	1350/1920 d.
Orchestra level to *cavea* first level	22/ 9	20	330/1920 d.
Cavea first level to top seat	35/32	30	390/1920 d.
Top seat to portico terminal cornice	30/12	30	630/1920 d.
Cavea rake	34°/27°	33°	30°

*Since Palladio includes two renderings of the *cavea*, the left number refers to the left-hand rendering and the right number refers to the right-hand rendering (see figure 46).

Table 4. Comparison of Palladio's Verona and Pola Theatre Drawings

	Verona	Pola
Orchestra diameter	Piede 140	Piede 149
Stage front to *cavea* line	0	15
Cavea radius (includes portico)	234	149
Cavea depth (excludes portico)	115	56
Portico depth	30	19
Frons-scenae length	140	149/175
Stage depth	20	26-6
Niche depth	18	none
Central portal width	9	29
Hospitalia width	9	10
Versurae opening width	7	10
Orchestra level to stage level	5	?
Frons-scenae height	98	?
First order height	42	?
Second order height	31	?
Third order height	25	?
Central portal height	17	?
Versurae opening height	15	?
Cavea total height	101	87
Orchestra to *cavea* first level	15	20
Cavea first level to top seat	43	32
Top seat to portico terminal cornice	43	35
Cavea rake	28.6°	28°

Table 5. Comparison of London Studio and Present Teatro Olimpico: *Cavea*

	London Studio* Left	London Studio* Right	Present Theatre Vicentine	Present Theatre Meters
Orchestra diameter	53.50	54.00	50.2	17.42
Orchestra radius (a = minor, b = major)	26.75	27.00	a 17.9	a 6.22
	—	—	b 25.1	b 8.71
Stage front to *cavea* line	—	—	2.57	.89
Outside radius of *cavea* (to exterior of wall)	58.50	50.25	30.43	11.30
Cavea depth (to top seat/portico front)	23.25	23.25	23.01	7.98
Depth seating superimposes over *frons-scenae*	13.00	13.00	lt. 6.62	lt. 2.54
	—	—	rt. 7.32	rt. 2.3
Portico depth (to exterior of wall)	9.25	8.60	none	none
Height, orchestra to first level *cavea*	8.25	8.25	4.69	1.63**
First level *cavea* to top seat	15.25	15.00	14.66	5.09
Top seat to terminal cornice (ceiling)	28.00	23.50	24.00	8.33
Shaft diameter, portico order = module	1.25	1.25	1.00	.35
Portico height (to top of statues)	22.25	21.50	21.52	7.47
Portico base + shaft + capital height	12.25	11.25	11.49	3.99
Portico entablature height	2.25	2.50	2.27	.79
Portico balustrade height	2.75	2.75	2.71	.95
Portico statue height	5.00	5.00	5.01	1.74
Cavea rake	34°	33°	33°	
Number of seating rows	13	12	13	

*The London Studio measurements are in Vicentine feet.
**The orchestra floor has been built up since its original construction. Originally this distance was 7'-9" Vicentine (2.69 meters).

Table 6. Comparison of London Studio and Present Teatro Olimpico: Stage

	London Studio* Left	London Studio* Right	Present Theatre Vicentine	Present Theatre Meters
Frons-scenae length (between *versurae* surfaces)	2×39.5	2×39.0	72.19	25.05
Stage depth	—	—	18.50	6.52
Central portal width	12.50	12.50	10.81	3.75
Hospitalia width	5.25	5.25	5.01	1.74
Versurae width	—	—	5.12	1.78
Orchestra to stage floor	33.75	3.75	1.87	.65**
Stage floor to terminal cornice	48.50	43.50	41.44	14.38
Central portal height	27.00	27.00	23.90	8.32
Hospitalia height	11.00	10.50	16.30	5.67
Versurae opening height	—	—	10.61	3.68

*The London Studio measurements are in Vicentine feet.
**The orchestra floor has been built up since its original construction. Originally this distance was 4'-6" Vicentine (1.56 meters).

Table 7. Comparison of London Studio and Present Teatro Olimpico: *Frons-Scenae* Orders

	London Studio*		Present Theatre	
	Left	Right	Vicentine	Meters
First order total height	20.00	20.00	18.80	6.53
shaft diameter = module	1.25	1.25	1.22	.43
pedestal height	4.00	4.00	4.00	1.39
base height	.75	.75	.83	.29
shaft height	11.00	11.00	10.05	3.49
capital height	1.75	1.75	1.44	.50
column height	14.25	14.25	12.33	4.28
entablature height	3.00	3.00	2.47	.86
Second order total height	15.50	15.25	14.66	5.09
shaft diameter = module	1.00	1.00	1.01	.35
pedestal height	2.75	2.75	2.53	.88
base height	.75	.75	.29	.10
shaft height	8.25	8.00	8.66	3.01
capital height	1.50	1.50	1.11	.39
column height	10.50	10.25	10.05	3.49
entablature height	2.25	2.25	2.02	.70
Third order total height	13.00	8.25	7.95	2.75
shaft diameter = module	.85	1.75	1.15	.40
pedestal height	2.00	.85	1.01	.35
base height	.75	.50	.49	.17
shaft height	6.50	5.50	5.42	1.88
capital height	1.25	.35	.29	.10
column height	8.50	6.25	6.19	2.15
entablature height	2.50	1.00	.75	.25

*The London Studio measurements are in Vicentine feet.

Table 8. Comparison of London Studio and Present Teatro Olimpico:
Frons-Scenae-Aediculae

| | London Studio* | | Present Theatre | |
	Left	Right	Vicentine	Meters
First order *aediculae*				
pedestal height	3.00	3.00	2.46	.85
order base height	.25	.25	.33	.12
order shaft height	5.50	5.50	5.05	1.75
order capital height	.75	.75	.95	.33
order entablature height	1.00	1.00	1.52	.53
column height	6.50	6.50	6.34	2.20
order shaft diameter = module	.75	.75	.65	.22
pediment height	2.00	2.00	1.83	.63
total height	12.50	12.50	12.15	4.22
pedestal width	6.50	6.50	5.53	1.91
pediment width	6.50	6.50	5.62	1.95
order intercolumnation	3.75	3.75	3.54	1.23
First order *frons-scenae*	8.00	8.00	7.29	2.53
intercolumnation				
Second order *aediculae*				
pedestal height	2.00	2.00	1.90	.66
order base height	.25	.25	.33	.12
order shaft height	4.50	4.50	4.32	1.50
order capital height	.75	.75	.96	.33
order entablature height	1.00	1.00	1.12	.39
column height	5.50	5.50	5.61	1.95
order shaft diameter = module	.75	.75	.57	.20
pediment height	1.75	1.75	1.41	.49
total height	10.25	10.25	10.05	3.49
pedestal width	6.50	6.50	5.53	1.91
pediment width	7.00	7.00	5.62	1.95
order intercolumnation	3.75	3.75	3.50	1.21
Second order *frons-scenae*	8.00	8.00	7.37	2.56
intercolumnation				

*The London Studio measurements are in Vicentine feet.

Table 9. Comparison of the Dimensions of the *Frons-Scenae* Plans in
the Right London Studio with the Present Theatre

	London Studio Vicentine	Present Theatre Vicentine	Meters
Stage left versurae surface--base line	0.00	0.00	0.00
Center, forward column	1.00	1.85	.64
aediculae	6.00	6.19	2.15
forward column	10.50	10.64	3.69
second order aediculae*	15.50	15.01	5.21
forward column	20.00	19.20	6.66
aediculae	25.00	23.59	8.18
forward column	29.50	27.95	9.70
arch column (pilaster in present theatre)	32.50	29.35	10.18
central portal	39.00	36.10	12.53
arch column	45.50	42.85	14.87
forward column	48.50	44.24	15.35
aediculae	53.00	48.61	16.87
forward column	58.00	53.01	18.39
second order *aediculae*	62.50	57.36	19.90
forward column	67.50	61.72	21.42
aediculae	72.00	66.09	22.93
forward column	77.00	70.45	24.45
Stage right *versurae* surface	78.00	72.19	25.05

*The *hospitalia* are not centered on the London Studio.

Appendix A

This is a complete transcription of Academician Paolo Chiapin's description of the Olimpic academy's 1562 production of *Sofonisba*. It is drawn from Bartolomeo Zigiotti, *Memoire dell'Accademia Olimpica*, MSS, Biblioteca Bertoliana, Vecenza, catalogued Gonzati 21.11.2. (pp. 21-22). As with the other citations from Zigiotti, the spelling and punctuation have not been modernized.

Fu incaricato dal Sign. Prencipe l'Accad°. Paolo Chiapin ad estenderne la descrizione di si nobilissimo spettacolo; e se n'è ritrovata poca parte, ma di molto corrosa, e mancante; buttavia se ne fà copia, perche riguarda all'Apparato sudt°.

. . . . Per entro la Porta a mano destra si scorgevano Case, che accompagnavano la maggior Prospettiva, e per quella a sinistra si vedeva una Campagna con molti Arbori, et nelle altre Porte dalle bande per testa erano altre Case, e tutto quello che si mostrava entro da esse Porte non era finito, ma perfuori, siccome uscivan dalla maggior Prospettiva, e tutte le porte avevano due delle già dette colonne per banda, computato anco uno di que'quatri, che serviva per colonna a l'una et a l'altra facciata con capitelli dorati, e con bassi rilievi, e piedestalli. Tra le quali colonne era un nicchio con statue di rilievo di tutto fondo, finto di bronzo, per ciascuno di grandezza umana, sopra il quale nicchio era un quadretto di pittura di chiaro scuro in color verde, finto di bronzo, et quest'ordine era da tutte le bande di esse Porte quadre, cioè tra le due colonne un nicchio con una Statua, e quel quadro di pittura di Mr. . . . . che vi erano sedeci quadri, et sedeci Statue. . . . . nella parte inferiore et superiore. Sopra i quadri . . . . un festone, che arrivana da una colonne all'altra. Con quest'ordine istesso era nella parte di sopra tra quelle colonne, che sostentavano. . . . . il fregio, et architrave, le quali erano composite . . . . quel loco dove nella parte di sotto era la porta grande . . . . di sopra era un quadro di pittura grande di chiaro scuro finto d'oro con figure eccellentissime d'umana grandezza fatte da Mr. Gio: Batta Veneziano, e da Mr. Gio: Antonio Fasolo Accademico. Sopra il cerchio dell'arco a porta maggiore erano dipinte due Vittorie nel soprad°. colore, e modo, e nel mezzo dell'arco pendeva l'impresa dell'Accademia dorata, ch'è delli Giuochi Olimpici, col motto HOC OPUS, HIC LABOR EST, et questo sia quanto all'ordine, e alla dispositione di esso Pariete. Il piano della Prospettiva era finto in un pavimento di quadri vaghissimo con certe fascie, i quali andavano minuendosi verso lo stringere di essa Prospettiva, onde portavano gli occhi de'riguardanti inoltre assaissimo, e tuttoche brevissimo spazio fosse, pareva all'occhio posto . . . .

Appendix B

The following is a chronological transcription of Olimpico academy and Vicenza City Council transactions relevant to the design of the Teatro Olimpico and the *Edippo* production. Unless otherwise noted, the transactions are from the first part of the Zigiotti manuscript and books "D" and "E" (marked "A") of the Zigiotti manuscript. Pagination refers to the manuscript. The spelling and punctuation have not been modernized.

1579

Pre-May 1 (p. 29).
L'intervennero anco li Clarissimi Ferigo Morosini Podestà, e Paolo Loredan Capit°, quali anche furono in d^{ta} Orazione laudati, e così gli altri Rettori, ch'erano intervenuti alle pubbliche Rappresentazioni sì Tragiche, che Comiche de Sig^{ri} Olimpici.

August 10 (pp. 149-50).
Adi X. Agosto 1579. nell'Accademia Olimpica—In Consiglio dove intervenero il Sig^{ri} Prencipe, Consiglieri—it Accademici in tutti al numero di 14.—Par che la Rappresenta-tione di Sofonisba Tragedia dell'Ecc^{mo} Sig^{re} Gio: Giorgio Trissino già nostro Patricia fatta l'anno 1561 [*sic*, old dating system] nel palazzo publico per la riuscita sua, non per sodisfazione, ma con mieraviglia di chi ne furono spettatori, habbia causato fin'hora in quest'Accademia un quasi continuo silentio a spettacoli publici, come che potendosi dificilmente sperare più da Lei impoese tanto illustri, fosse meglio per non declinare, non mettersi più, a recruna attione talle per l'avenire. Ma certamente essendo l'Accademia nostra fondata sopra i continue esercitij virtuosi dal'esperienza di molti anni essendo gia conosciuta tale, che può sperare sempre d'operare cose equali, almeno degne di se medesima e della Patria, non deve da questo troppo severo respetto lasciarsi impedire quel si lodevole corso, a cui dal genio suo, dallo stimolo virtuoso, dal debito della professione, dal desiderio, e dall'aspettatione altrie si sente eccitata onde anderà parte; che questo prossimo Carnasciale venturo sia recitata publicamente a casa dell'Accademia, con quella minora spesa che sia pussibile, attesa la dignità sua, una favola pastorale, come cosa nova, et non più fatta sin'ora da questa Accademia; quella cioè che sarà eletta dal Sig^{re} Prencipe nostro, et da 4. Accademici, che per questo Consiglio saranno a tal carico deputati—La qual parte passò alla banca et in Consiglio con tutti li voti.

August 10 (p. 30).
Furono eletti per trovar la Pastorale, et il loco da recitarla Paolo Chiapin, Cristoforo Barbaran, K^r, Girolamo Schio, e l'Angioletti. E qui il Sr Fabio Pace Accad° si diede a lavorare la sua Pastorale chiamata l'*Eugenio;* dalla quale trovasi scritto, che avesse origine in gran parte la fondazione del Teatro.

November 15 (p. 150).

15. 9tbre 1579 in Consiglio e essendo per parte presa sotto di X Agosto che sidovesse rappresentare una Pastorale nell'Accademia, e non potendosi per legitimi impedimenti effetuare questa deliberazione il prossimo carnasciale, l'andera partè che la sudetta attione sia diferita ad altro tempo più opportuno, come meglio parerà a questo consiglio.

1580

January 3 (p. 150-51).

Adi 3. Genero 1580. Fu presa parte in questo Consiglio a gli X Agosto prossimo passato dl recitare il prossimo Carnasciale una pastorale, e fu poi alli 15.9tbre sui sequente per ligitimi impedimenti diferita ad altro tempo più opportuno ma essendo paruto alla maggior parte degli Accademici, che non debba esse prolungata più oltre che per tutta la primavera 1580.

January 12 (p. 31).

12. Gen° in esecuzione del loro Statuto i Sig^{ri} Accademici per potersi esercitare ne studi di Matematica elessero per Lettore di quella Lodovico Lance, il quale fece una Lezione con soddisfazione di tutti gli astanti, e gli furono accordati D^{ti} 50 d'onorario all'anno. Furono eletti li Accademici Schio Pojana, e Valerio Barbarano sopra la fabbrica per la Rappresentazione della Pastorale—sopra gl'intermezzi li Co;Co: Pietro Conti, e Spinella Bissari, ed il Sr Onorio Belli.

February 15 (p. 31).

15 [Febo] Essendo venuto in pensieve al Sig^{re} Prencipe, e a molti altri Accademici, che il poter far l'apparato al coperto sarebbe di minor spesa, e di maggior soddisfazione, e che il poter farlo nel loco delle Prigioni vacchie sarebbe molto a propositi—L'andò parte di supplicare la Mag^{co} Città con quel modo che sarà piu conveniente, acciò concedesse detto loco per poter valersene per tal azione, e in ogni altra, ad eterna gloria della Città, e dell'Accademia, disegnando essi di venir alla fondazione del Teatro, secondo il modello già fatto del loro Concad° Palladio, e disegno parimenti delle Prospettive.

February 22 (Archivo di Torre, III, p. 312). Siccome l'Accademia degli Olimpici in diversi tempi ha con lodevoli azioni procurato d'illustrar se stessa, e la patria insieme; cosi non si sarebbe lasciata alle volte quasi addormentata, se di luogo opportuno a publici spettacoli non fosse fin'ora con molta sua scontentazza rimasa priva. Ora essendosi proposta di rappresentar nuovamente una Pastorale, e considerando che nella parte delle Prigioni vecchie di questa magnifica comunità si ritrova sito coperto, et parte scoperto, assai spazioso verso la fontana degle Angeli, inabitato et non adoperato nè in publico nè in privato servizio; del qual essa Accademia non solo in questa, ma in ogni altra sua occorrenza potrebbe valersi. Viene davanti le M.M.V.V. col mezzo di questa suplica pregandole che vogliano esser contente di prestarle questo particolar luogo, a beneplacito pero sempre di questa magnifica Communità in ogni caso che le bisognasse; con liberta all'Accademia di poterselo accomodare; le quale si offerisce all'incontro di restirurlo senza pretensione alcuna de miglioramento, et certo oltro che anco il luogo sara migliorato, et adornate et si adoperà in esercizii virtuosi; Elle saranno cauoa che quest'Accademia avrà un continuo stimolo, che la inciterà a publiche azioni onorate, con laude di se stessa, con esaltazione di questa Città, et con soddisfazione delle M.M.V.V. alla buono grazia delle quali riverentemente si raccomanda.

Admissa per M^{cos} D. Deputatos infrascriptos omnibus suffragiis cum cepitulis infrascriptis. D. Franciscum Tridentum, D. Galeatium Gurgo, D. Alexandrum de Valle, D. Baptistam de Monte, D. Joannem Saracenum, D. Jo. Baptistam Chieregatum, et D. Marium Capram.

Tenor Capitulorum antescriptae supplicationi appositorum.

1°. Che la concessione del loco antedetto habbia a durare solamente per anni dieci e non piu, i quali finit s'intenda esser anco finita la concessione, e volendo essi Accademici diman dar nuova concessione o confermatione siano obligati venir con nova suplica a questo consiglio nè possano ottenerla se non haveranno li due terzi delle ballotte, et interim a ogni beneplacito et voler di questa città, la qual possa torre esso loco con la metà delle ballotte del Consiglio.

2°. Che li predetti Accademici o altri suoi successori non possano mai dimandar pagamento di miglioramenti fatti per loro in detto loco siano di qual somma et di quanta importanza esser si voglia.

3°. Che li predetti Accademici non possano portar via legnami nè ferramenta nè altra sorte di materia la qual fosse stata messa per mantenimento et fortificatione di quel loco et particolarmente della coperta.

4°. Che non possano metter mano in disfare o distruggere o levar via quelli legnami di quel loco, se prima non haveranno fortificato la coperta di tutto quel loco in modo che non si possa dubitar che debba ruinare a giuditio de'periti da esser eletti per li m. deputati.

5°. Che a fine che in alcun tempo la città non sia per patir danno per tal concessione che tre delli predetti Academici in elettione delli m. deputati et suoi successori vengano a costituirsi piege principaliter et in solido et prometter che tutte le cose predette saranno inviolabilmente osservate sotto solenne obligatione in valida et solenne forma.

February 24 (p. 152).
Adi 24. Febraro 1580. In Consiglio (dell'Accademia) e. Havendo supplicato l'Accademia nostra ai Magnifici Deputati di questa Communità di Vicenza, che gli fosse prestato un loco parte coperto, e parte scoperto nella parte delle prigion Vecchie adoperata da essa magnifica Communità verso la fontana degli Angeli, et come in detta supplicatione, et essendo stata admessa con le conditioni et capitolationi hora intese per questo Consiglio dal sudetto Prencipe nostro. L'anderà parte, che dette conditioni apposte per essi Magnifici Deputadi ad essa supplica siano da questa Accademia accettate a fine che detta supplica possa esser porposta e ballotata ne Consiglio di essa Magnifica Communità, con questo però ch'esse Magnifici Deputadi stendano il numero deputado di anni cinque, in anni dieci.

February 25 (Archivo di Torre, III, p. 312v.)
Die Jovis 25 Februarii 1580. In eodem Consilio centum in quo interfuere etc. et consiliariis ad numerum onmibus computatis nanaginta quinque: proposita fuit infrascripta suplicatio jam sub die 22 dicti admissa per m. deputatos cum capitulis et condictionibus appositis per ipsos m. d. deputatos et cum itum fuisset in suffragia data et occulte reddita—obtinuit cum suffragiis pro 84. c. 14.

February 28 (p. 32).
28 [feb°.] diesi principio alla gran fabbrica, e furon eletti tre Accademici per ritrovar li recitanti, e furono Co: Co. Pompeo Trissino, Gunardo Thiene, et il Sig^{re} Girolamo Buso, or Bosio—sopra li vestimenti Sig^{ri} Lelio Pojana, Fabio Trissino, e Scilla Palladio.

March 15 (Archivo di Torre, III, p. 313).
1580. Die Martis 15 mensis Martii. Constitutis ad praesentiam M^m D^m Francisci de Tridento, et Hieronymi de Arnaldo Doctorum, et Baptistae de Monte, omnium trium de Numero M.D. Deputatorum ad Utilia civitatis. agentium, et stipulantium pro dicta civitate Vinc. M^{ci} D^{ui} Petrus q.m.d. Guidonis de Portis, Jo. Philippus a Banca, et Julius Pogiana, omnes tres academici in academia olimpicorum in hac civitate volentes et intendentes

nomine suo et aliorum nibilium academicorum d. academiae ad unguem observare omnia capitula posita in suplicatione per ipsos et alios academicos porecta superioribus diebus et in gravissimo consilio centum obtenta die 25 februarii proxime preteriti, ut in presenti libro partium, et praecipue captulum quintum de fide jubendo agentes per sese et suos haeredes et nomine aliorum nobilium academicorum collegarum suorum se se principaliter et in solidum reunitiantes et caet constituerunt fidejussores et plegois in omnibus et per omnia, pro ut continetur in dictus capitulis, obligantes sese personaliter, haeredes et bona sua tam habita, quam habenda in valida et solemni forma.

March 23 (p. 32).

[23. Marzo] Luigi Grotto, detto il Cieco d'Adria era stato destinato a recitar nella Pastorale, e però scrive a Gasparina Pittonia Vicentina celebre miniatrice, come confidente del Sig^{re} Gio: Bat^{ta} Maganza, acciò lo ringrazi perchè egli si era per pura sua cortesia mosso a trattar tal affare—lettere familiari a stampa del d^{to} Grotto c.40.

May 23 (p. 154).

Adi 23. Maggio 1580. in Consiglio e Essendosi dato principio, come sà tutto questo Consiglio alla fabbrica nel loco delle pregion vecchie, ove ha da esser l'habitatione dell'Accademia, et insieme Teatro, et Scena per pubblici Spettacoli a perpetua conservatione et essercizio di essa Accademia; et essendo necessario che tutti gli Accademici concorrino alla spesa di detta Fabbrica, l'anderà parte, che del numero degli Accademici sottoscritti alla solloscritione ordinaria, tuttiquelli che non sono sottoscritti al scritto per far detta Fabbrica si debbino in termine di girrni 15. sottoscrivere, obbligandosi di pagar quel tanto, che a ciascuno parerà. Adi detto nel Consiglio et perchè e molto convenevole, che facendosi spesa così honorata per cosa perpetua, vesti anco perpetua memoria di quegli Accademici che vi saranno concora, l'anderà parte, che ogni Accademico possa a spesa sua propria far fare la sua statue di stucco, con questo però, che siano tutte equali quanto alla spesa, con l'inscritione del suo nome, et con l'impresa, et arma, quali statue debbano esser poste nei piedestalli delle colonne, et nicchi dell'apparato sopradetto. Addi detto nel sopradetto Consiglio e Hora dovendosi fare sì come è stato stabilito le sopradette Statue per metterle nei lochi sopradetti a fine che alcuno non si possi dolere, l'andrerà parte, che degli quattro partiti, che ora saranno proposti quel sia il migliore che dalle nostre Signorie sarà con piu numero di suffragi approbato. Che gli Accademici di più età debbano haver i primi lochi. Che gli Accademice più antichi nell'Accademia debbano precedente. Che tai lochi si debbano dare a chi vorrà la sorte. Che i primi siano di quegli che in tal Fabbrica spendessero. Passo come superiore di voti il partito di quegli, che some più anni che sono in detta Accademia.

November 7 (p. 156).

Adi contrascritto in Consiglio e Perchè la fabbrica del nostro Teatro sin hora è ridotta a tal termine, che con pochi danari in breve tempo si possi metter in coperta con grandissimo honore et contento di tutta l'Accademia; ma perchè questi pochi danari non sono pronti, et il tardar saria troppo pericoloso, si propone di dar carico ad un gentilhuomo Accademico di trovar ad interene fin al numero di Ducati 550. per spendersi in detta attione.

1581

January 27 (p. 156).

Adi 27. Gennaro 1581. in Consiglio e Dovendosi per il Sig^{ri} Sila nostro Accademico, et figliuolo dell'eccellente q^{li} Andrea Palladio far ristampar gli libri di Architettura del detto suo padre ampliati di molti edificij sì antichi come moderni, et essendogli venuto in pensiero, per l'amore che porta a questa Accademia di farvi anco porre il disegno del Teatro nostro, et bisognandogli far fare le Tavole di pittura del Teatro nostro et intagliare, però l'anderà parte, che per intagliar le dette Tavole gli siano dati dalla nostra Accademia scudi 15 accio che possi haver fine cosi honorata opera passò con tutti i voti.

April 1 (p. 157).
Adi detto in Consiglio e Essendo di grandissimo danno alla nostra Accademia, che non vi sia alcuno, che stia sopra la fabbrica, che si far, si per rispetto di tanti operari, che tutto di vi lavorano, come per prede. sabion, et altra materia, che vi viene condotta, et non havendo partorito quel buon effetto che si sperava il far un soprastante con salario, come si ha fatto l'anno passato; l'andarà parte, che ogni Accadimico sia obbligato a venir per un giorno ad haver cura che le cose di detta fabbrica passino bene, et col maggior avvantaggio dell'Accademia sia posibile.

April 1 (p. 157).
Adi pᵒ Aprile 1581. in Consiglio e Essendo virtuè principalissi ma che l'uomo deve esser ricordevole di benefici ricevuti, però havendo la nostra Accademia recevuto il segnalato beneficio dalla magnifica nostra Città, il quale fu quando ella ci concesse il loco, dove hora, con honor di questa patria, et insieme con non poco splendor di detta nostra Accademia, si fabbrica tanto honorato Theatro, l'anderà parte, che si debba sopra la porta principale di detto Theatro mettervi l'arma della Magnifica Città, come benefatrice di noi tutti Accademici.

April 16 (Archivo di Torre, III, p. 345).
Molto Mᶜⁱ Sʳⁱ Deputati. Gravissimo Consiglio. Poco giovarebbe che da questa Magnifica Comunità fosse stato concesso all'Accademia degli Olimpici il loco delle pregioni vecchie, et che fosse ancho alla fabrica del teatro stato dato si gran principio in cosi breve tempo, se quella opera illustre non si conducesse al suo debito fine; anzi peggio sarebbe che non haverla incominciata. Ma essendo fin'hora stata spesa molta somma de denari, come ben può comprendere ogniuno, et essendo la contributione volontaria et non universale di tutti gli accademici, parte de'quali sono debili di forze, veramente il teatro corre manifesto pericolo di restar imperfetto, se dall'istessa mᶜᵃ comunità, che cosi prontamente consesse il loco, non è porto qualche importante ajuto. Già si sentono moltissimi cittadini commendar quella fabrica, e desiderare che si finisca non senza speranza che con notabile giovamento della novile gioventù v'abbia ad essere ancora un publico esercizio di azioni virtuose. Et l'Accademia che vede quello desiderio comune, e sente il suo proprio di giorno in giorno farsi maggiore va continuamente pensando di adempirlo. Onde riverentemente ricorda alle M.V. con modo facilissimo et convenevole senza diminuzione del danaro publico di favorire questa impresa; che è il crearsi da questa magnifica comunità per mezzo de' suoi consigli dodici cittadini ad istanza ed ajuto dell'Accademia, siccome è stato altre volte fatto in simili, e forse anche meno importanti occasioni; con applicare le tasse di ciascuna supplica particolarmente a questa fabrica del teatro. Cosi si accrescerà il numero dè vostri cittadini, così il teatro in breve spatio sarà finito, e cosi l'accademia membro pure di questa città adempirà il giusto desiderio di che con tutto l'affetto con ogni debita riverenza suplica alle M.V. et in buona grazia loro si raccomanda. Proposita ad Consilium, et ballotata obtinuit pro nonaginta duo et contra sexdecim.

April 18 (pp. 158-59).
Adi 18. Aprile 1581. in Consiglio. Desiderando l'Accademia nostra che con maggior diligenza che per il passato si attenda alla fabrica del Teatro nostro affine che più tosto si

giunga a così honorato fine. L'Andera parte che siano degli denari della cassa dell'Accademia nostra donati a Mr Silla figlio della bona memoria dell'Ecc^{mo} Palladio benemerito nostro Accademico scudi 3 d'oro al mese, et lui debba venire et esser soprastante alla sudetta fabrica, essendo però diligentissimo così in questa come in ogni altra cosa; et questo a beneplacito coiì di lui, come della nostra Accademia. Passò a tutti i voti.

April 26 (p. 36).
26 [Aprile]. L'Accademia supplicò novamente la Città d'altro terreno per far le Camere della Residenza, e per estendersi per le prospettive, esibendosi pagar l'affitto di casa al superstitie, e gli fu concessa.

April 26 (p. 36).
26 [Aprile]. L'Accademia supplicò novamente la Città d'altro terreno per far le Camere della Residenza, e per estendersi per le prospettive, esibendosi pagar l'affitto di casa al superstitie, e gli fu concessa.

May 23 (Archivo di Torre, III, p. 345).
Die Mercurii 1581 XXIIII Maii 1581 in mane. Perchè dalla admissione della suplica delli Magnifici Accademici Olimpici fatta per li magnifici vostri Deputati et ballotata in questo Consiglio sotto li 16 Aprile prossimo passato et massime ab illis verbis citra scilicet *cum hoc* usque in fine potria nascere qualche sinistra interpretatione contraria ancho alla libertà et giurisditioni di questa città, et alla mente et intentione di essi Magnifici Deputati et del Magnifico Consiglio, imperò per levar via ogni difficultà et a fine che resti sempre dichiarita la intention suddetta, Anderà parte che le parole predette se intendano sempre a questo modo scilicet che per il creare d'alcuno cittadino in fine della detta supplicatione non sia nè far si possa alcuno minimo pregiudition alli Comuni delle Podesterie et de Vicariati et ville di questo territorio quoad bona tantum di quello che fosse creato cittadino come è giusto et conveniente, nè alcuno si possa ballotare se non con questa espressa dechiaratione, con la quale però senza altro ogn'uno si possa poi ballotare si come per il passato sempre si è osservato. Admissa per M.M. Dominos Deputatos omnibus suffragiis. Proposita ad Consilium et ballotata obtinuit pro nonaginta duobus suffragiis et contra undecim.

June 3 (p. 36).
3 Giugno furon mandati sei scudi a Venezia per tre biglietti d'un Lotto, che colà facevasi per certi beni Dolfin—il p^{mo} col nome dell'*Accademia*—2do *Ercole Olimpico*—3^{zo} *il Teatro Olimpico*.

August 12 (p. 159).
Adi 12 Agosto 1581. in Consiglio e Havendo considerato che egli è molto discomodo alla nostra Accademia non haver Casa appresso il nostro Teatro, et considerando che non è possibile in breve tempo poter fabricarne una a nostra sodisfatione l'anderà parte che si debba supplicar alla magnifica nostra Communità che sii contenta concederne la casa dove hora habita M^r. Antonio Tavola con tutto quello che possede, obbligandosi però di dar D^{ti} 36 all'anno acciò possi trovar casa a sua sodisfatione.

August 28 (p. 36).
28 [Agosto] essendo giunto in Vicenza col Sig. Alvise Coronaro Giacomo Critonio Scozzese figl^o di Roberto della Real famiglia Stuarda il quale per le sue rarissime virtù ben meritava d'esser onorato da tutti, possedendo francamente dieci lingue, et in ogni esercizio cavalleresco universalmente giudicato un altro Pico della Mirandola, avendo pochi giorni

avanti tenute conclusioni in Venezia *de omni scibile* e come si ha da tutte l'Historie. l'andò Parte che se gli dovesse far un Banchetto nel Teatro per mostrars' il Sig^{ri} Olimpici grati alle sue divine virtù, e così fu esequito, creandolo Accademico Olimpico. Egli sostenne nel Teatro alcune pubblice Conclusioni con concorso di tutta la Città, e specialmente del Chir^{mo} Bardi Bembo Podesta, improvvisando in prosa, e verso latino.

Post-October 28 (p. 37).
Il Sig^{re} Don Angelo Ingegnieri propose all'Accademia una sua Pastorale intitolata la *Liminata,* ma il Sig^{re} Fabio Pace, et Sig^{re} Pagello si opposero, e fu in tal incontro proposto, che non si potesse rappresentar nell'Olimpico Teatro cose, che non fossero d'Autore Vicentine.

1582

January 11 (p. 160).
Adi XI. Gennaro 1582. in Consiglio e. Fu deliberato dall'Accademia nostra con parte presa sotto di 12. Agosto 1581 di supplicare alla magnifica Communità, che voglia concedere per nostra habitatione la Casa di essa Co^munità dove havita Mr Antonio dalla Favola con dare ad esso Mr Antonio Ducati 36 all'anno, come in quelia, et perchè l'effettuar questa deliberatione sarà di grandissimo commodo, et beneficio all'Accademia nostra; l'andarè parte, che siino eletti tre Gentilhuomini dell'Accademia, a quali sia dato carico di dar la supplica alli Magnifici Signori Deputati, et procurare, che sia presa nel Consiglio della Città, et anco di trattare col detto Tavola quanto fara bisogno, dando ancora alli detti tre Gentilhuomini libera auttorità di fare in questa materia tutto quello, che ad essi aparerà utile dell'Accademia.

January 28 (Archivo di Torre, III, p. 381).
Die Dominico 28 Januarii 1582. in consilio centum fuit proposita infrascripta pars per Magnificos Deputatos: Molto M.M. Signori Deputati, gravissimo consiglio. Poco gioverebbe che l'Accademia Olimpica con la famosa fabrica del Teatro, come anco per il buon numero degli Accademici che in essa finora si trovano fosse ridotta nella molta consideratione et fame nella quale si ritrova, se li vostri Accademici, secondo le occorrenze et bisogni, non havessero poi loco comodo et atto ove si potessero insieme ridurre, cosi per discorrere et trattare quanto alla gioventu è necessario non tanto per buonissima conservatione et esaltatione di essa accademia, quale per esercitarsi et ammaestrarsi in quelle virtù, con le quali si aggrandiscono e esaltano non solo le accademie ma le città et republiche insieme. Di qui è che non havendo, come ognuna delle M.V. sa, essa Accademia loco comodo et atto ove si possano ridurre li accademici, cosi per tutte le occupationi sudette, come anco per conservazion di quelle cose che parte Accademia si adoperano et anco per l'habitation del bidello. Suplicano le M.V. che si dignino concedergli et acomodargli, a beneplacito della citta, quelli lochi che al presente possiede il superstite di questa magnifica città, con tanto terreno che sarà bisogno per far la prospettiva, senza la quale non si potria dar ferfetion alla fabrica nelle prigioni vecchie; obligandosi essi accademici di pagar ogni anno al detto superstite quell'affitto che importerà una casa atta e comoda per la sua habitatione, et apresso dargli tutte quelle sodisfazione che in materia d'altro utile potesse pretendere, con l'intervento delli M.S. Deputati. Qual affitto et utile gli sarà dato ogn'anno un mese unnanzi S. Martino, cominciando la prima affittanza il detto Martino 1582. Il che le M.V. facendo, oltre che faranno cosa degna della loro solita benignita et liberalità, senza danno o pregiudizio di alcuno, tutti li Accademici si sforzeranno di far si che mai si troveranno pentiti delli molti favori et grazie ad essa

Accademia cosi prontamente concesse. 1º. Che la concessione del loco antedetto habbia a dura solamente per anni dieci et non più et ad beneplacitum Civitatis, i quali finiti s'intende anche finta la concessione, et volendo essi Accademici dimandar nova concessione o confirmatione siano obligati venir con nova suplica a questo Consiglio. 2º. Che li predetti Accademici o altri suoi successori non possano mai dimandar pagamento di miglioramenti fatti in detto loco, siano de qual summa et di quanta importanza esser si voglia. 3º. Che per cautione dell'affitto che essi Accademici s'obbligano a pagare al superstite di questa magnifica Città per il loco suddetto essi Accademici debbano per tutto il mese di Agosto ogn'anno haver fatta partita in una delle camere di questa città per li ducati quaranta che s'obbliga a pagare ad esso superstite. La qual partita non possi esser levata da esso superstite o altri per suo nome senza finito il giorno di 3. Martino prossimo subseguente, dovendo haver attione detto superstite caso che essa partita non fusse fatta, contro il Principe di essa Accademia che sara pro tempore, et la presente concessione non essendo stata fatta la partita sia et s'intendi esser nulla et di niun valore, et detti Accademici caschati dalla presente concessione potendo il superstite sensa altra contradizione andar al possesso del loco, come di sopra concesso ad essi Accademici. Balotata habuit in consilio pro 78. c. 35 et publicata quia obtinuit.

February 5 (pp. 161-62).

Giulio Pogliana Principe delli accademici Olimpici In herendo alla parte presa ne la nostra Accademia sotto di primo dell'instante in materia delle figure che s'hanno da far fare per li Accademici sia intimato a tutti gli infrascritti accademici come a quelli che di necessità bisogna che siino gli primi per havere il suo loco nel terzo Ordine, et che tutti ad un tempo faciano lavorare afine si levino via le Armadure et i ponti et insieme seguir de parte in parte dando una volta perfetione alla fronte della scena del Theatro. Che nel termine compreso nella parte debbano far fare le loro figure, altrimente cascheranno irremissiblilmente nella pena contenuta en essa parte. In quorum e—Dall Accademia Olimpica li 5 Febº 1582. D. Gerolamo Porto, D. Gio: Batta Lugo, alli s. del presente fu intimato il presente mandato al contras^{to} S^{re} Gio: Battista; D. Fausto Malchiavello adi 5. d$_o$ P^{mo} al contras^{to} S^{re} Fausto; D. Nicolo Tavola adi 5. dº P. al contras^{to} S^{re} Nocolo; D. Giovanni Monza, D. Honorio Belli; D. Paulo Piovene, Adi 5 del pre^{la} P. al contras^{to} S. Paulo; D. Paulo Chiappino, Adi s. dºP; D. Marcantonio Brogia, Adi 6 d^{to} P; D. Marco dalla Valle, adi 6. dºP.; D. Cesare Michiele; D. Gio: Battista Titoni, Adi 5. d^{to} P.; D. Girolamo Forni, et adi 5. detto P. P^{er} le statue.

April 1 (pp. 162-64).

Di Domenica pº Aprile 1582 in Consiglio e In proposto, che per la difficoltà nata nel dar essecutione alla parte già presa in materia delle statue per causa della diversità dei luoghi, e della capacità e incapacità delle imprese, delle armi, e dell iscrittioni, che per non far cosa contraria al decoro, et ornamento dell'edificio, siano eletti per questo Consiglio sei Accademici, due per ciascuno ordine del theatro, i quali insieme col Prencipe dell'Accademia tolto il parere (se cosi a loro parerà) di persone perite, et giudiciose habbiano autorita di dar esecutione alla detta parte, et di decidere ogni difficolta emergente, come sarà dalla maggior parte di essi giudicato più convenevole per servar quanto sarà possibile la equalità e l'ornamento dell'edificio: dichiarando che nella detta maggior parte degli eletti et del Prencipe vi debba concorrere uno almeno di ciascun di essi tre ordini: Pº ordine è quello delli 10 tabernacoli 2º quello delli nicchi e quariselli 3º e l'ordine superiore.

April 7 (p. 40).

Passò per Vicenza il Sig^{re} Giacomo Movelmino con gran seguito, portandosi come Ambasciatore dell'Imperator Moscovita al Sommo Pontefice Gregorio XIII. Fu con tutta la compagnia onorato dalli Sig^{ri} Olimpici in Teatro, tuttoche imperfetto, e gli furono recitate Composizioni in sua lode, ed una erudita Orazione. Gli diedero una lauta Colazione, alla quale intervennero li Clarissimi Sig^{ri} Rettori, e nolti Nobili Vicentini, e Forastieri — Itinerarium Italie R.P. Capugnani Lib. 2do—Castellini L.18.

April 24 (p. 165).
Di più fu proposto, che nel terzo ordine appresso il loco di D. Francesco Floriano Accademico sia posta la Statua di M. Andrea Palladio Accademico, et Architetto del Teatro con inscrizione debita alla sua virtù, da esser fatta fare a speza publica dell'Accademia; et fu preso con tutti i voti, che così si faccia. Paolo Chiappino Secretario.

July 29 (pp. 165-66).
Di Domenica 29 di Luglio 1582. In Consiglio—Fu proposta la parte infrascritta—Perchè il nostro Teatro si retrova condotto, come ognun vede, a buoni termini di compimento, con satisfazione et maraviglia di molti, et da ciò siamo astretti a dargli l'ultima mano, per non perder quella riputatione che dal molto progresso di quest' opera in sì poco statio di tempo ci abbiamo acquistato, mancandoci specialmente molte cose et importanti. L'anderà Parte, che ogni accademico sottoscritto nel libro dell'Accademia ordinario paghi ducati in due per ogni Ducato della sua sottoscritione in due rate, la prima fra termine di giorni quindici et l'altra per tutto il mese di Agosto prossimo venturo. La qual parte fu presa.

September 2 (p. 166).
Di Domenica 2. di Settembre 1582. Il Serenissimo Signor Giglielmo Gonzaga Duca di Mantove essendo alloggiato di passaggio in Vicenza, volse vedere il Teatro Olimpico et il giorno seguente che fu il 22 di Agosto MDLXXXII venuto all'Accademia udì nel Teatro una breve ma ornatissima et facondissima Oratione fattagli dal magnifico M. Antonio Maria Angiolello Academico nostro, alla quale precessero et sequirono diversi concerti di musica, et furono recitati diversi componimenti di poesia di M. Gio. Batt^a Maganza Academico nostro, così in lingua culta, come nella rustica Vicentina. Et Sua Altezza mostrando quanto sodisfacimento n'havesse havuto, creò publicamente nel tearo l'Angiolello suo Cavalliero postagli di sua mano una collana d'oro di cento scudi al collo, et fece far doni al Maganza et a Musici dell'Accademia. Paolo Chiapino Accademico et Segre^{to} dimand^o.

1583

January 2 (p. 42).
Il Sig^{re} Livio Pagello porpose alli Sig^{ri} Accademici la sua Tragedia intitolato l'*Eraclea;* e la Pastorale Eugenio del Sig^{re} Pace.

February 7 (p. 167).
Di Luni 7 Febraro. Si redusse il Consiglio—et fu proposta la infrascritta parte— Desiderando il Prencipe vostro et Consiglieri, che sia fatta deliberatione per questo Consiglio intorno alla rappresentazione di alcuno spetacolo publico come promette il Teatro nostro, et s'aspetta da questa, e dalle circonvicine Città e havendo già sentito che molti degli Academici inclinano a Comedia pastorale, et altri a Tragedia, et parendo loro che sia bene in questa difficolta prendere il parere e consiglio da persone intendenti fuori dell'Academia, non solo di questi ditta, ma di altre ancora, come di persone che non siano interessate, et c'habbiano a consigliar senza passione, a fine poi, che essendo consigliati a far

una di esse attioni, quegli Academici che desideravano l'altra, possano piu facilmente
acquestarsi a così maturo consiglio, et habbiano a prontamente concorrere alla rappresentatione di quell'attione che sarà in questo modo eletta. l'anderà parte che esso Prencipe
vostro et Consiglieri col Conservator delle leggi, debbano pigliar questo consiglio così in
questa Città come altrove da chi parerà loro essere più atti et intendenti. Fu ballottata et
presa. Paolo Chiapino Academico et Secretario.

February 19 (p. 167-68).
Di Sabbato 19 di Febraro 1583. Si ridusse il Consiglio e fu proposto l'infrascritta parte. Per
esecutione della parte presa in questo nostro Consiglio a 7 di Febraro corrente nella
difficultà di rappresentare o Comedia pastorale, o Tragedia, il Prencipe vostro, i
Consiglieri, et il Conservatore delle leggi hanno tolto il parere et il Consiglio di quattro
gentil'huomini della nostra Città giudicati da essi atti a consigliarse, et havendo essi quattor
consigliato che l'Academia nostra debba al presente tempo rappresentar piutosto
un'attione pastorale che tragica; esso Prencipe vostro et Consiglieri vi propongono: et cosi
anderà, che alla Pasca delle Pentecoste prossima ventura dell'anno 1584 si debba
rappresentare dall'Accademia nel Teatro la Pastorale già composta dall'eccellente D. Fabio
Pace Accademico nostro, se però essa Pastorale sarà conosciuta buona dalla Censori
dell'Accademia già eletti, o che fossero eletti, et ciò non ostante alcuna parte presa per
avanti in questa materia di Pastorale, la quale si habbia per nulla et di niun valore; overo al
medesimo tempo una Tragedia quella cioè d'alcun nostro Academico, ol d'altri, che sarà
giudicata buona dalli medesimi censori; et sia ballottato oguno di questi partiti da per se et
prima: Fu fatta la ballatatione della Pastorale udito il contradicente et altri Academici che
parlarono et per l'altro partito, et hebbe voti XV del Consiglio in favore et XVII contra. Et
dopo fu fatta la ballotatione della Tragedia, la quale hebbe voti XX in favore et XII contra;
et conseguentemente fu preso et deliberato, che si debba rappresentare una Tragedia, e così
per Segretario fu publicato in Consiglio. Paolo Chiappino Academico, e Secretario.

February 21, (pp. 168-69).
Lunidi 21 di Febraro 1583. Si ridusse di nuovo il Consiglio, et fu proposta l'infrascritta
parte. Essendo nata difficultà fra gli Academici sopra la deliberatione publicati in Consiglio
a 19 del corrente de rappresentar piu tosto una tragedia che la Pastorale, perciochè alcuni di
essi pretende vano che tal deliberatione non havendo havuto i due terzi delle palle come è
statuito per legge a C. 13 et alcuni pretendevano che o fosse legitimamente presa, o
dovendosi trattar sopra ciò si dovesse procedere per via d'intromissione del Conservator
delle leggi: il Prencipe vostro e Consiglieri per provedere ad ogni inconveniente che potesse
succedere et per acquetar questa difficultà, vi propongono et cosi anderà parte, che al tempo
delle Pentecoste del 1584 si debbano rappresentare dall'Academia nel Teatro prima una
tragedia di alcuno academico o d'altri, e dopo essa tragedia la Pastorale dell'eccellente M.
Fabio Pace, se pero l'una e l'altra saranno conosciute buone dalli Censori dell'Accademia già
eletti, o che fossero eletti, et approbate dal Consiglio nostro; la qual rappresentatione di
questi due spetacoli debba esser fatta a spesa volontaria di quelli Academici, che vi vorrano
concorrere, et questo non ostante alcuno statuto, et alcuna parte in contrario, alle quali
s'intenda per la presente parte derogato. Ballotata in Consiglio fu presa con voti 31 in favore
e 13 contra, et per me Secretatio puclicata per ligitimamente presa. Paolo Chiappino
Academico et Secretario.

Post-February 21 and pre-April 19 (pp. 42-43).
Percio si diedero li Sig.ri Accademici a far leggere più e varie fatiche di virtuosi soggetti, per
indi venire all'elezione di quella, che loro sembrasse più addattata; esaminarono percio La

Semiramide del S^(re) Muzio Manfredi Accad° Olimp°; *L'Eraclea* del Seg^(re) Livio Pagello Accad^(ci); *L'Aminta* del Sig^(re) Torquato Tasso; *L'Alessandro* del Sig^(re) Massaria Accad°; *L'Idalba* del Sig^(re) Maffio Venier; *La Plaudia* del Co: Luigi Valmarana; L'Alessio del Sig^(re) Girolamo Vida; Altra latina del Co: Antonio Loschi.

Post-February 21 (p. 43).
La Tragedia Pagello, tuttoche da lui diligentemente riformata ebbe nuove opposizioni, e scrissero ancora, il parer loro il Sig^(ri) Antonio Riccobuono Prof^(e) di Lettere in Padova, e K^(r) Guerini Accad° Olimp°, e Speron Speroni, Fu dimandato al Sig^(re) Pace se volea tradurre l'Edippo di Sofocle; e recusando portaron si due Accademici Pojana et Ragona in Venezia per udir l'Edippo del Sig^(re) Orsato Giustiniani.

February 23 (p. 169).
Al M Mag^(co) mio S^(ig) Oss^(mo) Il Sig^(re) Giulio Pogiana. Molto Magnifico mio Sig^(e). Sono stato per trovarla, et ho battuto alla sua Casa ma era troppo per tempo, volevo pregarla, et così la prego a far l'officio co i Signori Academici, che le ha conferito il Sig^(re) Antonio Maria et ciò in caso che si faccia Consiglio che io non vi possa giunger ad hora. La somma è che, con quel medisimo animo di far servitio all'Academia, col quale mi posi a far la Pastorale, col medesimo hor prego tutti, et particolar anche il signor Prencipe, che si contentino, che la non si rappresenti, che così io sono sodisfatto, che ho veduto il buon animo dell'Acadmia in favorirmi, et ho adempiuto il mio desiderio di non lasciar cosè facilmente publicar le cose mie, e tanto meno questa, così sono sodisfatti gli amici miei, i quali hanno havuto l'intentione sua et come io ho cercato compiacer loro di quanto m'hanno comandato cosi debbon condonare a me questo che io loro dimando in cortesia strettamente; così finalmente sonso sodisfatti quelli, che bramano altra sorte di poesia che Pastorale. Questo m'occorre dirle brevemente che V.S. sappia accompagnare col giudicio suo meglio che io non sò esprimere. Volevo io far questo officio, ma il bisogno, et preghi del Co. Lodovico Chieregato nostro Academico m'hanno impedito. Lo farò con la prima occasione. Ne lo feci prima nell'ultimo Consiglio, che si fece, per non esser forse di impedimento alla Parte che fu proposta, la quale io disiderava molto che passasse sì per ogni altro rispetto sì principalmente per la Tragedia, la quale doviamo favorire; si non veggio l'hora di vederne una gagliarda sottoscrittione, col mettere anch'io le mie debili forze. Di Casa il primo di Quaresima. Della V.S. M^(to) Mag^(ca) S^(re) Fabio Pace.

May 8 (p. 171).
In oltre al modo sopradetto habbiano carico, et autorità di far porre una convenevole inscrittione sopra l'arco del fronte della scena, intorno alla fabrica del Teatro, come parerà alla maggior parte del detto numero, et come è stato di sopra espresso.

August (pp. 43-44).
In questo mese (d'Agosto) venne a posta da Ferrara il Pre^(t) Prospero Malavolta a far un'Orazione in Teatro, ov e posta la musica nelle Prospettive, accomodata la Cattedra con c^(a) canto sedie, Scagni, ed altri banchi, con l'intervento di Monsig. Vescovo Prioli, delli Rettori, e Camerlengo Molin, a pien Teatro d^(to) P^(re) comincio scusarsi pesesser in così illustre Ridotto, laudando li Sig^(ri) Olimpici, e suo Teatro, volendo anch'egli sequire Ercole Olimpico, indirigo tutto il suo dire a Giove, ma che essend alla presenza de' Christiani trattar volea della scesa dal Cielo in Terra dal Verbo per vestir carne umana Trattò difusamente delle Idee con autorità di Filosofi, e de Poeti etrici. Venne poi alle lodi dell'Accademia, esortando a Lezioni, Rappresentazione, Corsi, Lotte bene furonvi molte Composizioni in sua lode.

November (p. 44).
In 9tbre fu terminata la fabbrica del Teatro, a riserva delle statue, le quali avean bisogno di riforma, non avendo avuto li Artefici altro pensiero, che di sodisfare il loro capriccio.

1584

January 1 (p. 171).
Di primo di Genaro 1584 dopo pranso qual fu fatte a simbolo nella nuova stanza dell'Academia.

Post-March 3 (p. 45).
Il Sig^{re} Giustiniani venne a Vicenza sendo molto contento, che si recitasse il suo Edippo tradotto, et il Sig^{re} Speron Speroni mandò agli Olimpici di propria mano alcuni avvertimenti circa la rappresentazione dellEddippo, e da Venezia scrisse alli stesse il Sig^{re} Alfonso Ragona, che li Sig^{re} Rettori non volevano che fosse recitato.

Post-march 5 (p. 46).
Il Sig^{re} Paolo Teja Modonese, che fu poi Accademico Olimpico, mando un inscrizione da porsi in Teatro; et il Sig^{re} Montagna da Ferrara mandò parimenti un Discorso circa l'illuminazione. Il Sig^{re} K^{r} Guerini scrisse a gli Olimpici porponendo loro il Sig^{re} Verati, e sua moglie per recitar nell'Edippo. Fu accordato, e sero loro venne il Sig^{re} Antonio Pasi Ingegnere del Sig^{re} Duca di Ferrara piu regolare l'illuminazione. Capitò pure Lettera alli Accademici cel Sig^{re} Filippo Monte, che dovea esser Musico principale nè Chori; questo ere virtuoso, e Prefetto della musica dell'Imperatore.

May 6 (pp. 173-77).
Di Domenica 6 di Maggio 1584. Nell'andetto Consiglio fu proposta la parte infrascritta. Appresso la provisione del denaro per la rappresentatione della Tragedia è bene che ad un medesimo tempo vada la distributione degli Officij et carichi necessarij a tale attione, acciochè le cose passino con ordine, et con la debita diligentia. Onde il Prencipe nostro et Consiglieri vi propongono et così anderà parte, che siano da questo Consiglio per scrutinio eletti, con più della metà dei voti, Accademici sei i quali insieme col Prencipe habbiano carico di ritrovar li recitanti, assegnar loro le parti della Tragedia, sollectitarli al mandarle per tempo a memoria sicurissima, et esercitargli, con autorità di spender ne'viaggi che facessero per haverne dì forestieri piu idonei, quella quantità del denaro destinato a questa attione, che serà necessaria. Ma per quel tempo, ch'essi recitanti forestieri si tratterranno in Vicenza per esser esercitati, et provati, siano alloggiati dagli Accademici, come parerà al Prencipe et Consigilieri, senza alcuna spesa del publico. Di piu essi eletti abbiano autorità di aggregarsi una persona sopraintendente con quella ricognizione, che parerà loro, cosi intorno a recitanti, et allo stabilimento della rappresentatione, come anco per determinare se fia meglio inserir concerti di musica vocale, et intrumentale in ciascuno dei ceri a fine che servano per intermedij, opur lasciare i cori interi, et la Tragedia continuata, introducendovi in altro modo la musica, nella qual deliberatione intervenir debbano anco gli eletti sopra essi cori. La qual parte ballottata fu presa - per esecutione della quale furono eletti gli infrascritti Accademici al Sopradetto carico sopra i recitante: D. Fabio Pace; D. Pompeo Trissino, D. Giullo Pollana; Glo, Batta Calderari; D. Alfonso Ragona; D. Pietro Porto. Che altri sei Accademici siano parimente eletti all'oltascritto modo, i quali habbiano carico primieramente di procurar d'havere dalla Sereneissima Signoria quella parte di terreno cinta di muri, che è vicina al teatro, et fabricarvi porta, et ciò che sarà necessario a spese dell'Accademia, et di far drizzare il proscenio, la scena di rilievo, et di pitture colle

prospettive, di far accomodar l'orchestra, cortine et tende, cielo, ovevo soffitto sopra il teatro, et siano sopra la inventione, et accomdatione de' lumi dentro et fuori della scena; et degli instrumetni bellici, che s'adoprano allo scoprir della scena; et finalmente habbiano piena autorità di oviar che non sia impedito il proscenio da persona veruna; et intorno altra cosa et dependente dalle sopradette, con facoltà di far accordi, e pagamenti del spradetto denaro agli operari, et esecutori delle cose, che essì commanderanno, se veramente occorrese che alcuno forestiere venisse in questa da essì condutto per trattare e divisare et anco operare intorno a tutto ciò, sia alloggiato al modo sopradetto senza spesa alcuna del publico quanto al solo allogiamento se per avventura non sarà fatta conventione sopra questo particolare. La qual parte ballottata fu presa-per esecutione della quale furono eletti gli infrascritti Accademici al sudetto carico: D. Pietro Capra; D. Angelo Caldogno; D. Giulio Pogliana; D. Hortensio di Loschi; D. Valerio Barbarani; D. Giacomo Magrè. Che siano eletti sei Accademici alla cura delle cose di musica, et sopra i cori della Tragedia, facendo comporre la musica sopra li cori con accomodata imitatione, con autorità di condur musici forestieri et di far accordi et pagamenti del denaro publico, che sarà in mano del Tesoriero nostro. Dovendo in essi accordi dè musici, che conduranno, comprender anche la spesa del viaggio, ma essi musici forastieri siano alloggiati, come di sopra, senza spesa del publico; ben siano rintegrati di quello spenderanno in viaggi, che essi Accademici o parte loro facessero in tale occasione. La qual ballottata fu presa-per esecutione della quale furono eletti gli infrascritti Accademici al sudetto carico sopra la musica. D. Gironimo Porto; D. Teodoro Tiene; D. Geronimo Caldogno; D. Geronimo Bosio; D. Gio. Batta Ghellino; D. Pietro Porto. Che altri sei Accademici siano eletti appresso il Prencipe et Soprantendente alla inventione de vestimenti, e degli habiti dè personaggi, che nell'attione interveranno, così nello stabilire la materia, et la foggia loro convenevole, come nel farli fare insieme con ogni debito ornamento, et requisito connesso, et dependente con autorità di spender l'occorrente quantità del denaro publico nelle cose sopradette, et nei viaggi, che essi Accademici eletti, o parte loro facessero. La qual parte ballottata fu presa per essecutione della quale furono eletti gl'infrascritti accademici sopra gli habiti, D. Gio. Batta Ghellino; D. Geronimo Schio; D. Gio. Batta Pellizzari; D. Spinella Bissaro; D. Tiburtio Marzari; D. Fausto Malchiavelli. Che dodici Accademici parimente s'elleggano alla custodia di tutte le porte per le quali si può entrar nell'Accademia del teatro, e alla Scena, con auttorità di far acconciare steccati, et riparar attorno esse porte, et di far in ciò qualunque altra opportuna provisione, e spesa del publico. La qual parte ballottata fu presa-per esecutione della quale furono eletti gl'infrascritti Accademici al sudetto carico sopra le porte: D. Pietro Capra; D. Christoforo Barbarano; D. Gironimo Schio; D. Angelo Caldogno; D. Hortensio Loschi; D. Lelio Pogliana; D. Giacomo Magre; D. Spinella Bissaro; D. Fabio Trissino; D. Francesco Floriano; D. Geronimo Porto; D. Giacomo Ragona; D. Pietro de Porti in suo [Ragoana] loco. Che altri dodici Accademici siano eletti di accomdoar gli huomini a luoghi loro. La qual parte fu presa per esecutione della quale furono eletti gli'infrascritti D. Torquato Monza; D. Gio. Batta Valmarana; D. Pietro de Conti; D. Vicenzo Giarzadori; D. Geronimo Caldogno; D. Francesco Caldogno; D. Nicola Tavola; D. Pietro Paolo Volpe; D. Mutio Monza; D. Giovanni Monza; D. Horation Velo. Che altrettanti siano eletti al carico d'introdur le donne alla orchestra. La qual parte fu presa, per esecutione di essa furono eletti gl'infrascritti Accademici. D. Christoforo Barbaran; D. Gio Batta Calderari; D. Lelio Pogliana; D. Pietro Porto; D. Lodovico Zuffato; D. Giulio Ghellino; D. Benedetto Sesso; F. Claudio Bissaro; D. Giacomo Ragona; D. Carlo Camozzo; D. Curio Orgiano. Che la maggior parte delli sopradetti deputati alli sopradetti carichi in ogni occasione di emergente difficoltà far quelli del medesimo numero possa deciderla e terminarla con l'intervento del Prencipe nostro. Che ogni Accademico possi esser eletto e ballottato a più do uno delli soprascritti carichi. Che il Soprantendente, et ciascuno dei recitanti sia et s'intenda fatto nostro Accademico, non ostante alcuna cosa in contrario.

Post-May 6 (p. 47).
Le Prospettive furono opera del Sig.^{re} Vicenzo Scamozio.

May 9 (p. 47).
9 Maggio il Sig.^{re} Prencipe con li eletti sopra la fabbrica del Teatro stipularono scrittura con la quale rimangono d'accordo con li Mr Mr Rugiero Brascase, e Domenico Fontana scultori dell'infrascritte opere. p.^{mo} di far le figure, o sian statue, che restano per scudi sette d'oro l'una. 2.do intagliar le Lettere, e colorirle, incastrar le pietre be. 3.^{zo} a racconciar tutte quelle, che sono diffettose, vestir la nude, mutar le Teste a quelle, che le hanno da donna be.

June 4 (p. 47).
4 Giugno. Per parte di Sig.^{ri} Accademici il Maganza scrisse a Luigi Groto in Adria invitandolo a sostener la parte di Tiresia.

November (p. 48).
Recitanti nella prova. Il Cav. Zabarella; Melchior Guilandini; Girolamo Mercuriale; Luigi Groto—Edippo [sic]; Christoforo Ferrari; Nicolo Rossi—Tiresia [sic]; Gio: Batt.^a Verato, e La Sig.^a sua Consorte.

November 14 (pp. 177-78).
Di piu propogono, et cosi andara parte, che perconvenienti rispetti niuno Accademico da quì innanzi fino al tempo della rappresentazione della tragedia possa introdur alcuna persona così terriera, come forestiera a veder le prospettive della scena, et quando essi Accademici vi verranno debbano lasciar fuori i loro servitori, et possano mostrar il teatro solo a persone forestiere, che desiderassero di vederlo. La qual ballotata fu presa.

1585

January 30 (pp. 178-79).
Di 3o Genaro 1585. Si ridusse il Consiglio e fu proposto la parte infrascritta—La parte che fu presa i mesì passati in questo Consiglio, che non si lasciasse entrar alcuno a veder le prospettive il quale non fosse Accademico, siccome allora non doveve prohibir l'adito al Teatro massime a persone forestiere; ma solamente la scena, che si faceva. La qual scena a quelli che fossero veniti nel teatro facilmente per se stessa essendo chiusa non si vedeva, così hora che detta scena è finita, et convien esser esercitata, et scoperta, deve esser aumentata con una totale prohibitione anco di esso Teatro, poichè ogni giorno importunamente vengono introdotte persone sopra i gradi con disturbo di coloro, che attendono di continui alle cose necessarie nella rappresentazione della Tragedia. Però si propone et così anderà parte che da qui innanzi niuno sia di qualsivoglia conditione, o terriero o forestiero possa esser intordotto nel teatro sotto qualsivoglia pretesto immaginabile, et accioche ciò piu fa ilmente si osservi, ogni Accademico, che sara in nome del Prencipe nostro ammonito, et richiesto, sia obbligato attender per un giorno alle porte del Teatro con la debita diligenza, non vi lasciando entrar altre persone forche gli operarij della fabrica, et a quelli che ad esso Prencipe pareranno esser di mestieri per le cose di essa rappresentatione —et balottata fu presa.

February 9 (p. 179).
Di 9 di Febbraio 1585. Nel Consiglio fu proposta la parte infrascritta. Parendo convenevole che al tempo della rappresentazione della Tragedia, non solamente gli Accademici ma anco le mogli loro habbiano loco distinto, et assegnato nel teatro et non debbano star

confusamente tra le altre persone senza ordine et differenza. Anderà parte, che sia consittuito ad essi Accademici loco particolare nell'orchestra, ove non sia concesso ad alcun altro il sedervi, et inoltre le mogli di tutti gli Accademici haver debbano in essa orchestra uno o due gradi dopo il primo, che sarà destinato alla clarissima Signora Capitania, et alle altre gentildonne Veneziane, et forestiere di conto, dovendo esse mogli degli Accademici andar in compagnia della Signora moglie del Prencipe nostro all'Accademia alquanto avanti la venuta della Clarissima Signore Captiania e delle altre gentildonne; per poter, come si conviene, ricever sua Signoria Clarissima, nè possa alcuna altra Gentildonna entrar in Teatro prima di essa moglie del Prencipe nostro, et sua compagnia. Quelli Accademici poi che non hanno mogli, possano dar loco insieme con le mogli degli altri, negli stessi gradi, ad altre Donne che siano loro di sangue congionte, facendo che esse vadano parimente a levar essa moglie del Prencipe a casa di lei; e se gli Accademici haveranno in casa gentildonnc forestiere possano tali gentildonnne andar insieme con le moglie et con le parenti di essi Accademici alevar essa moglie del Prencipe all'Accademia; dovendo pero esse Donne forestiere seder in altri gradi separati, con espressa prohibitione a donne et persone mascherate e travestite haver loco nell'orchestra, et meno in altra parte del teatro per convenienti rispetti.

March 5 (p. 50).
Fu recitato l'Edippo due volte, ed in un giorno di mezzo si portarono gli Olimpico a S. Rocco, ove fu solennemente cantata una Messa.

Appendix C

Because of the errors inherent in the illustrated history of the Olimpico, a detailed analysis of Palladio's design sources and motives has been much encumbered. The 1965 survey has removed this barrier. This appendix is intended as a brief examination of some of that iconography. It is neither exhaustive nor detailed and points out only the boldest of problems.

Bertotti Scamozzi's ground plan (figure 44) has a scale with a .50 meter margin of error. His elevation and partial section of the *frons-scenae* (figure 33) shows more of the perspectives than are actually visible from any single viewing point. His theatre section (figure 3) contains a bold error in that the drawing shows fifteen *cavea* seats instead of thirteen. The *cavea* section (figure 34) shows the proper number of *cavea* seats but neglects to illustrate the south wall notch. Figure 35 renders the *frons-scenae* and portico vocabulary within a tolerance of .10 meters. Giovanni Montenari, *Del Teatro Olimpico di Andrea Palladio in Vicenza* (Padoue: Gonzatti, 1733, and 2nd ed., Padova: Terrinario, 1749) published several curious designs. In figure 36, the theatre ground plan scale is not accurate, the orchestra curve is flattened in the middle, the number of seats is erroneously twelve, the *cavea* staircases are not accurately represented, the south wall notch is ignored, and the perspectives are only sketchily portrayed. Figure 1 shows Montenari's *cavea* section; he shows fourteen rows of seats, misplaced orchestra entrances, no south wall notch, distorted perspective, the wrong number of *cavea* windows, and no ceiling treatment. Gabriel Dumont's *Parallele de plans des plus belle salles de spectacles* (Paris: Chez Moutard, 1774), p. 7 (figure 37) ground plan is nearly as schematic as the Montenari ground plan. Giuseppe Bennasuti's *Del Teatro Olimpico di Vicenza* (Verona: Bisesti, 1826) has a ground plan (figure 38) with a useless scale and prints measurements which contradict Bertotti Scamozzi's. The south wall notch is not accurately represented. The *frons-scenae* elevation (figure 39) inaccurately places the *versurae*, schematizes the orders and features, leaves out Palladio's name on the plaque, and does not represent the Olimpico Stadium relief or the city coat of arms. Magrini, *Teatro Olimpico* (1847), illustrates his work with drawings derivative of Montenari and Bertotti Scamozzi (figure 40). Especially important are the collapsed orchestra curve and the ceiling shrouded with an awning. The danger of these illustrations appearing uncritically in the twentieth century is demonstrated by Valerio Mariani, who faithfully reproduces the Magrini ground plan complete with flattened orchestra curve in *Storia della scenografia Italiana* (Firenze: Renascimento del Libro, 1930), p. 41. Pierre Sonrel's illustrations in *Traite de scenographie* (Paris: Odette Lieutier, 1943), plate IV (here figures 41 through 43), repeat some earlier errors, make up some new ones, and also document a curious period in the Olimpico's history. Of the old errors, we see a Montenari-like ground plan (figure 36). The *frons-scenae* elevation (figure 41) and theatre sections (figure 43) show *versurae* as having windows with mullions—an impossibility. The *frons-scenae* elevation also shows an exterior perspective scene in the stage right *versurae* entrance. Sonrel's ground plan and theatre section do document an eighteenth century feature described by Montenari (1749), p. 72. Montenari claims that the orchestra was fitted with elevator jacks in 1747. Sonrel's illustrations confirm that feature, which is no longer a part of the theatre.

Notes

Chapter 1

1. Giacomo Marzari, *La historia di Vicenza* (Vicenza: Giorgio Greco, 1604), p. 117; "che tutti quei i quali ueggono hora questo superbo edificio, non per anchora a pienben fornito, neremangono non men sodisfatti che am mirati potendosi compare con qual unque altro, & antico & moderno Teatro per rappresentare edificato." Unless otherwise noted the translations are mine. No attempt has been made to modernize the spelling or punctuation of the original. The edition's colophon is dated 1590. While the first edition was not available for examination, the presence of the 1590 colophon suggests that the 1604 was only a reprinting of the 1590 edition.

2. Marzari, p. 117; "superbissimo Teatro da fondamenti in ouada forma."

3. Ibid., pp. 200 and 212-13.

4. Robin G. Collingwood, *The Idea of History* (Oxford: Clarendon Press, 1946), pp. 61-85 and 258-60.

5. To name only a few, Giovanni Montenari, *Del Teatro Olimpico di Andrea Palladio in Vicenza*, 1st ed. (Padova: Conzatti, 1733) and 2nd. ed. (Padova: Terrinario, 1749); Tommaso Temanza, *Vita di Andrea Palladio* (Venezia: Giambatista Pasquali, 1762); Enea L'Arnaldi, *Descrizione della architettura, pitture e scoltore di Vicenza*, 2 vols. (Vicenza: Vendramin Mosca, 1779); Ottavio Bertotti Scamozzi, *L'Origin dell'Accademia Olimpica di Vicenza con un breve descrizion del suo teatro* (Vicenza: Giovanni Rossi, 1790); and Bertotti Scamozzi, *Le fabbriche e i disegni di Andrea Palladio*, 4 vols. (Vicenza: Giovanni Rossi, 1796).

6. Montenari (1749), p. 5; "Questo theatre è stato formato secondo le idee, che ne abbiamo da Vitruvio."

7. Ibid., pp. 11-15.

8. Ibid., pp 73-75. Unless otherwise noted, textual references to Vitruvius are from *Vitruvius on Architecture*, trans. and ed. Frank Granger (Loeb Classical Library; London: William Heinemann, Ltd., 1931). Throughout this study, references will be to modern divisions.

9. Montenari (1749), p. 8, notes that the initial piece of property allocated by the Vicenza Commune for the theatre measured 92 × 85 Vicentine feet (a Vicentine foot or "piede" = .347 m. = 13.66 inches U.S.); later in 1582 additional property was granted for the construction of the perspectives, the atrium, and odeo. Montenari's figures are problematic. There is no document contemporary to the building of the Olimpico which states the initial

property size. Scholars are in general agreement, however, that the lot was rectangular and they use the figures 116 × 65 piede because of encroaching buildings on the north, south and east sides and a public street to the west and because Palladio appears to have built to his maximum limits. A survey in July 1965 yields an initial lot of 40.25 × 22.5 meters (converted into Vicentine feet, 116′-0″ × 64′-8″).

10. Montenari (1749), p. 8; Montenari cites from the Philandri edition of 1534.

11. Ibid., p. 11; "Egli non ci ha lasciato le memorie del come si sia diretto, ma ci ha lasciato vedere il maraviglioso frutto del suo sapere di far risultare da una figura Elliptica tutta quelle parte del teatro Romano colle stesse proporzione prese da Vitruvio dalla circolare."

12. Daniel Barbaro, *I dieci libri dell architettura de Vitruvio* (Venice: Francesco Marcolini, 1556).

13. *Marci Vitruvii Pollionis Viri Suae Professionis Peritissimi di Architectura Libri Decem Cum Notis Philandri et Sexte Frontini* (Strasburgo: Knoblochiana, 1543).

14. Montenari (1749), p. 10; he admits his confusion over the matter of Vitruvian interpretation differences, saying he will "leave the question to the mathematicians" ("lascio la questione ai Matematici"). In the Giovanni Poleni rebuttal of Montenari's rebuttal of Poleni's *Degli antichi teatri, e amfiteatri* (Vicenza, 1735), and printed as an appendix to Montenari's 1749 ed., Poleni is quick to point out Montenari's erudition getting in the way of critical analysis.

15. See also Montenari (1749), p. 5, who says Federigo prepared "twelve large statues" ("dodeci statue grandi") for Palladio's Venice Theatre (1565); his source, Vasari, calls them "twelve large stories" ("dodici storie grandi") and explains that they were two-dimensional panels; Giorgio Vasari, *Le vite di più eccelenti pittori ed architettori,* Gaetano Milanesi, ed. (Firenze: G.C. Sansoni, Editore, 1881), VII, 100.

16. Montenari (1749), p. 89. *Titio Livio,* book 99, "L. Roscius tribunus plebis legum tulit, ut equitibus Romanis in Theatris quatuor decim gradus proximi assignarentur."

17. Curiously, Montenari's work receives undue attention in the twentieth century. Helene Laclerc (*Les Origines italiennes de l'architecture théâtrale moderne.* Paris: Librairie E. Droz, 1949), Leo Schrade (*La Representation d'Edipo Tiranno au Teatro Olimpico.* Paris: Centre National de la Recherche Scientifique, 1960), and Harold E. Bergman ("The Teatro Olimpico of Vicenza, Italy." Unpublished M.A. thesis, Florida State University, 1955) use the work as a chief source of information without testing its validity.

18. Ottavio Bertotti Scamozzi, *Fabbriche,* pp. 30-33.

19. Ibid., pp. 47-48.

20. Ibid., pp. 31-32.

21. Bertotti Scamozzi's assertion (*Fabbriche,* I, 29-30) is not documentable. There are no instructions of the sort; we can only infer, circumstantially, from the finished product, that this was Palladio's goal and that the goal was commensurate with the academy's expectations.

22. Bertotti Scamozzi, *Fabbriche,* I, 43-35, "Se al Palladio fosse stato assegnato un ampio spazio di terreno per piantarvi un Teatro, probabilmente egli avrebbe camminato sulle linee della Pianta Vitruviana."

23. Ibid., I, 35; "Ma se nella ristrettezza ed irregularita del terreno, che gli venne destinato, avess'egli dato alla sua Pianta una figura circolare perfetta secondo le prescrizioni di

Vitruvio, non ne sarebbe riuscito, come riflette giudiciosamente il Co: Montenari, ne un sufficiente, ne un comodo Teatro, non solo per le popolazione di Vicenza, ma neppure per un luogo meno popolato del nostro."

24. Montenari could not decide whether to inscribe Vitruvius' triangles in the *cavea* circle or the orchestra circle (see note 14). Bertotti Scamozzi has favored the Barbaro edition interpretation for good reason; Palladio helped with the interpretation and commentary.

25. Bertotti Scamotti, *Fabbrichi,* I, 35-36.

26. Citations of measurements are from Bertotti Scamozzi, *Fabbrichi,* and are in Vicentine feet and inches (see note 9). There is a difference between the Bertotti Scamozzi measurements and the 1965 survey of the theatre. In most cases the differences can not be blamed on restorations, since restorations have been minimal (mainly the seating and stage proper) and since the structural stonework has not changed and determines the theatre's shape; one must conclude that either we do not specifically understand the precise points from which Bertotti Scamozzi measured or Bertotti Scamozzi was not being accurate in his measurements. For example, Bertotti Scamozzi says the *frons-scenae* length was 70'-4" Vicentine; the 1965 survey yields a dimension of 25.05 meters (converted, 72.19' Vicentine). In subsequent chapters the 1965 survey will be considered the most reputable authority.

27. Bertotti Scamozzi, *Fabbrichi,* I, 37; "Con qual regola il Palladio siasi determinato a stabilire la lunghezza della Scena, che abbia relazione col diametro dell'Orchestra, e col semi-diametro, ella non è cosa sì agevole da indovinare."

28. Ibid., I, 37-38. Using the 1965 survey figures, the sum of the major axis and half the minor axis is more than a meter short of the *frons-scenae* length (17.42 + 6.22 = 23.64m.).

29. Ibid., "La differenza d'un piede in circa potrebbe essere derivata da un qualche sbaglio nell'esecuzione: differenze, che non induce o niuna o pochissima alterazione nell proporzion delle parti."

30. Ibid., I, 33-34; "quegli avra superate le naturali difficolta facendole servire al Disegno." See also I, 46.

31. Ibid., I, 42.

32. See Heinz Kindermann, *Theatergeschichte Europas, Das Theater der Renaissance* (Salzburg: Otto Muller Verlag, 1959), II, pp. 64, 74-75, 78, 84, and 87-88; Leon Moussinac, *Le Théâtre* (Paris: Flammarion Editeur, 1966), pp. 78-80; and Thomas E. Lawrenson, *The French Stage in the XVIIIth Century* (Manchester: Manchester University Press, 1957), pp. 16-19.

33. Kindermann, II, pp. 78, 84-85.

34. Cf. the Barbaro ed. of Vitruvius (1556) elevation of the *frons-scenae* (figure 50); the Chiapin description in this study, appendix A, derived from Bartolomeo Zigiotti, *Memorie dell'Accademia Olimpica* (MSS of the 19th century held by Biblioteca civica di Vicenza, catalogued, Gonzati 21.11.2), pp. 21-22; and Zigiotti, p. 31; "secondo il modello gia fatto dal loro Concado Palladio, e disegno parimente delle prospettive."

35. Lawrenson, *The French Stage,* p. 18.

36. Ibid., p. 19.

37. Ibid., p. 18.

38. Ibid., p. 17.

39. Ibid., p. 18, note 3.

40. George Kernodle, *From Art to Theatre* (Chicago: University Press, 1944), p. 167.

41. Ibid., pp. 170-171.

42. Ibid., p. 167.

43. See Allesandro d'Ancona, *Origini del teatro italiano*, 2 vols. (Torino: Lowscher, 1891), for the most detailed examination and documentation.

44. Thomas E. Lawrenson and Helen Purkis, "Les Éditions Illustrées des Terence Dans L'Histoire du Theatre, Spectacles Dans un Fauteuil?," in Jean Jacquot, ed., *Le Lieu théâtrale a la Renaissance* (Paris: Editions du Centre National de la recherche scientifique, 1964), pp. 1-23.

45. Kernodle, p. 169.

46. Ibid., p. 170.

47. Antonio M. Dalla Pozza, *Palladio* (Vicenza: Edizione del Pellicano, 1943), pp. 190-91; "Il problem della derivazione dell'Olimpico dal teatro latino non e d'oggi negli studi d'architettura: e ancor oggi è vivo e attuale, pur se la critica idealistica lo affronta con intendimenti ormai diversi, ponendolo più sotto l'aspetto di una curiosita dotta che come un ver problema d'arte." "Il richiamo che suolfarsi a questo o qual monumento, nella fallace speranza di potervi riconoscere più che un precedente un modello, conserva sempre un alto interesse di cultura."

48. Ibid., p. 193; "Non e difficile tuttavia rintracciare nell'Olimpico precedenti strutturali e forme desunte o derivate da monumenti congeneri dell'antichità; ma voler riconoscere nel teatro di Berga o in altri teatri romani un modello quasi necessario ci sembra fatica per gran parte oziosa." Franco Fausto, "Il teatro Romano dell'antica Berga e la genesis del Teatro Olimpico," *Atti dell III Convegno Razionale di Storia dell'Architettura* (Rome, 1941), pp. 171-182, argues for the Berga theatre as "indispensible model."

49. Dalla Pozza, p. 193; "ormai è chiaro per tutti che il teatro Olimpico non e una erudita riesumazione archeologica ma una maniera di rivivere l'antichita secondo lo spirito artistico e il sogno del Rinascimento. Il Palladio voleva ricostruire non un teatro antico, ma fare un teatro al modo degli antichi. In senso large quindi, planimetria e membrature e strutture antichi vengono adottate per l'Olimpico, ma trasfigurate e fatte per così dire obbedienti alla sensibilità individuale dell'artista, non diversamente da quanto egli fece in qualunque altro edificio, di sua ideazione, espresso coll'impiego degli ordini."

50. The "London Studio" is a preliminary design of the Olimpico *frons-scenae* which includes a section of the *cavea*. It indicates a stage of design different from the finished product and indicates two solutions to the height of the *frons-scenae*. The design probably predates the selection of the Olimpico building site; it is in Palladio's hand. As evidence, the Studio will be examined more closely in chapter 4.

51. Dalla Pozza, p. 197; "la scansione degli spazi esercitata dalla colonne aveva un titimo piuttosto lento che avrebbe consentito troppa evidenza, con danno dell'insieme, alle forme plastiche inserite negli intercolunni."

52. Ibid.,; "L'attico, occupato da una serie di bassorilievi scanditi da lesene, diveniva come una zone di riposo necessaria dopo tanta folla di linee ascendenti."

53. Ibid., pp. 197, 199.

54. Ibid., pp. 199-200; "membrature dunque di una plastità marcata, le quali nella esecuzione vengono sostituite con semplici e lineari lesene scanalate, di valore squisitamente pittorico."

55. Ibid., pp. 200-1; "Ora quelle colonne ai finachi con il vario comportarsi della luce sulla superfice ricurva dei fusti, avrebbero ritardato il passaggio di tono tra la luminosita delle masse murarie e l'oscuro profondo dell'arcata. Nella esecuzione le colonne vengono perciò eliminate, e l'arco resta imposto direttamente sul muro, bene mascherato sui due lati in vista, da lesene corinzie. In tal maniera l'effetto di contrasto tra bianchi e neri attraverso il limite deciso dei piedritti a spigolo vivo si moltiplica e quel gran vuoto centrale che regge artisticamente l'intera costruzione puo assumere la sua funzione di collegarla al libero spazio."

56. Rudolf Wittkower, *Architectural Principles in the Age of Humanism,* Columbia University Studies in Art and Archaeology, No. 1 (New York: Random House, 1965), has firmly established Palladio's aesthetic as organistic.

57. Dalla Pozza, pp. 201-2.

58. Ibid., p. 202; "Anche la speciale struttura a semiellisse impressa alla cavea, giustificata dai più con le angustie del luogo, riflette a nostro avviso—consapevole o meno l'architetto—l'ansia sua di superare ogni posizione statica nel movimento, di evadere dal finito suggerendo l'infinito: che e il dramma vissuto dal l'artista; e percettibile in tutte le sue opere migliori dove e sempre protagonista lo spazio."

59. Licisco Magagnato, "The Genesis of the *Teatro Olimpico,*" *Journal of the Warburg and Courtauld Institutes,* XIV (1951), pp. 209-20; and Magagnato, *Teatri Italiani del cinquecento* (Venezia: Neri Pozza, Editore, 1954), pp. 50-75.

60. Magagnato, "Genesis," p. 211. Italics mine.

61. "Genesis," p. 212.

62. Ibid., pp. 213-14.

63. Ibid., p. 214.

64. Ibid.

65. "Genesis," p. 209.

66. *Teatri,* pp. 50-51; "creder che proprio l'ambizione di questa maggior chiarezza d'idee sulle strutture del teatro romano, la coscienza dei chiarimenti apportati alla lettera di Vitruvio, dovettero aver non piccola parte nello stimolarlo a proporsi senza equivoci la costruzione dei suoi vari teatri ad imitazione di quelli antichi."

67. Ibid., pp. 50-53.

68. Ibid., pp. 54, 63, *et passim.*

69. "Genesis," p. 213, note 4. "The Olimpico arched *scenae* door is copied from the Cesariano (1521) edition of Vitruvius."

70. "Genesis," p. 216 and *Teatri,* pp. 67-69.

71. *Teatri,* p. 69; "Così nel bagaglio delle forme architettoniche del cosiddetto manierismo, il Palladio sceglieva ancora una volta quello che faceva al suo caso; nell'arco trionfale trovava un motivo di richiamo a quel mondo classico ciu ere romanticamente legato, ma soprattutto un elemento architettonico che meglio dell'arco scenico si prestava a diventare una delle pareti di quel grande spazio interno."

72. "Genesis," p. 215, note 1.

73. Ibid., p. 217.

74. *Teatri*, pp. 69-70; Magagnato is quick to point out that while Palladio had apparently intended real scenery behind the *frons-scenae*, property limits did not allow this conception during Palladio's lifetime.

75. *Teatri*, p. 72; "in questo momento si nota in lui un'accentuazione lievemente scenografica di quegli incartri di spazi entro spazi."

76. Ibid., p. 72, and "Genesis," p. 218.

77. *Teatri*, pp. 64-65; "Come ogni vera architettura l'Olimpico era ambiente nato per vivere nella luce diurna."

78. Ibid., p. 72; "Questa genesi ci sembra esemplare per cogliere lo spirito della poesia de Palladio."

79. Sebastiano Serlio, *Il secondo libro d'architettura* (Venitia: per Pietro di Nicolini de Sabbio, 1551), pp. 26v-31r.

80. Magagnato, "Genesis," p. 216.

81. *Teatri*, p. 63; "anziche perderci nella ricerca astratta delle fronti della sua creazione."

82. Roberto Pane, *Andrea Palladio* (Torino: Giulio Einaudi, Editore, 1961) and Lionello Puppi, *Il Teatro Olimpico* (Vicenza: Neri Pozza, 1963).

83. Pane, p. 366.

84. Puppi, p. 39.

85. Pane, p. 366; "lo spirito classicistico da una parte e quello razionalistico dall'altra."

86. Puppi, p. 39; "L'architetto pare sia decisamente venuto affermando una sua forma, nella quale si risusciata il teatro classico non come pedante ricomposizione di relitti archeologici, ma come recupero attuale, fondato, garantito e condizionato da una consaperole scelta culturale, nel quadro di una autentica problematica architettonica; come conquista, in una singolare e originale concezione dello spazio."

87. Pane, p. 363, note 35; "Una speciedi timore reverenziale sembra avere impedito alcune semplice constatazioni."

88. Ibid., p. 364; "A rigore, anzi, qui si tratta di que spazi e non di uno, dato che la cavea e il palcoscenico si fronteggiano senza unirsi, pur essendo l'una in continuità dell'altro. I due muri trasversali, contro i quali termina il semiellisse della gradinata, sono la chiave del compromesso, che si conclude, in alto, con i due diversi soffitti."

89. Ibid., p. 362.

90. Ibid., p. 363; "Le prospettive di Scamozzi, manieristicamente divertenti e curiose."

91. Ibid., p. 364; "la densa ed estrosa successione di episodi diversi che Scamozzi si compiacque poi di allineare."

92. Ibid.

93. Ibid., p. 363; "Un semplice sguardo alla struttura dell'Olimpico è sufficiente a rilevare l'enorme sporporzione tra lo spazio assegnato agli spettatori, cosí angusto da costringere l'architetto a far ricorso allo svolgimento ellittico della cavea, e quello del proscenio e delle prospettive."

94. Ibid.

95. Ibid., p. 364; "quello cioè di dar vita ad un finizione.

96. Ibid., pp. 364-66. Pane's analysis of the fictional problems in the Olimpico is contained on these pages.

97. Pane notes, p. 365, that the style of the portico niches is the same as the *versurae* niches; they are different than the *frons-scenae* niches.

98. Ibid., p. 365; "Dunque abbiamo indizi sicuri per potere affermare che quel liscio spessore del muro esprime l'intenzione meramente intellettualistica di separare le due immagini."

99. Ibid.

100. Puppi, pp. 49-51.

101. Ibid., p. 51; "Tuttavia, l'elemento che, nell'attuale struttura dell'Olimpico, tende a compromettere, nel modo più stridente, la possibilità di un'unificazione in un organismo spaziale senza dissonanze, è nel risalto che acquistano le prospettive, la cui evidenza illusionistica, oltre i vani e l'arco che si è portati a sentire in qualche modo come cornice, vien accresciuta dalla distribuzione divergente, rispetto all'asse ottico della cavea, di quelle laterali, C'e di più: l'affermazione delle prospettive in una loro realta, avulsa dal restante contesto spaziale, non è scindibile dall'introduzion di quell'altre presenze, che abbiamo denunciato: sicché, l'individuazione di colui che le progettò implica, *tout court,* l'individuazione della mente estranea, che freno l'integrale realizzazione dell'idea palladiana."

102. Ibid., pp. 51, 55-56.

103. Ibid., pp. 55-56.

104. Arguing for Palladio as designer is Giangiorgio Zorzi in "Le prospettive del Teatro Olimpico nei disegni degli Uffizi di Firenze e nei documenti del 'Ambrosiana' di Milano," *Arte Lombarda,* X (1965), pp. 70-97, and *Le ville e i teatri di Andrea Palladio* (Venezio: Neri Pozza, 1969), pp. 293-303; arguing for Vicenzo Scamozzi as designer is Lionello Puppi in *Il Teatro Olimpico,* pp. 54-56, and "Prospettive dell'Olimpico, documenti del'Ambrosiana e altre cose: argomenti per una replica," *Arte Lombarda,* XI (1966), pp. 26-32. The details of the argument will be discussed in chapter 4.

105. Zigiotti, pp. 78-79, 200, is used as the source for the confirmation of these *principe*-ships and to complete the name spellings. See Zigiotti, p. 91, for the dates of the productions.

106. Magagnato, "Genesis," p. 217.

107. Zigiotti, pp. 21-22.

108. Dalla Pozza, p. 196; "Che egli abbia lavorato di sola fantasia ci sembra sia da escludere, poiche quegli episodi si volemano dipinti per sonservarne la memoria nella storia; e l'asseneza di ogni riferimento al vero avrebbe urtato la suscettibilità di quei contemporanei—e i superstiti dovevano essere ancora moltissimi—che avevano assistito o collaborato agli spettacoli, ed erano in grado perciò di ricordare."

109. Puppi, p.37

110. Ibid., pp. 55-56.

111. Magagnato, *Teatri,* p. 55, and Puppi. pp. 32-33.

112. Antonio Magrini, *Memorie intorno la vita e le opere di Andrea Palladio* (Padova: Tipografia del Seminario, 1845), pp. 43-44.

113.   Zigiotti, p. 4; The manuscript is 200 pages long, followed by 7 pages of addenda, 2 loose pages, and 9 blank pages bound with the MSS.

114.   Ibid., p. 5; "più autentici Summari." Italics mine.

115.   Ibid., p. 5; "che possono dar più dignità, e riputazione a detta Accademia."

116.   Zorzi, *I disegni delle antichità di Andrea Palladio* (Venezia: Neri Pozza, 1959).

117.   The U.S. published paperback appeared in 1965 under the title *Architectural Principles in the Age of Humanism.*

118.   Wittkower, p. 101.

119.   See especially Plato *Timaeus* 35B-36B.

120.   Wittkower, p. 158.

Chapter 2

1.   No simple explanation exists for the Italian Renaissance and associated humanism and no small amount of modern publications has made important contributions to its study. The hallmark of modern inquiry into the Italian Renaissance was Jakob Burkhardt's *The Civilization of the Renaissance in Italy,* trans. S.G.G. Middlemore (The Modern Library; New York: Random House, 1954), first published in Leipzig, 1860, under the title, *Die Cultur der Renaissance in Italien.* In this study I have followed Burkhardt's 'sense' of the Renaissance and humanism. Much as Burkhardt has done, my use of the terms Renaissance and humanism refer to those time-bound activities that were antimedieval in character and that venerated the classic. At the same time we must not lose sight of the forest because of the trees. Art and architecture are only a small part of the larger phenomenon encompassing politics, religion, the sciences, literature, and many other more or less dependent disciplines. And Andrea Palladio is just a small part of archaeological humanism and Renaissance architecture.

2.   "Vita di Andrea Palladio scritta da Paolo Gualdo," first published in Giovanni Montenari, *Del Teatro Olimpico,* 2nd ed. (Padove: Terrinario, 1749), pp. vii-xii. The Palladian biography is sketchy at most. His contemporary biographer, Paolo Gualdo, dates his birth and death only. Gualdo does narrate a progression of confirmable events but makes enough factual errors to give suspicion to his work. The best biography and the one followed most closely by modern writers is Tommaso Temanza, *Vità di Andrea Palladio* (Venezia: Giambatista Pasquali, 1762). Even though excellently documented, he has argued from a portrait of Palladio (by Licino) dated 1541 which says Palladio was then twenty-three years old (p. 1); Temanza thus arrives at the 1518 birth date. Giangiorgio Zorzi, "La vera origine e la giovinessa di Andrea Palladio," *Archivo Veneto-Tridentino,* II (1922), pp. 120-50, has argued for the 1508 date convincingly. While Gualdo (p. vii) claims Vicenza as Palladio's birthplace, Padua has been established by Antonio M. Dalla Pozza, *Palladio* (Vicenza: Edigioni del Pellican, 1943), pp. 22-24.

3.   James S. Ackerman, *Palladio* (Baltimore: Penguin Books, Inc., 1966), p. 20. The details of this summary are enumerated in Temanza, Dalla Pozza, and Giangiorgio Zorzi, *I disegni delle antichità di Andrea Palladio* (Venezia: Neri Pozza Editore, 1959), pp. 3-4.

4.   See my brief discussion of the Trissino Academy in chapter 3. For details see Bernardo Morsolin, *Giangiorgio Trissino* (Vicenza: Tip. Gir. Burato, 1878), pp. 232ff. See Zorzi,

Disegni, p. 111, for the archive documentation of Palladio and Trissino's familiarity dating February 19, 1538. Palladio cites Trissino as "the splendor of our times" in his preface to *Quattro libri della architettura*. In this study citations from the *Quattro libri* (hereafter *QL*) will be drawn from the best English translation, *The Four Books of Andrea Palladio's Architecture*, trans. Isaac Ware (London: Isaac Ware, 1738). Dover Publications, New York, issued a reprint in 1964.

5.   Ackerman, p. 21.

6.   Gian Giorgio Trissio, *Dell'architettura*, Frammento con l'aggiunta di due epigrammi latini (Vicenza: Nozze Feserico-Bertidini, 1878). Cited in Zorzi, *Disegni*, p. 111 and note 1.

7.   See Ackerman, pp. 21-22 and Zorzi, *Disegni*, p. 4 and note 23. Palladio documents his knowledge of the Loggia Cornaro, Padua, in *QL*, I, 28.

8.   Regarding Serlio's presence in Vicenza in 1539, see my discussion, chapter 3, of the theatre he erected in Vicenza while consulting on the Basilica.

9.   Sebastiano Serlio, *Regole generali di architettura sopra le cinque maniere de gli edifici* (Venice, 1537). This volume, *Book IV*, in the Venice, 1551, collected edition of Books I-V, was the first published of his proposed seven books. See William B. Densmore, "The Literary Remains of Sebastiano Serlio," *Art Bulletin*, XXIV (1942), pp. 55-91 and 115-54, for the most scholarly discussion of Serlio's works. Regarding Palladio's design for the Vicenza Basilica, see Ackerman, pp. 90-92, and Zorzi, *Disegni*, p. 5.

10.   Located in the central Vicenza piazza, it is certainly attention-getting. The arcade of a series of arches generated from essentially blind imposts, supported by a minor order with a larger order superimposed over the impost, comes to be known as one of the Palladian motifs. Palladio never repeats the motif, except adaptively in the Teatro Olimpico; Inigo Jones and Christopher Wren popularize it in England in the seventeenth century.

11.   Most of the early Palladio designs are not exactly datable. I will use the most generally accepted datings as followed by Ackerman, p. 14, which are for the most part reflected in the stylistic analysis of Rudolf Wittkower, *Architectural Principles in the Age of Humanism*, Columbia University Studies in Art History and Archaeology, Number 1 (New York: Random House, 1965).

12.   *Il tergo libro di Sebastiano Serlio Bolognese, nel qual si figurano, e descrinono le antiquita di Roma, e le altre che sono in Italia, e fuori d'Italia* (Venice, 1540).

13.   Daniel Barbaro, *I dieci libri dell architettura di Vitruvio* (Venise: per Francesco Marcolini, 1556).

14.   Morsolin, pp. 286-87.

15.   Ibid., pp. 321-23.

16.   Ibid., pp. 331-32.

17.   Ibid., p. 322.

18.   Zorzi, *Disegni*, Index of Monuments, pp. 199-202.

19.   Morsolin, p. 330 and note.

20.   Gualdo, p. vii.

21.   Andrea Palladio, *L'antichità di Roma* (Rome: Vincenzo Lucrino, 1554).

22.   Wittkower, p. 62.

23.   *QL,* preface. Palladio confirms but does not enumerate his travels.

24.   *QL,* I, 14.

25.   See Wittkower, p. 64 and note 4 regarding the history of these designs.

26.   Burlington's holdings are now at the Royal Institute of British Architects. Other drawings are now in the Museo Civico and the Biblioteca Bertoliana, Vicenza.

27.   Cf. *QL,* IV, 12, pl. 27, with Zorzi, *Disegni,* pl. 156 (Tempo di Giove Serapide, Rome), and *QL,* IV, 16, pl. 42, with Zorzi, *Disegni,* pl. 183 (Battistero di Costantino a S. Giovanni Laterano, Rome).

28.   Cf. *QL,* III, 19, pl. 17, with Barbaro (1556), V. i, (pp. 129-31). Palladio acknowledges Barbaro in *QL,* III, 19. While the *QL* publication date is 1570 and does not include palazzi done by Palladio just before the publication (see for example, *QL,* II, 3, pls. 15-16 for Palazzo Barbarano), there is reason to believe that Palladio had expected earlier publication. Barbaro (1556), VI, xi (p. 179), refers to the book when he writes "presto venirà in luce un libro delli case private, composto e disegnato del Palladio." See Zorzi, *Disegni,* pp. 147-156 concerning the extant fragment of the early manuscript to *QL.*

29.   See Carol H. Krinsky, "Seventy-eight Vitruvius Manuscripts," *Journal of the Warburg and Courauld Institutes,* XXX (1967), pp. 36-70. It is highly improbable that Trissino owned a Vitruvius codice. Without evidence to support a Trissino associated codice, we must assume that Palladio's readings were from one of the many available sixteenth century editions.

30.   The illustrations for the early editions of Vitruvius serve as clues to their derivation. Before *M. Vitruvius Per Jocundum So Lito Castiga Tier Factus Cum Figuris Et Tabula Ut Iam Legi Et Intelligi Possit* (Venetiis, 1511) there appeared three unillustrated editions: *Lucii Vitruvii Pollionis De Architectura Libri Decem, Detta Anche Sulpiciana da Giov. Sulpicio da Veroli Che In Unione A Pomponio Leto* (Roma, 1486), *Lucii Vitruvii Pollonis De Architectura Libri Decem Sexti Iulii Frontini de Aquaeductibis Liber Unus Angeli Politiani Opuscolum* (Florentie, MCCCCLXXXXVI), and *Marci Vitruvii Pollionis De Architectura Libri Decem, Accedunt Cleodidae Harmonicum Introductorium Frontini De Aquaeductibus, Policiani Opuscula* (Venetiis: Simonem Papiensem, MCCCLXXXXVII). After the 1511 Jocundus an unauthorized reprint of Jocundus appeared in Florence, 1513. *Di Lucio Vitruvio Pollione de Architectura Libri Dece Traducti de Latino in Vulgare Affi Gurati Commentati da Cesare Cesariano* (Como: Magistro Gotardo de Ponte, 1521) was followed by a Latin edition in 1522 (Florence). Two Italian editions followed whose illustrations were plagiarized from Jocundus (Florence, 1523, and Venetia, 1524). A plagiarism of a Cesariano appeared in the *Architettura con il suo commento et figure Vetruvio in Volgare lingua raportato per M. Giambatista Caporali di Perugia* (Perugia: Conte Jano Bigazzini, 1536); this edition included only the first five books. Subsequent references to these and other editions will be entered as follows: editor, date in parentheses, modern book and chapter number (following Granger's divisions), and parenthetical foliation or pagination of the original. The reader is directed to the bibliography for a complete listing of the editions consulted. See also B. Ebhardt, *Die Zehn Bücher der Architektur des Vitruv und ihre Herausgeber seit 1484* (Berlin: Grunewald, 1918) and Georgii Loukomski, *I maestri della architettura classica* (Milano: Ulrico Hoepli, 1933) for thorough listings of Vitruvius editions since the *princeps.*

31.   We do know of Trissino's knowledge of Alberti as documented by Trissino's reference to Alberti in *Dell'architettura.* See note 6, this chapter.

32. While Palladio's final theoretical statement on the ancient Roman theatre is contained in the Barbaro (1556), V.ii and ff., chapter 3 of this study dwells on several practical statements by Palladio in the form of temporary theatres of apparent antique modelling, built in Vicenza and Venice in 1561, 1562, and 1565.

33. Of course a "faithful" translation is a relative concept. Barbaro seems to have translated from a Latin edition, apparently ignoring other Italian renderings by Cesariano, Durantino, and Caporali. This conclusion is at most speculative, however, since an increased Italian vocabulary allows more alternative translations—each one "faithfully" representing the sense of the Latin. In Barbaro (1556), V.i (p. 130), he cites Filandro as an authority on the basilica at Fano. In the absence of references to other Latin editions, we must assume that Barbaro was translating from the Philandri (Filandro) edition of 1543, 1544, 1550, or 1552. Since Barbaro's work was in progress in 1547 (see X.xvi, p. 274), we must favor the 1543 or the 1544 editions. The available Latin editions were quite free of interpretative variants. The Philandri (1543) is substantially the same as the Jocundus (1511). To return, then, to the problem of "faithful" translations, only major variants are visible in any rendering since the discovery process involves the translation of the Italian into English and then comparison of that English with the literal English of a Latin translation. One ends up learning more about the Italian language than about the meaning of the text. For this reason, we rely on the editions' illustrations as a more meaningful "translation" of the texts.

34. Barbaro (1556), I.vi (p. 40). I quote from Wittkower's translation, p. 65.

35. Morgan (1914), V.vi.1 (p. 146).

36. Philandri, (1543), V.vi (p. 128).

37. C. Perrault, *Les Dix Livres d'Architectura de Vitruve* (Paris: Coignard, 1673).

38. Granger (1934), V.vi.1 (I, p. 283).

39. Barbaro (1556), V.vi, (pp. 150 and 155). The Latin is from Philandri (1543), V.vi, (pp. 128-29). Vitruvius is consistent in his usage of various theatrical terms. *Pulpitum,* and variants, is the stage platform. *Scenae,* and variants, is the whole stage proper including the *frons-scenae; frons-scenae* is the formal background of the stage *(scenae). Proscaenii* is the front surface and delimited line or edge of the stage platform.

40. Morgan (1914), V.vi.3 (pp. 146, 148).

41. Barbaro (1556), V.vi (p. 151).

42. V.vi.8 improves on our understanding of the *versurae.* "Next to these [*periaktoi*-scenic machines] the walls run out which contain the entrances to the stage, one from the public square [audience's right] and the other from the country [audience's left]." The Granger translation interpolates "entrance" as a distinct opening. Barbaro renders the passage accurately; his translation conflicts with the placement of the *versurae* on the same plane as the other openings (1556), V.vi (p. 155) Cf. with figure 49.

43. The reader will note an undescribed feature in Barbaro's Roman stage. In the plan (figure 51) joining the *versurae* openings to the *cavea* side is a substructure. In the *frons-scenae* elevation (figure 49) we see a section of a parapet surmounted with balusters in front of the *versurae* opening (which is thereby partly covered). The meaning of this feature is unknown.

44. Barbaro (1556), V.vi, (p. 155). This passage contains definite clues that Barbaro worked from a Jocundus derived Latin edition. In translating "lower seats" ("seggi inferiori"), he follows the Jocundus Latin ("inferiores sedes") and not the text of the root codices—"interiores sedes"—G. and H. G. and H. are, respectively, the Wolfenbüttel 11th century MS

and the London Harleian 8th century MS. See Granger, I, pp. xvi-xxxiii and Valentinus Rose, ed., *Vitruvii de Architectura* (Lipsiae: B. G. Teubneri, 1867), pp. ix-xii, for codice bibliography and apparatus.

45.   Alberti (1485), VIII.vii, (pp. 149v-150r).

46.   Barbaro (1556), V.vi, (p. 155).

47.   English from Granger (1934), V.vi.8 (I, p. 289). The Latin is from Philandri (1543), V.vi (p. 131). Barbaro's commentary (1556), V.vi (p. 167), calls them "machine triangolari versatili." Although no text has been cut, the 1556 printing has skipped pages 158 through 166.

48.   Barbaro (1556), V.vi (p. 155).

49.   Barbaro's commentary extends the use of the *periaktoi* beyond Vitruvius. He says that in Sophocles' *Ajax* a god is made to appear by the revolving of the machine. While Barbaro is familiar with the existence of the Greek *episkene,* as instanced in the commentary in V.vi (p. 155), here he participates in the popular confusion of the Greek *Theologeion* and the *periaktoi* function. This slight notice leads us to believe that Barbaro had read Pollus' *Onomasticon.* See Julius Pollus, *Onomasticon,* Immannelio Bekkeri, ed. (Berlin: Friderici Nicolai, 1846), IV 126-130 (pp. 172-73).

50.   The use of *periaktoi* by Palladio in his Vicenza and Venice theatres is not documentable. See the conclusions about Palladio's scenic applications in chapter 3. Chapter 4 will briefly address the arguments, pro and con, for *periaktoi* in the Teatro Olimpico.

51.   English from Granger (1934), V.vi.6 (I, p. 287). See Barbaro (1556), V.vi (p. 155).

52.   Barbaro (1556), V.vi (p. 155)

53.   Barbaro (1556), V.vii (p. 167). The relevance of this and other ruins will be analyzed in a later part of this chapter.

54.   Barbaro (1556), V.vi (pp. 157-167).

55.   Barbaro (1556), V.vi (p. 155).

56.   Barbaro (1556), V.vii (p. 167).

57.   The Jocundus Latin edition (1511), V.vii (p. 52r), starts the inversion. It is continued by Cesariano (1521), V.vii (p. LXXXIIIIr); Durantino (1524), V.vii (p. 52r); Caporali (1536), V.vii (p. 120r); and Philandri (1543), V.vii (p. 132). The codices G. and H. are the sources for the inversion error. See Rose, p. 120, note. It is worth noting that Vitruvius is here describing his concept of a Greek theatre, with its Hellenized, less than full-circle orchestra.

58.   In the case of the applied classical vocabulary on the *frons-scenae,* there are distinct differences between the Barbaro translation and Palladio's drawings. Since Vitruvius and Barbaro's translation are so abundantly clear about the precise physical nature of the *frons-scenae* orders, Palladio's drawn deviations are surprising. Looking somewhat ahead to chapter 4, we will discover that the Teatro Olimpico initial and final designs of the *frons-scenae* do not use Vitruvian instructions or Palladio's deviations as the source for their physical proportions. Rather Palladio clearly seems to be applying his own stylistic concept of classical order proportions in deviation from Vitruvius. The Palladian *frons-scenae* deviations are a historical curiosity in their own right. They may be rendering errors since there are even differences between the 1556 edition's drawing of the *frons-scenae* (figure 45) and the 1584 edition's drawing of the same features. We can note below the x/1920 differences between the Barbaro translation, the 1556 Palladio drawing, and the 1584 drawing (1d. = orchestra diameter). All measurements are in reference to heights.

Frons-scenae	Barbaro tr.	Palladio, 1556	Palladio, 1584
	1248/1920 d.	1290/1920 d.	1275/1920 d.
First order	736/1920 d.	770/1920 d.	750/1920 d.
pedestal	160/1920 d.	165/1920 d.	165/1920 d.
column	480/1920 d.	500/1920 d.	480/1920 d.
entablature	96/1920 d.	105/1920 d.	105/1920 d.
Second order	512/1920 d.	520/1920 d.	525/1920 d.
pedestal	80/1920 d.	80/1920 d.	75/1920 d.
column	360/1920 d.	375/1920 d.	375/1920 d.
entablature	72/1920 d.	75/1920 d.	75/1920 d.

Each feature, taken separately, has such a small deviation (except for the 1556 first order column height which has a 1'-8" increase) that rendering error may be the cause. On the other hand, the differences in the total *frons-scenae* heights suggest *conscious* deviation. Since no available system of architectural order proportions allows the explanation of Palladio's apparent deviations, we must conclude that they are the result of either rendering errors or Palladio unsystematically toying with the proportions. The latter will gain credence as we discover that Palladio experimented with order proportions in the last years of his career. For these reasons only Barbaro's translation of the *frons-scenae* features will be treated as a viable design source.

59.   Referring to the Palladio *frons-scenae* (figure 45), the pedestal height is defined from the stage floor to the bottom of the column base; the column height includes the column base plus the shaft plus the capital; the entablature height is defined between the top of the capital and the bottom of the next pedestal. The entablature includes, in ascending order, a slightly corniced stringcourse architrave, a pulvinated frieze, and a cornice.

60.   Even though we have ascertained that Barbaro's source text was Jocundus or a Jocundus-derived text, we have no documentation to support Barbaro's knowledge of specific editions. If the Teatro Olimpico had an exterior appearance commensurate with the multi-ordered, arched facades of the numerous editions' illustrations, it might be fruitful to examine these pre-Barbaro editions to discover their relevance to the Barbaro edition. The same applies to Alberti, who includes an extensive description (1485), VIII.vii (pp. 151r-151v), of the porticos that encase the *cavea* on the exterior. But since the Olimpico exterior is stucco over brick with no applied classical vocabulary, there is no point in examining this aspect of Roman theatre construction. There is no record concerning the design of the Teatro Olimpico exterior; we can only speculate on the reasons behind its plain exterior appearance. In all likelihood Palladio did not treat the Olimpico exterior to look like the exterior of a Roman theatre (for example, see figure 14) because of space limitations and finances. We will see in chapter 4 that the original Olimpico building was encased on three sides by older, medieval buildings thus disallowing any extensive decoration. Finances became a burden in the building project; only after the building had been erected did a few wealthy contributors save the academy from debt. A third and highly speculative reason is that the rectangular Olimpico would not decorate, recognizably, as a curved Roman theatre.

61.   In fact Palladio would probably have found Alberti's methods eccentric and obscure. For example, Alberti does not generate the plan of the theatre from inscribed triangles, does not use the orchestra diameter as a prime module, nor does he detail the *frons-scenae*. He does posit an ideal 30° *cavea* rake and essentially generates his theatre from the implied ratios in a pythagorean triangle. No enlightened study of Alberti's theatre exists. See the 1966 Orlandi and Portoghesi ed. of the 1485 *princeps* for the relevant text of book VIII.vii (pp. 149v and ff.).

62. The Peruzzi and Sangallo drawings are housed in the Uffizi (Gabinetto desegni e stampe) and are reproduced from Lukomaki, *Maestri*, pp. 163 and 219. The Ligorio drawing is reproduced from Jean Jacquot, ed., *Le Lieu théâtrale*, p. 57, and plate IV, fig. 7.

63. Serlio, book III (1551), p. XVVII.

64. Ibid., p. XLVI.

65. The most complete collection of Palladio's archaeological drawings was published in Zorzi, *Disegni*. The Royal Institute of British Architects (R.I.B.A.) holds the majority of the originals.

66. Barbaro (1556), V.vii (p. 167). "Nella pianta del Latino, nella Scena havemo fatto tre porte, & in çia scuna un Triangolo versatile, perche si accompagnasse di prospettiva la facciata di mezzo, & ancho à diverso modo havemo congiunto la scena col Theatro, come si vede dalla pianta, non niego però, che ancho ad altro modo non si possa conguignere, & ancho dissegnare la Scena: ma con grande pensamento consultando questa cosa dellaquale nº ne havemo essempio antico, insieme col nostro Palladio si ha giudica to questa esser convenientissima forma & di più siano stati aiutati dalle ruine d'un Theatro antico, che si trova in Vicenza tra gli horti, & le case d'alcuni Cittadini, dove si scorgono tre Nichi della Scena, la dove noi havemo posto le tre porte, & il Nichio di mezzo è bello, e grande."

67. The Palladian authenticity of the drawings used in this study has been established by Zorzi, *Disegni*, pp. 25-27. Zorzi's method is to compare the autographic handwriting of certain Palladian letters and receipts with the handwriting on the extant drawings. Another method is to compare the "P" in Palladio (on the letters and receipts) with the characteristic "P" of *piede* (foot) used in the drawing measurements. Instances of Palladio's publication of his own drawings is documented in notes 28 and 29 of this chapter. There is no evidence to suggest that Palladio was merely adding measurements to drawings in other's hands, in the drawings used in this study. The measurements on the Palladian drawings are in Veronese or Vicentine feet and inches (1 *piede* Veronese = .343 meters = 13.5 inches U.S.; and 1 *piede* Vicentine = .347 meters = 13.66 inches U.S.). For the sake of simplified comparison and in an effort to avoid conversion errors, I will reproduce measurements according to the original scales. Two exceptions will be allowed. The measurements, in meters, on tables 1 and 2 will eventually be used for comparison to the Olimpico measurements, in meters, in the chapter 4 survey of that theatre. The relative accuracy of Palladio's drawings is not an important consideration in this study. Here we are interested in what Palladio documents that he saw and not how accuately he saw it. Two points are worth mentioning. First, Palladio's plans are quite accurate. Aldo Neppi Modona, *Gli edifici teatrali Greci e Romani* (Firenze: Leo S. Olschki Editore, 1961), p. 121, confirms Palladio's measurements in the Pola theatre and I have personally confirmed Palladio's measurements in the Verona theatre. Second, Palladio's elevations have a tendency to be inventive; this is symptomatic of archaeological research of the period due to structure deterioration. We can see Palladio's inventiveness operating especially in his drawings of various Roman *thermae*, the Temple of Fortuna, and even the theatre designs. See Zorzi, *Disegni*, for reproductions. There have been two attempts to reconstruct the Berga theatre in an effort to confirm Palladio's accuracy. See Ortensio Zago, "Disegni Autografi del Teatro Berga, nel MSS: Della Maravigliosa grotta...di Costozza e del Teatro Berga," 17th century MS., in Biblioteca Bertoliana, Vicenza, and Giovanni Megleoranza, *Prima relazione intorno gli scavi intrapresi per l'illustrazione dell'antico teatro di Berga* (Padova: Tip. Sicca, 1838). The value of these studies is limited since the archaeological remains available to them were minimal and since they appear not to have reconstructed independently of Palladio's work.

68. Palladio's drafting of an open-faced square in the middle of the stage area is not a case of invention but an example of rendering something not from real archaeological knowledge but from previous Vitruvius editions or second-hand archaeological information. That open-faced square is a *pulpito* and can be seen in Jocundus and Serlio, for example. See the Jocundus (1511), V.vi (p. 50v), Roman theatre plan, and Serlio, *Book III* (1551), p. LI, plan of the theatre at Pola for delineations of a pulpito.

69. This ruin has never been identified as a theatre scene. See Zorzi, *Disegni*, p. 60, and Zorzi, *Ville e i teatri di Andrea Palladio* (Venezio: Neri Pozza, 1969), p. 240.

70. This conclusion further supports the probability of drawing errors in the Vitruvius *frons-scenae*. See note 59.

71. The Verona and Pola theatre drawings have some problems in terms of internal consistency and problematic measurements. The Verona drawing has been measured with a scale other than the Vicentine unit; since we know that the maximum diameter of the orchestra (not through the generating center of the orchestra but measuring between the maximum arc of the erected *cavea*-orchestra junction) is 45.5 meters, the probable conversion unit is the Veronese *piede* which equals .343 meters. (Thus, for example, the *frons-scenae* length, P. 140, equals 49.02 meters.) Palladio was not very consistent in his drafting since, while his Verona plan is archaeologically correct (figure 50), he illustrates inconsistent orchestra dimensions in the two sections (figures 51-52). It is as if Palladio forgot where the generating center was for the orchestra-*cavea* curves. I might note that the temple and associated levels above the *cavea* are largely conjectural and are indicative of Palladio's inventive tendency with elevations. See note 68. The Pola drawing was executed in two scales: the *piede* and the *pertiche*. The *piede* is in the Vicentine unit; the *pertiche* is a "rod" of about 6 *piedi* in length. Both of the theatres' drawings have several out-of-scale measurements, unlike the Berga, so that I use the measurements, particularly those from the elevations, with some reservations.

72. Palladio does illustrate several arched *cavea* porticos in his amphitheatre drawings. See Zorzi, *Disegni*.

73. Meyer Schapiro, "Style," *Anthropology Today*, A.L. Kroeber, ed. (Chicago: University of Chicago Press, 1953), p. 288.

74. Ibid., 287.

75. The most authoritative statement on Palladian vocabulary is the *First Book* of Palladio's *Quattro libri*. There he outlines the proportions of the five classical orders according to a system of modules. The features of a given order are all generated from a single module (the column shaft diameter at the base). For example, one of Palladio's earliest buildings using classical orders was the Vicenza basilica (1549); its Doric first order (*QL*, II, 20, pl. 20) has a shaft diameter (module) at its base of 1'-6" Vicentine and a column height of 12'-0" Vicentine. According to the Doric canon (*QL*, I, 15) the column height should be eight times the module. The basilica order conforms precisely. The Palazzo Chiericati (1550; *QL*, II, 3, pl. 3), has both a Doric and an Ionic order; each conforms to the *QL* canon (I, 15 and 16). After 1560, Palladio essentially abandons the use of all orders except the Corinthian. While the *QL* (1570) establishes the Corinthian order as having a column height of 9 1/2 modules, a pedestal height of 1/4 the column height and an entablature height of 1/5 the column height (I, 17), we can observe Palladio using a 1:10 column height ratio in the Carità design (1561; *QL*, II, 6, pl. 21), the Palazzo Valmarana (1565-66; *QL*, II, 3, pls. 11-12) and the Palazzo Schio-Angaran (pre-1566; *QL*, II, 17, pl. 17). This 1:10 ratio is an example of Palladio's late style deviation from classical decorum. Counter to the expectation that Palladio would revert to a more decorous handling of the Olimpico, we will observe the 1:10 vocabulary ratio applied in the Olimpico.

76. Ackerman, p. 43.

77. Wittkower, pp. 87 and 89.

78. Ackerman, p. 109.

79. See *QL,* I, 20, on psychology as an important architectural consideration.

80. Ackerman, p. 182.

81. Wittkower, pp. 57-100 and 126-42.

82. My dependence on Wittkower is total. Needless to say my outlines of Palladio's system of harmonic proportion is only a condensation of Wittkower's analysis.

83. Wittkower, pp. 66 67 and 69.

84. Barbaro (1556), II, preface (p. 58).

85. *QL,* IV, 5.

86. Wittkower, p. 15.

87. Plato *Timeaus* 33B. Quoted from Francis M. Cornford, *Plato's Cosmology* (London: Kegan Paul, Trench, Trubner & Co., Ltd., 1937), p. 54.

88. Plato *Timeaus* 35B-36B, and Wittkower, p. 103, note 2.

89. Wittkower, p. 101.

90. Alberti (1485), IX.vi (p. 166v).

91. Wittkower, p. 103.

92. Alberti (1485), IX.v (pp. 164-167).

93. Wittkower, pp. 103-104.

94. Translated by Wittkower in his Appendix I, p. 155.

95. Wittkower, p. 61.

96. Silvio Belli, *Della proportione et proportinalità* (Venetia: Elesanta, 1573).

97. *QL,* I, 21 and 23, and II, 2.

98. Wittkower, p. 129.

Chapter 3

1. Edward Conradi, *Learned Societies and Academies in Early Times,* reprinted in *Pedagogical Seminary,* II (December, 1905), p. 16.

2. See Giangiorgio Zorzi's documented discussion, *Le ville e i teatri di Andrea Palladio* (Venezio: Neri pozza, 1969), pp. 244-45, and Bernardo Morsolin, *Giangiorgio Trissino* (Vicena: Tip. Gir. Burato, 1878), pp. 137 ff.

3. Rudolf Wittkower, *Architectural Principles in the Age of Humanism,* Columbia University Studies in Art History and Archaeology, Number 1 (New York: Random House, 1965), p. 58.

4. Morsolin, Appendix LXIII (pp. 498-500).

5. Wittkower, p. 60.

6. See Zorzi, *Ville e i teatri,* p. 244, Wittkower, p. 60, and Morsolin, p. 180.

7. Bartolomeo Zigiotti, *Memoire dell'Accademia Olimpica,* MSS, pp. 7-8; the 1555 charter date is derived from the statement that the officers and initial *statuti* should be created in three months. On the first of March 1556 these procedures were accomplished.

8. See Antonio Magrini, *Il Teatro Olimpico* (Padova: Tip. del Semenario, 1847), p. 13, and Zigiotti, *passim,* for confirmation of these occupations.

9. Zigiotti, p. 103; "Gli Academici Olimpici hanno tutti uno animo, et uno volere: Onde non è maraviglia, se tutti parimente tendono ad un fine solo: et questo è, che ogn'uno di quelli desidera di imparare tutte le scientie, et specialmente le Matematiche, le quali sono il vero ornamento di tutti coloro, che hanno l'animo nobile, et virtuoso." The academy's use of the term "Matematiche" is obscure in this context. I think its use here has a meaning broader than simply the science of numbers. We recall from the background discussion of Palladio's aesthetic in chapter 2 that Greek mathcmatics and its relation to cosmology found its way into Renaissance theology and cosmology through neo-Platonic humanistic study. Apparently the academy saw in "Matematiche" the foundations for all sciences and the means for achieving the ideal that they perceived in the ancients.

10. Ibid., p. 110.

11. Confirmed by Daniel Barbaro's *Dalla eloquenza* (Venezia: Valgrisio, 1557), which mentions the Costanti.

12. Longiano da Fausto, *Del modo di tradurre* (Venetia, 1556), "Dedica."

13. Giacomo Marzari, *La historia di Vicenza* 2nd ed. (Vicenza: Giorgio Greco, 1604), Parte II. For the dissolution see Zigiotti, pp. 122-23.

14. Zigiotti, p. 108. See Silvio Belli, *Della proportione et proportionalità* (Venetia: Elesanta, 1573) as an example of Belli's learning.

15. Ibid., p. 9.

16. Ibid., pp. 91-93.

17. Ibid., p. 12; "23 do. [ditto = "xtbre"; December, 1556] fu presa parte di recitare una Comedia sotto il nome dell'Accademia, con facoltà ad ogni Accademico di poter condur seco alla recita tre persone, e fu dapoi instituita un Mansionerià per loro commodo, e docoro con onorario al Capetlano [*sic?*]."

18. Ibid., p. 11; "Adi 24 Genaro M.D. LVII. E andata la parte, che, reservata ogn'altra parte a questa non contraria, si debba recitar la comedia principiata a imparare dalli Academici, con consenso, et sotto nome della Academia, Pro 41. contra 4."

19. Ibid., pp. 110-11; "Adi 25 Genaro 1557. Volendo il Mag^{co} principe nostro il S^{ig} Daniel Loscho; l'ex^{te} Mon. Alessandro Massaria; il S^{ig} Hieronimo Schio eletti il giorno da heri a dar ordine circa le cose della comedia; hanno deliberato che Il S^{ig} Giacomo Pagiello; Il S^{ig} Valerio Barbarano; M. Gio Antonio Fasolo; M. Battista Marangon, q. M^o Gugielmo; M. Lorenzo Schultore; Habbino cura di far provesion et ordinare la scena et le cose pertinente a quella. Che il S^{ig} Horatio Almerico; Il S^{ig} Cavalier Capra; Il S^{ig} Cavalier Manfredo da Porto; Il S^{ig} Cavalier Christophoro Barbarano; Habbino cur di trovar, et esser sopra li vestiment et habiti. Che Il S^{ig} Alessandro Milano, habbi cura di concerti a musica et che puossi ordinar, et comandar a quelli che parerano a lui siano al proposito circa il redur musici, et altre cose reservandosi ells S^{ig} Principe, e collega la autorita di poter aggiongere, et minuire, et far quanto li parera, secondo li e sta concesso per il consiglio."

20.   Ibid., p. 111; "A di detto Il S^{ig} Principe con li collega destinati all provisione della comedia hanno elletto per locho idoneo la salla di S. Marcello picciola dove hora è il fromento del monte di S. Joanne, ne quale si habbi a metter in ordine la Scena a quel meglior modo che parera alli soprastanti elletti a questo, con il consenso de i sopradetti."

21.   Ibid.

22.   Ibid., pp. 112-13; "Adi 23. Febraro 1557. È andata parte che li quatro deputadi sopra la comedia con penna de esseo cassi siano obligati di far si che niuno non entri ne nella scena, ne nello apparato fino al giorno deputado."

23.   Ibid., p. 13; "26 do. [Febraro] fu data ampla facoltà al S^{ig} Girolamo da Schio di far col consenso delli Clarissimi Si^{gri} Girolamo Mocenigo Podestà, e Benedetto da Lezze tutte quelle provisioni possibili e necessarie, acciochè la Comedia fosse recitata pacificamente."

24.   Ibid., "Negli ultimi di Carnovale, essendo Vice Principe il S^{ig} Elio Belli, fu dagli Accademici fatta, recitar la Comedia la quale era fatica del S^{ig} Ac^{co} Alessandro Massaria, fu la traduzione in italiano dell' *Andria* di Terenzio, e fu eseguita con molta sodisfazione, e contento di tutta l'Udienza."

25.   Ibid., p. 116; "Adi ditto [24 Febraro 1558] Essendo l'accademia debitrice a Mr. Hieronimo di Forni di troni settanta doi per alcuni legnami per la comedia de l'anno passato. L'andarà parte che detti denari si debbano pagare della entrata ordinaria de l'accademia in tre rate cioè sotto tre Principe Cominzando la prima rata sotto il Principe futiero alli p^o Aprille proximo, et cossi successive fiu alla integra satisfatione. Pro 32. C^o 2. Idem Carolus secret."

26.   See Sabastiano Serlio, *Il secondo libro d'architettura* (Venetia: Pietro di Nicolini de Sabbio, 1551), pp. 26v and 27r, for this distinction. Serlio's use of the term *theatro* means stage platform, *apparato* means scenery, and *scena* means stage platform and all that is on it. To identify the platform specifically he used the term *suolo*.

27.   Lionello Puppi, *Il Teatro Olimpico* (Vicenza: Neri Pozza, 1963), p. 31.

28.   Zigiotti, p. 16; "Nella Residenza in questo anno [1560] fu recitata la Comedia del S^{ig} Alessandro Piccolomini Sanese—cioè *l'Alessandro*."

29.   Ibid., pp. 122-23; "1560. Adi primo Decembrio. Havendo gli Academici disiderio et volontà infinita di rapresentare questo carneval prox^a la bella et honoratissima comedia del S^{ig} Alessandro Piccolomini intitolata l'Amor Costante, et essendo bisogon di ritrovare denari per la spesa che occorerà fare per recitar detta Comedia, con miner dano et incomodo de gli academici che sia possibile... Adi sopra d^o fu balottati diversi acad^{ei} per thesorieri del danaro che si riscoterà per occasion come nella sudetta parte et resto M. Valerio Barbarano con voti quatordeci a favore, et contra cinque. Item sono sono [*sic*] stati eletti li sottoscritti, i quali habbino insieme col Principe et m^o Andrea Palladio il carico di dar fuori le parti della comedia a chi parerà loro atti recitare e di farle imparare et provare, et apresso academia che si possi. M. Lunardo Thieni pro 19, contra 1; M. Bernardin da Mosto pro 16, cont. 4; M. Giac^o Pagiello Pro 16. cont. 4. Prosp^o Fraina Segret$_o$."

30.   Ibid., p. 123, December 13, 1560; see aslo Zigiotti, 129-30, February 2, 1561.

31.   Ibid., p. 124; "[27 Decembre 1560] Perche non si può ritrovare cosa di maggior dignità per la essaltatione dalla nostra, ne che sia più conforme alla grandezza de gli Accademici, che il continuo essercito delle attioni virtuose si sono immaginati gli Academici, che hanno tutti buona voluntà, che saria universale nostro grandissimo honore, et infinita nostra contentezza se nel medesimo ricco bello, et leggiadrissimo apparecchio che sarà tosto all'ordine per recitare la comedia dell'Amor Costante si rappresentasse. doppo ancora la

Sophonisba tragedia ecco^ma et massimamente perche hanno discorsa, che ella si potrà recitre facilmente, et sopra tutto senza fare alcuna altra spesa, ma con grandissima sodisfattione di tutta questa Città et se bene essi Academici hanno già determinato, et concluso di voler la fare in ogni modo, non di meno per accrescere maggior gratia, et reputatione a questa loro honoratissima deliberatio ne co'l mezo sell'autorità, et del favore di tutti gli Academici universalmente. L'andarà parte che questo Carnevale doppo che si havrà rappresentata la Comedia, sia recitata ancora per gli stessi Academici nostri la Sophonisba Tragedia dignissima, et bellissima, la qual fu già composta dal Sor Gio: Giorgio Trissino gentil'huomo benemeritissimo della patria nostra Pro 23. C. 3. Paolo Chiappino Vice secretario dell' Academia Olimpica."

32. Ibid., pp. 124-25; "Adi detto [29 Decembre 1560] è stato per il consiglio nostro eletti gli infrascritti per dispensar la parte della Tragiedia, et insiemme con il Principe habbino carico di farle imparare et provare. M. Valerio Chieregatto Caval^r Pro 29, contra 4; M. Batta da Porto Pro 24, contra 10; M. Anto. Maria Angiolelo Pro 27, contra 6. Adi detto, fu eletti parimente per il consiglio nostro gli infrascritti li quali insieme con il Principe, habbino il carico de gli intermedij della comedia, et della Tragedia. M. Montan Barbaran Caval^r Pro 29, contra 5; M. Horatio Almerico Pro 24. contra 10; M. Silvio di Belli Pro 23, contra 12. Prospero Farina Segreto."

33. Zigiotti, pp. 126-27.

34. Vicenza, Archivio di Torre, book 94, marked 38; "1561, 26 febjo; habe due facchini ha disbarato lo pozolo per poterandar a arco lo palazo per lo trabicolo della comedia, qual facchini porto la roba, legnami, fagoti ere su dicto pozolo in la casa meta . . . lire 1.05.6 . . . e poso dopo: adi 27 habe m. Alvise Sepzzapria per pagar fachini porto il legname grosso dal dito pozolo, ch'ha cosi comanda li signori deputa 1.2.0.0." One wonders why the city had to get involved in his cartage problem; conceivably the academy had been negligent.

35. Zigiotti, p. 17; "Scielto da Sig^re Accademici il gran Salone del pubblica Palazzo per una Rappresentazione da recitarsi nel Carnovale di quest' anno [1561]; l'Accademico Palladio per tal occasione disegnò un Teatro di legname, e fu innalzato con tante diligenza, ch'era in tutto simile a quello degli antichi Romani."

36. *L'Amor costante comedia del S. Stordito Intronato, Composta per la venuta, De l'Imperatore in Siena L'Anno del XXXVI.* In Venetia al Segno del Pozzo, 1550. [del Alessandro Piccolomini.] See the prologue, pp. 2v and ff. The title claims that the play was first performed in [15]36 before the "Imperatore" (Charles V—Holy Roman Emperor) in Siena.

37. Zigiotti, p. 17, and Antonio Maria Angiolelli, *La Lidia* (Brescia: Ludovico Britanico, 1561).

38. Zigiotti, p. 128; "Adi 22 Febraro 1561. È andata la parte, che siano eletti quattro Academici che habbino ad ordinar, et regular i chori della Tragedia, e trovar persone atte a recitarli, et vestimenti da vestir li, et far circa ciò quello, che farà bisogno in essecution della qual parte sono sta eletti—M. Aloigi da Porto, M. Franc^o Ghellino; M. Luigi Trissino; M. Antonio Thiene Dottore; Pro 27. Ct^ra O. Giambatta Losco Secret. Adi detto. È andata parte che quelli che havevano il carico della scena nella comedia habbino l'istesso della scena nella tragedia, in mutarla, e variarla, me loro parera, e non lasciarvi star alcuno, et haver custodia del Theatro, et qual tanto, che occorrera necessario in tal cosa. Pro 24, ct^ra O. Giabatta Losco Secret^o Adi detto. Item che il carico de mutar la scena e di esserle soprastante sia del S^ig Giacomo Pagello, et il S^ig Bernard^o da Mosto, e del S^ig Leonardo Thiene, e del S^ig Andrea Palladio, e similmente della custodia del palazzo della scena, et Theatro non habbia danno, con ogni ampla autorità pro 23. ct^ra 1. Giabatta Losco secret^o."

39.   Ibid., pp. 130-31; "1561 adi 7 April. Messa, et proposta parte per il S^{ig} Principe, et Consiliarij, se si diveva dar licentia a privati Academici di far la Tragedia loro a nome di Academia, et questo a fine, che si proceda avanti... come in un manuscritto a ciò formato. à voce et per fiat tutti de trentatre che erano à voce eccetto duoi contentorno Giambatta Losco vice secret°."

40.   Ibid., p. 130.

41.   Ibid., pp. 17-18; "1562. Sig^i Olimpico si dovea nel carnovale di quest'anno far recitare la *Sofonisba.*"

42.   Ibid., p. 149.

43.   See note 38.

44.   See Licisco Magagnato, *Teatro italiani del cinquecento* (Venezia: Neri Pozza, 1954), p. 55, Puppi, pp. 32-33, 38-39, and Zorzi, *Ville e i teatri,* p. 269. Recall the discussion in chapter 1 of the monochromes and their apparent lack of authority.

45.   Magrini, *Teatro Olimpico,* p. 16.

46.   Antonio Magrini, *Memoire intorno la vita e le opere di Andrea Palladio* (Padova: Tip. del Seminario, 1845), pp. 43-44. See note 34.

47.   Zigiotti, p. 20, citing the MS of Silvestro Castellini's Libro VIII: Silvestro Castellini, *Storia della Città di Vicenza* (Vicenza: Tip. Parise Editore, 1822).

48.   Marzari, p. 60.

49.   Zigiotti, p. 18.

50.   Ibid., p. 21.

51.   Giangiorgio Trissino, *Sofonisba,* Franco Paglierani, ed. (Bologna: Bresso Gaetano Romagnoli, 1884).

52.   Marvin T. Herrick, *Italian Tragedy in the Renaissance* (Urbana: University of Illinois Press, 1965), pp. 45 ff. and 76.

53.   Filippo Pigafetta, *Due lettere descrittive,* Leonardo Trissino, ed. (Padova: Valentio Crescini, 1830), p. 28.

54.   See appendix A for the text of the Chiapin description of *Sofonisba* (1562).

55.   The letter is quoted in Zorzi, *Ville e i teatri,* p. 281. "Anchora che io credo che inanzi che acaderà far cosa alcuna, io sero a Vicenza perchè ho fornito di far questo benedetto theatro nel quale ho fatto la penitentia de quanta peccati ho fatti e son per fare. Marti prossimo si reciterà la tragedia, quando V.S. potesse udirla, io la esorterei a venir perchè si spiera che debbia esser cosa rara. Nostro Signor Dio la conservi e faccia felice. Di Venetia alli XXIII Febraro. Di, S.D.V.S. El Palladio."

56.   Giorgio Vasari, *Le vite di più eccellenti pittori, scultori ed architettori,* Gaetano Milanesi, ed. (Firenze: G.S. Sansoni, Editorie, 1881), VII, p. 100: "Ora Federigo [Zucchero], se bene era solleci tatto a tornarsene da Vinezia, non potè non compiacere e non starsi quel carnovale in quella città in compagnia d'Andrea Palladio architetto; il quale avendo fatto alli signori della Compagnia della Calza um mezzo teatro di legname a uso di Colosseo, nel quale si aveva da recitare una tragedia fece fare nell'apparato a Federigo dodici storie grandi, di sette piedi e mezzo l'una per ogni verso, con altre infinite cose di fatti d'Ircano re di Ierusalem, secondi il soggetto della tragedia: nella quale opera acuqistò Federigo onore

assai, per la bonta di quella e prestezza con la quale la condusse."Zucchero painted a theatre curtain in Florence in 1565 for the performance of Francesco d'Ambra's comedy *La Confanaria* in celebration of the wedding of Giovanni of Austria to Francesco, son of Cosimo I. Alois M. Nagler, *Theatre Festivals of the Medici, 1539-1637* (New Haven: Yale University Press, 1964), p. 16. Nagler documents this eyewitness account from the Mellini description.

57.   Tommaso Temanza, *Vite dei più celebri architetti e scultori Veneziani* (Venice: C. Palese, 1778), p. 312.

58.   Leone Battista Alberti, *L'Architettura,* Latin text and Italian trans. by Giovanni Orlandi (Milano: Edizione il Polifilo, 1966), VIII.vii (149r). The Latin text is based on the 1485 edition and the Vatican codices. Textual references to Alberti are to the 1485 foliation. See also Daniel Barbaro, *I dieci libri dell'architettura di Vitruvio* (Venecia: Francesco Marcolini, 1556), V.iii (p. 138).

59.   See Andrea Palladio, *Quattro libri dell'architettura,* II, 6, plate 20, for the plan and elevation for the Carità. Palladio designed the building in 1561.

60.   Zigiotti, p. 22, cites the publication of the work, Conte de Monte, *Antigono* (Venezia: Comin da Trino, 1565). The publication was licensed for ten years of sale in Venice; Archivo Stato Senato Terra, Reg. N. 45, p. 107.

61.   Giovanni Montenari, *Del Teatro Olimpico di Andrea Palladio in Vicenza* (Padova: Terrinario, 1749), p. 5.

62.   Vito Pandolfi, *La commedia dell'arte,* 5 vol. (Firenze: Edizione Sansoni Antiquariata, 1957), makes no documentation of their existence.

63.   Zigiotti, p. 22; "privatamente senza apparato."

64.   Magrini, *Teatro Olimpico,* p. 18.

65.   Zigiotti, p. 25.

66.   Ibid, p. 14.

67.   Zigiotti, pp. 14-15.

68.   Magrini, *Teatro Olimpico,* p. 19.

69.   Pompeo Gherardo Molmenti, *Venice: The Golden Age,* Pt. II., trans. Horatio F. Brown (Chicago: A. C. McClurg and Co., 1907), I, pp. 87-89.

70.   The Vicentino painting is held by the Museo Correr, Sala Delle Quattro Porte of the Ducal Palace, Venice. The other drawing is reproduced by A. Chastel, "Palladio et l'art des fêtes," *Bollettino centro internazionale di studi d'architettura Andrea Palladio,* II (1960), pp. 29-33 and figure 26.

71.   Serlio (1551), *Book II,* p. 26v.

72.   For a more thorough discussion of the development of Italian theatre architecture the reader is directed to the works by the following authors listed in the bibliography: Eckert, Kernodle, Larson, Lawrenson, and Nagler. A good English summary with a few factual and inference errors can be found in Sir Edmund K. Chambers, *The Elizabethan Stage* (Oxford: Clarendon Press, 1923), III, chapter I. Foreign language works of merit are Borcherdt, D'Ancona, Kinderman, Leclerc, and Magagnato.

73.   See note 58.

74. The Eunuchus was translated by Hans Mithart and printed by C. Dinckmut in Ulm, 1486.

75. Alberti (1485), VIII.vii, (pp. 150r-150v).

76. See Kenneth J. Conant, "Afterlife of Vitruvius in the Middle Ages," *Journal of the Society of Architectural Historians,* XXVII (March 1968), pp. 33-38, and Carol H. Krinsky, "Seventy-eight Vitruvius Manuscripts," *Journal of the Warburg and Courtauld Institutes,* XXX (1967), pp. 36-70 for a discussion of the many codices of Vitruvius that were available before the mid-fifteenth century. Their studies substantially destroy the myth that Vitruvius was rediscovered in 1415 by the humanist Poggio in St. Gall.

77. See Magagnato, *Teatri,* p. 25, for text: "Tu etiam primus picturatae scenae faciem quum Pomponiani Comoediam agerent, nostro saeculo ostendisti: quare a te quoque theatrum novum tota Urbs magnis votis exptectat."

78. See Chambers, III, p. 3.

79. Richard Krautheimer, "The Tragic and the Comic Scene of the Renaissance, The Baltimore and Urbino Panels," *Gazette des Beaux Arts* CLIX (1948), p. 343.

80. Ibid., pp. 341-42.

81. Alesandro D'Ancona, *Origini del teatro italiano* (2nd ed.; Torino: Loescher, 1891), II, pp. 128-29; from the *Diario Ferrarese,* "con case v merlade, con una fenestra e uscio per ciascuna."

82. Krautheimer, pp. 340-41.

83. Ibid.

84. Ibid., p. 328.

85. Ibid., p. 337 *et eq.*

86. Printed by Johannes Trechsel, Lyons, 1493.

87. Printed by Lazarus Soardus, Venice, 1497. A second edition appeared in 1499.

88. D'Ancona, II, p. 130.

89. Julia Cartwright Ady, *Beatrice d'Este, Duchess of Milan, 1475-97* (London: J.M. Dent, 1903), p. 124, and Chambers, III, p. 9.

90. D'Ancona, II, 102; "La scena poi era finta una città bellissima con le strade, palazzi, chiese, torri, strade vere, e ogni cosa di rilevo, ma ajuta ancora da bonissima pintura e prospettiva bene intesa. Fra le altre cose ci era un tempio a otto facce di mezzo rilevo."

91. Vasari (Milanesi ed.), IV, p. 600.

92. William B. Dinsmoor, "The Literary Remains of Sebastiano Serlio," *Art Bulletin,* XXIV (1942), pp. 55-91 and pp. 115-54.

93. Serlio (1551), *Book II,* pp. 26v-31r.

94. Alois M. Nagler, *Theatre Festival of the Medici, 1539-1637.*

Chapter 4

1. Appendix B, 1579, 29. See appendix B for descriptive note. (Hereafter, "B," date, and MS page number.)

2.   B, August 10, 1579, 149-50.

3.   B, August 10, 1579, 30.

4.   B, November 15, 1579, 150.

5.   B, January 3, 1580, 150-151.

6.   B, January 12, 1580, 31.

7.   B. February 15, 1580, 31.

8.   B, Feburary 22, 1580, Archivo di Torre, III, p. 312.

9.   B, *Ibid.*

10.   B, February 24, 1580, 152.

11.   B, February 25, 1580, Archivo di Torre, III, p. 312.

12.   B, March 15, 1580, Archivo di Torre, III, p. 313.

13.   B, February 28, 1580, 32.

14.   B, March 23, 1580, 32.

15.   B, May 23, 1580, 154.

16.   B, November 7, 1580, 156.

17.   B, April 1, 1581, 157.

18.   B, April 1, 1581, 157.

19.   B, April 18, 1581, 158-59.

20.   B, April 16, 1581, and May 23, 1581, Archivo di Torre, III, p. 345. While financial problems initially forestalled the completion of the Olimpico and academician contributions did not fully satisfy construction needs, the completion of the theatre and the satisfactory mounting of the *Edippo* were achieved by special contributions from a few donors: Academician Leonardo Valmarana contributed a total of 1633.4.3 ducats; Monte de Verona, 1000 ducats; Signora Claudia Piovene, 1400 ducats; plus four additional contributions totalling 890 ducats. See B, May 5, 1585, 180. Since the financial records of the Olimpico construction are so minimal and since financial problems were finally removed by major contributions, the practicalities of finance cannot be considered a viable factor in the Olimpico design. While not confirmed by a contemporary document, Antonio Magrini, *Il Teatro Olimpico* (Padova: Tip. del Seminario, 1847), p. 26, says the theatre cost 18,000 ducats to build and the perspectives cost 1500 ducats.

21.   B, April 26, 1581, 36.

22.   B, June 3, 1581, 36.

23.   B, August 12, 1581, 159.

24.   B, *Ibid.*

25.   B, August 28, 1581, 36.

26.   B, post-October 28, 1581, 37.

27.   B, January 11, 1582, 160.

28.   B, January 28, 1582, Archivo di Torre, III, p. 381.

29. B, February 5, 1582, 161-62.

30. B, April 1, 1582, 165.

31. B, April 24, 1582, 165.

32. B, February 5, 1582, 161-62.

33. See Magrini, *Teatro Olimpico*, p. 45. The final list of statues for the third order was, from the stage right *versurae* to the stage left *versurae*, Gio. Battista Gorgo, Orazio Velo, Giovanni Monza, Gio. Battista Titoni, Girolamo Forni, Marco Valle, Paolo Piovene, Fausto Macchiavelli, Onorio Belli, M. Antonio Broglia, Paolo Chiapin, Francesco Florian, Micola Tavola, and Cirolamo Porto. This list has been confirmed by the Centro Internazionale di Studi d'Architettura Andrea Palladio, Vicenza. Although the decision to complete the final thirty-two statues was made in 1751 (Magrini, p. 42), they were not dedicated until 1847 (Magrini, p. 76).

34. B, July 29, 1582, 165-66.

35. B, September 2, 1582, 166.

36. B, January 2, 1583, 42.

37. B, February 7, 1583, 42.

38. B, February 19, 1583, 167-68.

39. B, February 21, 1583, 168-69.

40. B, February 23, 1583, 169.

41. B, May 8, 1583, 171.

42. B, post-February 21 and pre-April 19, 1583, 42-43.

43. B, post-February 21, 1583, 43.

44. B, post-March 5, 1584, 45.

45. B, August, 1583, 43-44.

46. B, November, 1584, 44.

47. B, Ibid.

48. B, January 1, 1584, 171.

49. B, post-March 5, 1584, 46.

50. B, May 6, 1584, 173-77.

51. B, post-May 6, 1584, 47.

52. B, May 9, 1584, 47. See also Giangiorgio Zorzi, *Le ville e i teatri di Andrea Palladio* (Venezia: Neri Pozza, 1969), p. 327, for documentation of autographic contracts held in the Biblioteca Bertoliana, Vicenza, catalogued Gonzati, 5.1.5-E146 n. 84.

53. B, June 4, 1584, 47.

54   B, Ibid.

55. B, November 14, 1584, 177-78. See also, B, January 30, 1585, 178-79.

56. B, November, 1584, 48.

57. Nicolo Rossi wrote *Discorsi intorno la commedia* (Vicenza: Dalla Noce, 1589) and *Discorsi intorno la tragedia* (Vicenza: Greco, 1590.

58. B, February 9, 1585, 179.

59. B, March 5, 1585, 50-51.

60. This map is an enlargement of the central portion of Vicenza, encompassed by the oldest of the city's walls. It is taken from Georg Braun and Franciscus Hogenberg, *Civitates Orbis Terrarum* [2nd ed., 1574], R.A. Skelton, intro. (Cleveland: World Publishing Co., 1966), pt. 4, pp. 45 ff. The map was drawn from the north, looking south. The artist used an imaginary viewing point. The date of the map is problematic. At #22, the "Piazza Magiore," the artist has rendered the civic basilica as it appeared before Palladio's renovations were begun in 1549. Two blocks north of the "Piazza Magiore" on the northern edge of the block are two buildings between which is a long and low unbroken structure. This building may be the Palazzo Thiene, built by Palladio ca. 1540-50. In all probability the map dates between 1540 and 1550. The map's accuracy is suspect with regard to detailed renderings. The major east-west street, marked #29, called then the Strada di Angelo (now the Corso Andrea Palladio), ran from #84, "Porta de Castel," to the Bridge of Piero, #53 ("Ponte di S. Piero"). The old prison property (#25), on which the Olimpico was built, was on the north side of the Strada di Angelo and not, as the map suggests, to the south of the Strada. The Bridge of Piero (#53) is shown with only two arches; as Palladio implies in *Quattro libri*, III, 12, the bridge always had three arches. Palladio says the bridge is "near the Church of S. Maria degli Angioli," marked #28 on the key ("S. Maria di Angeii"); the map fails to locate a #28. The Church of S. Maria degli Angeli was located at the western end of the old Prison and the bridge.

61. B, January 28, 1582, 160.

62. B, January 27, 1581, 156. There is no doubt that the London Studio is in Palladio's hand or that it predates the acquisition of the old prison property. There are Palladian autograph measurements on the drawing, as well as the already mentioned *frons-scenae* height instruction. The statuary is in a style comparable to his other designs which contained statuary. However, we have no method for discovering whether this design was part of a series or what part it plays in the initial design procedure. The design is certainly an early one, and the only extant one; my terming it the preliminary design implies only that it was not the final design and that it experienced revision.

63. Some discussion in chapter 2 has already addressed Palladio's normative architecture. It was observed that Palladio established rules for his use of classically derived vocabulary. Specifically noted were the differences between Palladio's use of a 1:9.5 and 1:10 module to column height ratio. A tolerance of *more* than 2% eliminates these ratios as distinct norms. It bears repeating that most of Palladio's designs were executed precisely according to those rules. Comparisons can be made between the published designs in the *Quattro libri,* the survey drawings in Ottavio Bertotti Scamozzi, *Le fabbriche e i disegni di Andrea Palladio* (Vicenza: Giovanni Rossi, 1796), and the current surveys available at the Centro Internazionale di Studi d'Architettura Andrea Palladio. These comparisons confirm Palladio's rigor. In the instances where the surveys document a deviation from the norm, the deviation is generally within a 2% tolerance. See for example the deviation in the Palazzo Schio-Angaran (pre-1556) as documented in Bertotti Scamozzi, *Fabbriche,* I, pl. XLIV. In this palace the major Corinthian order has a module of .56 meters and a column height of 5.51 meters. According to the 1:10 ratio the column height is short by .09 meters or within the 2% error tolerance.

64. *QL,* I, 17.

65. *QL,* I, 14. Palladio does not use a Tuscan order in any of his post-1560 designs. The only referable system must be that detailed in the *QL.*

66. For the Pantheon, see *QL,* IV, 20 (pl. 58); for the San Giorgio Maggiore, see Bertotti Scamozzi, *Fabbriche,* IV, pl. 8.

67. For the Basilica, see *QL,* III, 20 (pls. 19 and 20); for the Carità, see *QL,* II, 6 (pl. 21) and for Iseppo Porto see *QL,* II. 3 (pl. 6).

68. In the analysis of Palladio's practice of harmonic proportion it is frequently necessary to round off or adjust given quantities so that they can participate in the aesthetic. As Wittkower (p. 136 *et passim*) demonstrates, there are slight differences between the *Quattro libri* stated dimensions for a building and the executed dimensions. The dimensions in the *Quattro libri* are generally rounded off so that they will be commensurate quantities. In the Palazzo Chiericati (Vicenza, 1551-54; *Ql,* II, 3, pls. 2-4), for example, practicalities forced Palladio into an adjustment of one room size. The rooms have the following ratios in Vicentine feet: 12′ × 18′, 18′ × 18′, 18′ × 30′, and 16′ × 54′. With the exception of the width of the large hall (16′ × 54′), all the dimensions are multiples of 6′. If Palladio had executed the palazzo large hall with an 18′ width, the vault of the room would have been pushed up into the second story. Idealized, the above room dimensions have the following musical ratios: 2:3 (diapenti), 1:1 (octave), 3:5 (major sixth), 1: (two octaves). In the analyses which follow, I will adhere to Wittkower's practice of applying ratios to only the bold features and quantities.

69. See James A. Ackerman's excellent analysis of Gothic and Renaissance building practice in "'Ars Sine Scientia Nihil Est': Gothic Theory of Architecture at the Cathedral of Milan," *Art Bulletin,* XXXI (1949), pp. 84-111, and "Architectural Practice in the Italian Renaissance," *Journal of the Society of Architectural Historians,* XIII (October 1954), pp. 3-11.

70. Magrini, *Teatro Olimpico,* p. 30.

71. The Bertotti Scamozzi (1796, I, pls. 1-5) drawings executed by Antonio Mugnon in 1788 are to be found in figure 44 (ground plan), figure 3 (theatre section), and figures 33 through 35.

72. See Guglielmo de Angelis d'Ossat, "War Damage to the Monuments of Vicenza," *The Burlington Magazine,* XC (May 3, 1948), pp. 14-43. D'Ossat documents heavy bombing raids on Vicenza on May 14, 1944, and March 18, 1945 (p. 141). While much of the property around the theatre was demolished during these raids, the theatre proper was not. The Centro Internazionale di Studi d'Architettura Andrea Palladio has an extensive collection of photographs taken of the theatre in 1944 before it was disassembled and during its dismantling.

73. The survey figures are in the form of 28 triangulations from two fixed points at the corner of the stage piers on the *cavea* side (distance between the fixed points = 22.26 meters). The flexible point and intersections of the triangulations were 28 points along the back (riser) of the 12th *cavea* seat.

74. The focal points of a plane ellipse are found by subtracting the square of half the length of the ellipse's minor axis from the square of half the length of the ellipse's major axis; the square root of the subtraction is the distance along the major axis (in both directions) from the intersection of the two axes. The points fixed by the distance are the foci.

75. The margin of error is as much as .90 meters for the sum of the foci triangulations. On the assumption that Palladio had generated his orchestra and *cavea* ellipses from the stage front as major axis, another set of foci were extracted from the new minor semiaxis; these produced an even larger margin of error in their triangulations—1.20 meters.

76. See David Eugene Smith, *History of Mathematics* (Boston: Ginn and Co., 1923), I, pp. 92, 114, and 171.

77. The oval (admittedly, the ellipse is a geometrically pure oval) was a little used shape in Renaissance architecture. Barbaro (1556) V.i. (p. 136) has an ovoid curve in the plan of the basilica at Fano. Serlio's *Fifth Book* (1547) shows nine centralized church plans, one of which is ovoid. See Wittkower, pl. 6.

78. Serlio, *First Book* (Venice, 1551), pp. 13r-13v.

79. *Ibid.*, p. 13r. The method involves the striking of two 120° arcs at the ends of the major axis from two centers along the major axis. These 120° arcs form the ends of the oval. Then the curves between the legs of the 120° arcs are generated from centers along the minor axis; the minor axis centers are equidistant from the two major axis centers. As Serlio describes the four generation centers, they are the four angles of a rhombus made from two equilateral triangles, the common side of which is the distance between the two major axis centers.

80. No satisfactory explanation is available for the stage depth's .30 meter deviation from the speculative rationale.

81. By the very fact that Palladio has designed the original building without consideration of the then unavailable space for the perspectives, the recognized expectation for three-dimensional scenery as documented in the *Sofonisba* (1562) design and the academy's reference to the "prospettive" designed by Palladio for the Olimpico (February 15, 1880), we must assume that Palladio envisioned subsequent acquisition of the needed perspective property.

82. Roberto Pane, *Andrea Palladio* (Torino: Einaudi Editore, 1961), pp. 364-65.

83. If Palladio had followed Vitruvian canon for the present *frons-scenae* vocabulary, for example on the first order, he would have generated an order with the following measurements:

	Vitruvian Canon	Expected	Executed
Orchestra diameter	1 d.	17.42	17.42
Column height	1/4 d.	4.35	4.28
Pedestal height	1/12 d.	1.45	1.39
Entablature height	1/20 d.	.87	.86

If Palladio had followed the *Quatro libri* (1:9.5) canon on the first order, for example, he would have generated an order with the following dimensions:

	QL Canon	Expected	Executed
Column module	1 mo.	.425	.425
Column height	9 1/2 mo.	4.04	4.28
Pedestal height	1/4 (9 1/2 mo.)	1.01	1.39
Entablature height	1/5 (9 1/2 mo.)	.81	.86

84. See James A. Ackerman, *Palladio* (Baltimore: Penguin Books, Inc., 1966), pp. 64, 66-67, and 124-125 for his discussion of Palladio's decorative vocabulary. For the identification of the bas-reliefs and statuary see Magrini, *Teatro Olimpico*, pp. 33-34 and 41-46.

85. Licisco Magagnato, *Teatri italiani del cinguecento* (Venezia: Neri Pozza Editore, 1954), p. 69. Magagnato extends the argument to draw an analogy between the whole of the *frons-scenae* and the triumphal arch. See chapter 1 for my rejection of this argument.

86.   Palladio and Barbaro's misplacement of the Roman theatre scenic machine *(periaktoi)* behind the *frons-scenae* openings has led some critics to believe that Palladio intended to use *periaktoi* behind the Olimpico openings. See Pierre Patte, *Essai sur l'architecture théâtrale* (Paris: Chez Moutard, Libraire-Imprimeur de la Reine, 1782), p. 60; Orville Kurth Larson, "Italian Stage Machinery, 1500-1700" (Unpublished Ph.D. dissertation, University of Illinois, 1956), pp. 72-73. Certainly Palladio was familiar with the scenic potential of *periaktoi* although he appears to have adapted their scenic placement with scenery in the manner of Peruzzi-Serlio for the *Sofonisba* theatre. See the discussion of Italian Renaissance use of *periaktoi* by Franz Rapp, "Notes on Little-Known Materials for the History of the Theatre," *Theatre Annual*, III (1944), pp. 60-61. Rapp cites Aristotle da San Gallo's use of them in 1543 and their treatment in Vignola's *Le due regole della prospettive pratica,* 1583. A.M. Nagler has argued convincingly for their limited use at the Medici Court in 1569, "*Periaktoi* at the Medici Court," *Theatre Annual* XIV (1956), pp. 28-36.

87.   Lionello Puppi, "Prospettive del Olimpico, documenti dell'Ambrosiana e altre cose: argomenti per una replica," *Arte Lombarda,* XI (1966), pp. 26-32; Giangiorgio Zorzi, "Le prospettive del Teatro Olimpico nei disegni degli Uffizi di Firenze e nei documenti dell' 'Ambrosiana' di Milano," *Arte Lombarda* X (1965), pp. 70-97; and Zorzi, *Ville e i teatri,* pp. 295-303. Tomaso Buzzi's argument in "Il Teatro al' antica di Vicenzo Scamozzi a Sabbioneta," *Dedalo,* II (1928), p. 512, that Scamozzi used the same design in his Sabbioneta theatre that he used behind the Olimpico central portal is patently ridiculous. See also Howard Gregory Myers, "Andrea Palladio: Activities with the Accademia Olimpica," (Unpublished Ph.D. dissertation, Kent State University, 1978), pp. 97 and ff. Myers argues that Palladio conceived of three-dimensional scenery behind the *frons-scenae* for his designs for *L'Amor costante* (1561) and *Sofonisba* (1562), and that three-dimensional scenery would have been a logical design notion for the Olimpico. He provides the same supporting evidence as Zorzi in *Ville e i teatri* for the design attribution of the inaugural (and present) scenery to Andrea Palladio. It is Myers' contention that Silla Palladio merely executed his father's designs; Vicenzo Scamozzi had no role in the design or execution of the Olimpico scenery. Myers does not address the chronology issues where Palladio dies (1) before the additional property for the scenery was acquired and (2) before the inaugural play *(Edippo)* was chosen, thus precluding the predeath design of the "Theban" scenery. He, with Zorzi, excludes Scamozzi's role with some specious arguments; Myers provides no new evidence or enlightening interpretations beyond those provided by Zorzi. Myers' appendices contain English translations of the Zigiotti MS.

88.   Vicenzo Scamozzi, *Dell'idea della architettura universale* (Venetia: Presso l'Autore, 1615), book VIII, dedication.

89.   The Chatsworth designs are far more detailed than the Uffizi holdings. The autograph is confirmed by the Scamozzi autographic designs for the theatre at Sabbioneta, also held by the Uffizi.

90.   Zorzi gives no method for his discovery of this fact. It seems quite arbitrary that Zorzi selected these entries as interpolations when he had no doubts about any of the other academy records.

91.   Giacomo Marzari, *La historia di Vicenza* (Vicenza: Giorgio Greco, 1590/1604), II, pp. 212-13.

92.   In 1838 a cyclorama effect was erected over the perspectives. Magrini, *Teatro Olimpico,* p. 50.

93.   Vicenzo Scamozzi, p. 118.

94.   See Magrini, *Teatro Olimpico,* pp. 53-58, for the identification of these murals and the name listings on the plaques.

95.   Ackerman, *Palladio,* pp. 34-35 and 180.

96.   Appendix B, May 6, 1584, 174-75.

97.   Marzari, 1590/1604, I, pp. 116-17.

98.   Magrini, *Teatro Olimpico,* pp. 47-49.

99.   Ibid., pp. 46-49.

100.   Conte Enea Arnaldi, *Idea di un teatro* (Vicenza: Antonio Veronese, 1762).

101.   Ottone Calderari, *Discorso intorno la copertura da farsi al pulpito del Teatro Olimpico de Vicenza* (Padova: Tip. di Seminario, 1762).

102.   Georgi K. Lukomski, *Andrea Palladio* (Paris: Auguste Vincent & Cie., 1927), p. 72.

Bibliography

Ackerman, James S. "Architectural Practice in the Italian Renaissance," *Society of Architectural Historians*, XIII (October, 1954), 3-11.

_____. "'Ars Sine Scientia Nihil Est': Gothic Theory of Architecture at the Cathedral of Milan," *Art Bulletin*, XXXI (1949), 84-111.

_____. *Palladio*. Harmondsworth: Penguin Books Ltd., 1966.

Ady, Julia Cartwright. *Beatrice d'Este, Duchess of Milan 1475-97*. 2d ed. London: J. M. Dent, 1903.

Alberti, Leone Battista. *De re aedificatoria*. Latin and Italian texts translated by Giovanni Orlandi with an introduction and notes by Paolo Portoghesi. Milano: Edizioni il Polifilo, 1966.

Ancona, Allesandro d'. *Origini del teatro italiano*. 2 vols. Torino: Loescher, 1891.

Archivo di Torre, Vicenza, Italy. Selected references from Libro III.

Arnaldi, Conte Enea L'. *Descrizione delle architettura, pitture e scoltore de Vicenza*. 2 vols. Vicenza: Vendramin Mosca, 1779.

_____. *Idea di un teatro*. Vicenza: Antonio Veronese, 1762.

Ashby, Thomas (ed.). *Topographical Study in Rome in 1581: A Series of Views with a Fragmentary Text by Etienne du Pérac*. London: J. B. Nichols and Sons, 1916.

Barbaro, Daniel. *Della eloquenza*. Venezia: Valgrisio, 1557.

_____. *Di Marco Vitruvio Pollione i dieci libri commentati da Mons. Barbaro*. Venecia: Francesco Marcolini, 1556.

Beccanuvoli, Lucrezio. *Tutte le donne maritale vedone e dongelle*. Vicenza, 1539. MS in Biblioteca Bertoliana, Vicenza.

Belli, Silvio. *Della proportione et proportionalità*. Venetia: Elesanta, 1573.

Bennasuti, Giuseppe. *Del Teatro Olimpico di Vicenza*. Verona: Bisesti, 1826.

Bergman, Harold E. "The Teatro Olimpico of Vicenza, Italy." Unpublished Master's thesis, Florida State University, 1955.

Bertotti Scamozzi, Ottavio. *Le fabbriche e i disegni di Andrea Palladio raccolti ed illustrati*. 4 vols. Vicenza: Giovanni Rossi, 1796.

_____. *L'origin dell'Accademia Olimpica di Vicenza*. Vicenza: Giovanni Rossi, 1790.

Borcherdt, Hans Heinrich. *Das europäische Theater in Mittelalter und in der Renaissance*. Leipzig: Verlag buchhandlung von J. J. Weber, 1935.

Braun, Georg and Franciscus Hogenberg. *Civitates Orbis Terrarum*. 3 vols. Introduction by R.A. Skelton. Cleveland: World Publishing Co., 1966.

Burkhardt, Jakob. *The Civilization of the Renaissance in Italy*. The Modern Library. New York: Random House, 1954.

Buzzi, Tomasso. "Il teatro all'antica di Vincenzo Scamozzi a Sabbioneta," *Dedalo*, II (1928), 488-524.

Calderari, Ottone. *Discorso sopra la copertura da farsi al pulpito del teatro Olimpico di Vicenza*. Padova: Tip. di Seminario, 1762.

Caporali, Giambatista. *Architettura con il suo commento et figure, Vetruvio in volgar lingua raportato per M. Giambatista Caporali di Perugia.* Perugia: Conte Jano Bigazzini, 1536.

Cappelli, Adriano. *Cronografia e calendario perpetuo.* Milano: Ulrico Hoepli, 1930.

Cesariano, Cesare. *Di Lucio Vitruvio Pollione de Architectura Libri Dece Traducti de Latino in Vulgare Affi Gurati: Commentati: E Con Mirando Ordine Insigniti: Per Il Quale Facilmente Potrai Trovare La Multitudine De Li Abstrusi et Reconditi Vo Cabuli A Li Soi Loci Et In Epsa Tabula Con Summo Studio Expositi Et Enucleati Ad Immensa Utilitate De Ciascuno Studioso Et Benivolo De Epsa Opera.* Como: Magistro Gotardo, 1521.

Chambers, Sir Edmund K. *The Elizabethan Stage.* 4 vols. Oxford: Clarendon Press, 1923.

Chastel, Andrè. "Palladio et l'art des fêtes," *Bollettino centro internazionale di studi d'architettura Andrea Palladio,* II (1960), 29-33.

Collingwood, Robin G. *The Idea of History.* Oxford: Clarendon Press, 1946.

Conant, Kenneth J. "Afterlife of Vitruvius in the Middle Ages," *Society of Architectural Historians,* XXVII (March, 1968), 33-38.

Conradi, Edward. *Learned Societies and Academies in Early Times.* Reprinted in *Pedagogical Seminary,* II (December, 1905), 12-43.

Cornford, Francis M. *Plato's Cosmology.* London: Kegan Paul, Tranch, Trubner and Co., Ltd., 1937.

Dinsmoor, William B. "The Literary Remains of Sebastiano Serlio," *Art Bulletin,* XXIV (1942), 55-91 and 115-54.

Dumont, Gabriel. *Parallèle de plans des plus belle salles de spetacles.* Paris: Chez Moutard, 1774.

Durantino, Francesco Lutio. *Marci Luci Vitruvii Pollionis De Architectura.* Venetia: Joane Antonio et Piero Fratelli de Sabio, 1524.

Durm, Josef and Hermann Ende. *Handbuch der Architektur, Die Baustile.* 2 vols. Stuttgart: Alfred Kröner Verlag, 1905.

Ebhardt, B. *Die Zehn Bücher der Architektur des Vitruv und ihre Herausgeber seit 1484.* Berlin: Grunewald, 1918.

Eckert, William D. "The Renaissance Stage in Italy." Unpublished Ph.D. dissertation, University of Iowa, 1961.

Ferrari, Giulio. *La Scenografia, cenni storici dall'evo classico ai nostri giorni.* Milano: Ulrico Hoepli, 1902.

Franco, Fausto. "Il teatro romano del antica Berga e la genesi del Teatro Olimpico," *Atti del III convegno nazionale di storia dell'architettura,* Rome, 1941.

Gallo, Alberto. *La prima rappresentazione al Teatro Olimpico.* Milano: Editioni Il Polofilo, 1973.

Gardner, Edmund G. *The King of Court Poets.* New York: Haskell House Publishers, 1906.

———. *The Painters of the School of Ferrara.* London: Duckworth and Co., 1911.

Granger, Frank. *Vitruvius on Architecture.* 2 vols. Loeb Classical Library. London: William Heinemann, Ltd., 1931.

Gregor, Joseph. "Das Theater des Vitruv nach den Handschriften und Drucken der National Bibliothek in Wien," *Philobiblon,* IX (1936), 285-99.

Harrison, William. *The Description of England.* Edited by George Edelin. Ithaca, New York: Cornell University Press, 1968.

Herrick, Marvin T. *Italian Tragedy in the Renaissance.* Urbana: University of Illinois Press, 1965.

Jacquot, Jean (ed.). *Le Lieu Théâtrale a la Renaissance.* Paris: Éditions du Centre National de la recherche scientifique, 1964.

Jocundum. *M. Vitruvius Per Iocundum So Lito Castiga Tior Factus Cum Figuris Et Tabula Ut Iam Legi Et Intelligi Possit.* Venetiis: Ioannis de Tridino alias Tacuino, 1511.

Kennard, Joseph Spencer. *The Italian Theatre.* 2 vols. New York: W. E. Rudge, 1932.

Kernodle, George. *From Art to Theatre.* Chicago: University of Chicago Press, 1944.

Kindermann, Heinz. *Theatergeschichte Europas.* 8 vols. Salzburg: Otto Muller Verlag, 1959.

Krautheimer, Richard. "The Tragic and the Comic Scene of the Renaissance, The Baltimore and Urbino Panels," *Gazette des Beaux-Arts,* CLIX (1948), 327-46.

Krinsky, Carol Herselle. "Cesare Cesariano and the Como Vitruvius Edition of 1521." Unpublished Ph.D. dissertation, New York University, 1956.

———. "Seventy-eight Vitruvius Manuscripts," *Journal of the Warburg and Courtauld Institutes.* XXX (1967), 36-70.

Larson, Orville Kurth. "Italian Stage Machinery, 1500-1700." Unpublished Ph.D. dissertation, University of Illinois, 1956.

Lawrenson, Thomas E. and Helen Purkis. "Les Éditions Illustrées de Terence dans l'histoire du theatre, spectacles dans un fauteuil?" in *Le Lieu théâtrale a la Renaissance.* Paris: Éditions du Centre National de la recherche scientifique, 1964.

Lawrenson, Thomas E. *The French Stage in the XVII Century.* Manchester, England: Manchester University Press, 1957.

Leclerc, Helene. *Les Origines italiennes de l'architecture théâtrale.* Paris: Librarie E. Droz, 1946.

Lugli, Giuseppe. *The Classical Monuments of Rome and Its Vicinity.* Translated by Gilbert Bagnani. 2 vols. Roma: Libreria di Scienze e Lettere, 1929.

Lukomski, Georgi K. *Andrea Palladio.* Paris: Auguste Vicente & Cie, 1927.

———. *I maestri della architettura classica da Vitruvio allo Scamozzi.* Milano: Ulrico Hoepli, 1933.

Magagnato, Licisco. "The Genesis of the *Teatro Olimpico,*" *Journal of the Warburg and Courtauld Institutes,* XIV (1951), 209-20.

———. *Teatri Italiani del cinquecento.* Venezia: Neri Pozza, Editore, 1954.

Magrini, Antonio. *Il Teatro Olimpico nouvamente descritto ed illustrato.* Padova: Tip. del Seminario, 1847.

———. *Memorie intorno la vita e le opere di Andrea Palladio.* Padova: Tip. del Seminario, 1845.

Mariani, Valerio. *Storia della scenografia italiana.* Firenze: Rinascimento del libro, Tip. Classica, 1930.

Marzari, Giacomo. *La historia di Vicenza.* 2d ed. Vicenza: Giorgio Greco, 1604.

Megleoranza, Giovanni. *Prima relazione intorno gli scavi intrapresi per l'illustrazione dell'antico teatro di Berga.* Padova: Tip. Sicca, 1838.

Montenari, Giovanni. *Del Teatro Olimpico di Andrea Palladio in Vicenza, discorso del signor conte Giovanni Montenari.* 2d ed. Padova: Terrinario, 1749.

Morgan, Morris Hicky. *Vitruvius, The Ten Books on Architecture.* New York: Dover Publications Inc., 1960.

Morsolin, Bernardo. *Giangiorgio Trissino, o Monografia di un letterato nel secolo XVI.* Vincenza: G. Burato, 1878.

Moussinac, Leon. *Le Théâtre, des origines a nos jours.* Paris: Flammarion, Editeur, 1966.

Myers, Howard Gregory. "Andrea Palladio: Activities with the Accademia Olimpica." Unpublished Ph.D. dissertation, Kent State University, 1978.

Nagler, A.M. "Periaktoi at the Medici Court?" *Theatre Annual,* XIV (1956), 28-36.

———. *Theatre Festivals of the Medici, 1539-1637.* New Haven: Yale University Press, 1964.

Nash, Ernest. *Pictorial Dictionary of Ancient Rome.* 2 vols. New York: Frederick A. Praeger, 1962.

Neppi Modona, Aldo. *Gli edifici teatrali Greci e Romani.* Firenze: Leo S. Olschki Editore, 1961.

Niemeyer, Charles. "The Evolution of Baroque Theatre Design in Italy," *Theatre Annual,* I (1942), 36-42.

Nogara, Gino. *Cronache degli spettacoli di Vicenza dal 1585 al 1970.* Vicenza: Accademia Olimpica, 1972.

Ossat, Guglielmo de Angelis d'. "War Damage to the Monuments of Vicenza," *The Burlington Magazine,* XC (May 3, 1948), 140-43.

Palladio, Andrea. *L'antichità di Roma.* Rome: Vincenzo Lucrino, 1554.

_____. *The Four Books of Andrea Palladio's Architecture.* Translated by Isaac Ware. London: Isaac Ware, 1738.

Pandolfi, Vito. *Le commedia dell'arte.* 5 vols. Firenze: Edizione Sansoni Antiquariata, 1957.

Pane, Roberto. *Andrea Palladio.* Torino: Giulio Einaudi Editore, 1961.

Patte, Pierre. *Essai sur l'architecture théâtrale.* Paris: Libraire-Imprimeur de la Reine, 1782.

Perrault, C. *Les Dix Livres d'Architecture de Vitruve.* Paris: Coignard, 1673.

Philandri, Guglielmi. *Marci Vitruvii Pollionis Vivi Suae Professionis Peritissimi De Architectura Libri Decem Cum Notis Philandri et Sexti Frontini de Aquaeductibus Liber, et Nicolai Cusani de Staticis Experimentis.* Strasburgo: Knoblochiana, 1543.

Piccolomini, Alessandro. *L'Amor costante comedia del S. Stordito Intronato, composta per la venuta de l' Imperatore in Siena l'anno dell XXXVI.* Venetia: Segnodel Pozza, 1550.

Pigafetta, Filippo. *Due lettere descrittive l'una del l'ingresso a Vicenza della Imperatrice Maria d'Austria nell'anno 1581. L'altra della recita nel Teatro Olimpico dell'Edippo di Sofocle nel 1585.* Edited with introduction by Leonardo Trissino. Padova: Valentino Grescini, 1830.

Policiani. *Marci Vitruvii Pollionis De Architectura Libri Decem, Accedunt Cleonidae Harmonicum Introductorium, Frontini de Aquaeductibus, Policiani Opuscula.* Venetiis: Per Simonem Papiensem, 1497.

_____.[Politiani, Angeli.] *Lucii Vitruvii Pollionis De Architectura Libri Decem Sexti Iulii Frontini de Aquaeductibus Liber Unus Angeli Politiani Opusculum.* Florentie: n.p., 1496.

Pollux, Julius. *Onomasticon.* Edited by Immanneleo Bekkeri. Berlin: Friderici Nicolai, 1846.

Pozza, Antonio M. Dalla. *Palladio.* Vicenza: Edizioni del Pellicano, 1943.

Puppi, Lionello. *Andrea Palladio.* Milano: Electa, 1973.

_____. *Il Teatro Olimpico.* Vicenza: Neri Pozza, 1963.

Rapp, Franz. "Renaissance *Periaktoi,*" in "Notes on Little-Known Materials for the History of the Theatre," *Theatre Annual,* III (1944), 60-78.

Rose, Valentinus. *Vitruvii de Architectura.* Leipzig: B. G. Teubneri, 1867.

Rossi, Nicolo. *Discorsi intorno la commedia.* Vicenza: Dalla Noce, 1589.

_____. *Discorsi intorno la tragedia.* Vicenza: Greco, 1590.

Scamozzi, Vincenzo. *L'idea della architettura universale.* Venetia: Presso l'Artore, 1615.

Schapiro, Meyer. "Style," in *Anthropology Today.* Edited by A.L. Kroeber. Chicago: University of Chicago Press, 1953.

Scholfield, P.H. *The Theory of Proportion in Architecture.* Cambridge, England: University Press, 1958.

Schrade, Leo. *La Représentation d'Edipo Tiranno au Teatro Olimpico (Vicence, 1585).* Paris: Editions du Centre National de la recherche scientifique, 1960.

Serlio, Sebastiano. *Il primo [a quinto] libro d'architettura.* Venetia: Pietro di Nicolini de Sabbio, 1551.

Smith, David Eugene. *History of Mathematics.* 2 vols. Boston: Ginn and Co., 1923.

Sonrel, Pierre. *Traité de scénographie.* Paris: Odette Lieutier, 1943.

Sulpicio, Giovanni. *Lucii Vitruvii Pollionis De Architectura Libri Decem. Detta Anche Sulpiciana, Da Giovanni Sulpicio da Veroli, Che, In Unione A Pomponio Leto, La Curo.* Roma: n.p., 1486.

Temanza, Tommaso. *Vite dei più celebri architetti e scultori Veneziani.* Venice: C. Palese, 1778.

_____. *Vita di Andrea Palladio.* Venezia: Giambattista Pasquali, 1762.

Trissino, Giangiorgio. *La Sofonisba.* Edited by Franco Paglierani. Bologna: Presso Gaetano Romagnoli, 1884.

Vasari, Giorgio. *Le vite di più eccellenti pittori scultori ed architettori.* Edited and annotated by Gaetano Milanesi. 9 vols. Firenze: G. C. Sansoni, Editore, 1881.

Venturi, Angelo. *Storia dell'arte italiani.* 15 vols. Milano: Ulrico Hoepli, 1920.

Vitruvius Pollionis, Marcus. For editions used in this study see the editors: Barbaro, Caporali,

Durantino, Granger, Jocundum, Morgan, Perrault, Philandri, Policiani, Rose, and Sulpicio.

Wittkower, Rudolf. *Architectural Principles in the Age of Humanism.* 3d ed. revised. Columbia University Studies in Art History and Archaeology, No. 1. New York: Random House, 1965.

Zago, Ortensio. "Disegni autografi del Teatro Berga, nel MSS.: Della maravigliosa grotta di Costozza e del Teatro Berga." 17th century MS in Biblioteca Bertoliana, Vicenza.

Zigiotti, Bartolomeo. *Memorie dell'Accademia Olimpica.* 19th century MSS in Biblioteca Bertoliana, Vicenza. Catalogued, 21.11.2.

Zorzi, Giangiorgio. *Le chiese e i ponti di Andrea Palladio.* Venezia: Neri Pozza, 1967.

—————. *I disegni delle antichità di Andrea Palladio.* Venezia: Neri Pozza, 1959.

—————. "Le prospettive del Teatro Olimpico nei disegni degli Uffizi di Firenze e nei documenti dell' 'Ambrosiana' di Milano," *Arte Lombarda,* X (1965), 70-97.

—————. "La vera origine e la giovinezza di Andrea Palladio," *Archivo Veneto 'Tridentino,* II (1922), 120-50.

—————. *Le ville e i teatri di Andrea Palladio.* Venezia: Neri Pozza, 1969.

Index

Academies: Accademia dei Constanti, 103;
    Accademia dei Sociniani, 101-102;
    Academia di Vicenze, 102; Accademia
    Trissiana, 28, 30, 102; humanism in the, 11,
    14, 102-103; Olimpic Academy, 101-103;
    suppression of the, 101.
Accademia Olimpica. *See* Olimpic Academy.
Albanese, Giovanni Battista, 131, 134.
Alberti, Leone Battista, 7, 28-30, 33, 49-50,
    110-114.
Aleotti, Giambattista: Teatro Farnese in
    Parma, 1-2, 8, 114; theatre in Ferrara, 114.
Arnaldi, Enea, 142.

Barbaro, Daniel: Vitruvius edition with
    Roman theatre plan by, 4, 11, 29-30, 32-34,
    37-38, 108-110, 142, 147.
Bertoliana Library in Vicenza, 25.
Bertotti Scamozzi, Ottavio, 3-7, 17, 24, 131-
    132.

Calderari, Ottone, 142.
Centro Internazionale di Studi di
    Archetettura: survey of the Teatro
    Olimpico, 132.
Chiapin, Paolo, 22-23, 107-109; description
    of *Sofonisba* production by, 106-109.
Classical imitation, 2, 4-5, 7-8, 45-46, 105-
    110.
Conradi, Edward, 101.
Cornaro, Alvise, 28-45.

Dalla Pozza, Antonio M., 11-13, 22, 147.

Edippo re, 1, 19, 22, 107, 119-120, 131, 141,
    142, 148: *See also* Teatro Olimpico;
    inaugural production for.

Giorgi, Francesco, 50.
Greek theatre plan, 3.

Harmonic aesthetic. *See* Teatro Olimpico:
    Harmonic aesthetic used in.

Ingegneri, Angelo, 117-119, 147.

Jones, Inigo, 29.

Kernodle, George, 8-10, 115; and Terence
    school tradition, 9, 113.
Krautheimer, Richard, 112-113.

Lawrenson, Thomas E., 7, 132, 145.
London Studio, 11-12, 24, 44, 123-130, 132-
    139.

Magagnato, Licisco, 13-16, 22, 106, 139, 145,
    147.
Magrini, Antonio, 106, 110, 141.
Marcellus theatre in Rome, 36; drawn by
    Sangallo, 36; drawn by Ligorio, 36; drawn
    by Peruzzi, 36.
Marzari, Giacomo, 2, 141.
Montenari, Giovanni, 3-5, 24.

Olimpic Academy, 1; academicians in, 102-
    103; as architect's client, 19-20;
    development of, 101-104; guests at
    productions by, 107; pre-production plans
    by, 115-120; productions in Vicenza
    Basilica, 105-110; production of *L'Amor
    costante* by, 21-23, 104-106, 109;
    production of Andria by, 104-105;
    production of *Edippo re* by, 1, 19, 22, 119-
    120, 131, 141, 142, 148; production of
    Eunuch by, 110-111; production of
    intermezzi, *La lidia* by, 105; production of
    La Mandragola by, 110, 115; production of
    Sofonisba by, 7, 15, 17, 22-23, 105-110, 114-
    115, 130, 140, 142 (*see also* Chiapin
    description); proposed production of *La
    Clizia* by, 104, 111; and recitation of
    L'Alessandro by, 104.
Orefice, Otavio, 131, 134, 142.

Palladio, Andrea: archaeological research by,
    14, 28-29, 46-47, 142-143; at Berga theatre,

8, 11, 30, 34, 37-41, at Pola theatre, 7, 37, 41-43, 47, 135, at Verona theatre, 37, 40-43, in Rome, 36-37; architectural practice, 44-48, architectural vocabulary, 14-16, 42-51, 125, 136, 142; biography, 27-30; corinthian order used, 125-126, 131, 136-138; design of theatres for Olimpic Academy by, 105-111; design of theatre in Venice for production of *Antigono,* 110; education, 27-30, 48; preference against illusionistic theatre, 111-114; *Quattro libri* by, 29, 44-47, 50, 125, 130, 137; Vitruvius canon studied by, 3-4, 28-29, 101, 123-125, 129, 136, 139, 142-143; Vitruvius edition work by, 30-42, 48; works of, Casa Civena, 28, 45, Chapel at Maser, 44, Loggia del Capitaneato, 44-46, 139, Monastery of the Carita, 129, Pallazzo Barbarano, 44-46, 139, Palazzo Chiericati, 44-46, Palazzo Iseppo Porto, 44-45, 129, Palazzo Porto Breganza, 46, Palazzo Thiene, 28, 45, 138, Palazzo Valmarana, 44-46, 51, 129, 138, Il Redentore, 12, 15, 135, San Giorgio Maggiore, 12, 15, 128, 135, Vicenza Civic Basilica, 7, 21, 129, Villa Badoer, 47, Villa Godi, 129, and Villa Trisino, 47.

Palladio, Silla (son), 1, 118; as construction supervisor of Teatro Olimpico, 118.

Pane, Roberto, 17-19, 136.

Periaktoi, 33, 37.

Peruzzi, Baldassare, 7, 14, 36.

Piccolomini, Alessandro, 104; *L'Amor costante* by, 21-23.

Pomponius Laetus' productions in Rome, 112.

Puppi, Lionello, 17-20, 106, 141, 147.

Renaissance theatre archaeology, 13.

Renaissance illusionistic theatre, 2, 8-9, 13-14, 111-114; Baldassare Peruzzi designs for, 113; Baltimore and Urbino panels for, 112-113; Bramante designs for, 113; Castiglione description of, 113.

Romano, Giulio, 28.

Royal Institute of British Architects, 25, 131.

Sangallo, Antonio da, 36.

Sanmichele, Michele, 28.

Sansovino, Jacop, 28.

Scamozzi, Vicenzo, 29; perspective scenery in Teatro Olimpico by, 7-8, 17, 19-20, 120, 134, 142-143, 147; theatre at Sabbioneta by, 1-2, 114.

Schrade, Leo, 148.

Serlio, Sebastiano, 28, 37, 133; theatre design by, 113-114; scenic illusionism by, 7, 14, 113-114.

Sofonisba, 7, 15-17, 22-23, 102, 105, 110-111, 114; *frons-scenae* for, 106-110.

Teatro Olimpico: archaeological research as design source for, 128-129; atrium of, 21, 119-121, 141; *cavea* of, 30-33, 36-45, 117-118, 129, 132-136, 139; *cavea* portico of, 36-48, 122-124, 129-130, 132, 135; ceiling design for, 141; committee to pick inaugural play for, 119-120; design source analysis of, 115-143; elliptical auditorium, 4-5, 8, 13, 132; exterior, 43; frescoes at, 21-22; *frons-scenae* in, 3, 7, 9-12, 14-16, 22, 24, 32-45, 106-111, 114, 116-119, 122-124, 128-130, 132-140; *frons-scenae aediculae* in, 125, 127, 130-131, 135-138, 140; harmonic aesthetic used in, 6, 26, 47-51, 123, 128-130, 133, 139-140, 142; inaugural production company assembled for, 119-120; inaugural production of *Edippo re* for, 1, 19, 22, 107, 119-120, 131, 141, 142, 148; London Studio design for, 12-13, 24, 44, 123-130, 132-139; odeo of, 4, 119-120, 141; periaktoi planned for, 7, 15; perspective scenery for, 115, 118-121, 131, 140, 142; pre-construction production plans for, 115-121, to produce a pastoral, 116, to produce Giusteniani's *Edippo re,* 119, to produce Ingegneri's *Limonata,* 117, to produce Loschi's *L'Achille,* 119, to produce Manfredi's *Semiramide,* 119, to produce Masaria's *L'Allessandro,* 119, to produce Pace's *Eugenio,* 115, 117, to produce Pagello's *Eraclea,* 118, to produce Tasso's *L'Aminto,* 119, to produce Valmarana's *La Placidia,* 119, to produce Vernier's *L'Idalba,* 119, to produce Vida's *L'Alessio,* 119; property granted by city council for, 115-116; property limits on design of, 3-4, 5-7, 118, 120-121, 123-124, 130-134, 142-143; property requested for, 115-116; as Roman model, 2-10; semi-ovoid auditorium in, 133; as tempered by renaissance culture in design of, 10-19; triumphal arch as design source for, 14-15; *versurae* in, 18, 22, 23, 39, 118, 122, 135, 139; Vitruvius model in *cavea* portico, 31-32, 36-45, 122, *cavea* shape, 133, and *frons-scenae,* 106-110, 114, 122, 127

Trissino, Giangiorgio: academy of, 27-29, 102; *Sofonisba,* 7, 15-17, 21-23, 102, 105-111, 114-115, 130, 140, 142-143.

Trissino, Leonardo, 24.

Triumphal arch, 111; as *frons-scenae,* 110; for royal entries, 111.

Uffizi Library, 25.

Vasari, Giorgio, 13, 110, 113-114.

Vicenza City Council, 24.
Vicenza Civic Museum, 25.
Vitruvius editions, 7, 28-30, 43; Daniel
   Barbaro, 5, 11, 29-31, 32-34, 37-38, 108-
   110; Cesare Cesariano, 30, 36; Frank
   Granger, 32; Fra Jocondus, 30; Morris
   Hickey Morgan, 32; Charles Perrault, 32;

Guglielmi Philandri, 4; Sulpitius
   Verulanus, 112.

Wittkower, Rudolf, 25, 148.

Zigiotti, Bartolomeo manuscript, 22-24, 107.
Zorzi, Giangiorgio, 20, 25, 106-107, 141.